RED AND BLACK
THE DEBTOR/CREDITOR RELATIONSHIP

by

Barbara E. Kirby, Esq.

Pearson Publications Company
Dallas, Texas

ISBN 0-929563-41-7

ACKNOWLEDGMENTS

"True ease in writing comes from art, not chance,
As those move easiest who have learned to dance." Alexander Pope

There is so much to learn about writing a book, and I want to express my sincere gratitude to those who helped me along the way. My thanks to Susan Stoner, who encouraged me to teach and provided the opportunity. My thanks to Frances Beall Whiteside and Diane Baldwin, who encouraged me to write this book, and extra thanks to Diane for reviewing the text prior to publication. I give this thanks to Frances and Diane, even though they deceived me into thinking that writing this book would be easy.

A special thank-you to Robert Geis and Thomas Roll, my Xerox legal counterparts in Florida and California, for their assistance and insights regarding the laws of their respective states, and also for the much-needed therapy sessions they have provided over the years. Additional thanks go to Dora Lew and Michael W. Youdin for reviewing the text, and to George F. McElreath and Katherine Kazanas for the bankruptcy forms contained in the appendix. I am especially grateful to Sherry L. Hartman of Pearson Publications Co. for her help and encouragement throughout this unfamiliar process. Finally, special thanks to publisher Enika Pearson Schulze, who created a window of opportunity for me and then had the patience to keep the window open while I squeezed through it.

Barbara Kirby

DEDICATION

This book is lovingly dedicated to three people whose constant support has been the foundation of my success as an attorney, an author, and a human being. I owe them a debt that I can never adequately repay:

Jane D. Kirby, my mother;
Sid Burall, my husband; and
Chuck Corrigan, my paralegal.

TABLE OF CONTENTS

PREFACE

An Overview of the Debtor/Creditor Relationship

Many view the areas of bankruptcy and the debtor-creditor relationship as specialized practices. Actually, these are areas of law that touch a variety of people on an individual basis. As Polonius advised Laertes, "Neither a borrower nor a lender be." (*Hamlet*, Act I, Scene iii) This is difficult advice to follow in the modern age. Upon reaching college age, the average person cannot avoid becoming a debtor. We all hope, someday, to become creditors. The debtor-creditor relationship will be an important one for every person who becomes an active participant in the free market economy.

There are numerous contexts in which knowledge of the debtor-creditor relationship ranges from useful to absolutely necessary. Most of an attorney's clients are participating in the mainstream of business and commerce. Many paralegals will seek employment in this mainstream. Knowledge of the various bodies of law that govern the debtor-creditor relationship creates a level of understanding of the ground rules under which clients operate, regardless of the type of legal problem presented. In addition, many jobs involving credit management, collection of accounts receivable, and bankruptcy coordination and management are available in corporations.

In the legal context, a basic understanding of debtor-creditor issues is essential in order to effectively assist clients. These clients may be consumers who, due to some catastrophic illness or disaster, are unable to pay their bills, or large corporations seeking counsel regarding customers who have not paid for goods or services. Even if you never counsel a client regarding payment or collection of money, the knowledge contained in this text will be useful in every area of legal practice. How can this be so? If you handle only plaintiff's personal injury cases, and you obtain a judgment for your client, it has absolutely no tangible value unless it can be converted to cash. In this book, you will learn which assets are protected from collection efforts of creditors, and the procedures you can use to get assets out of the hands of debtors, both before and after final judgment.

Often paralegals find lucrative jobs as law office managers or administrators. You may find that, as the only paralegal in a small office, day-to-day management chores may fall into your lap. Remember (and lawyers often do not) that the practice of law is also a business. Someone has to assure that accounts are paid and that any disputes that may exist regarding those accounts are resolved. This book will give you some of the tools needed to collect accounts in a manner that is sensitive to clients and customers, and also in compliance with state and federal laws that govern debt collection.

An additional incentive for study of the debtor-creditor relationship exists on a very personal level. As individual participants in a free-market economy, we are all at some point debtors, creditors, or both. It is important to know your rights as they relate to the extension of credit and the collection of payments, as well as potential remedies should it be necessary to proceed from an individual basis to collect a debt. There are numerous consumer protection statutes that apply to each of us as we utilize credit to purchase goods and services for our personal, family and household purposes.

Finally, although this is not intended to be a comprehensive text on bankruptcy law, you will find some basic information regarding the ability of debtors to obtain a "fresh start" through the different chapters of the Bankruptcy Code. The main purpose of this book is to give a basic understanding of the laws that apply to debtors and creditors, as a foundation to unraveling the intricacies of the bankruptcy process. Many texts concentrate solely on the bankruptcy process. Unfortunately, students often do not have the basic knowledge of the legal relationships that existed long before the bankruptcy proceeding was filed. It is much like skipping to calculus when you have not mastered basic mathematics. I hope this book lays a foundation that lessens the anxiety that may be encountered upon delving into a more substantive study of bankruptcy law and procedure.

Barbara Kirby

Chapter One

KEY CONCEPTS

A Basic Vocabulary

A **debtor** is a person who owes a debt that is due or will become due. A **creditor** is a person who has a legal right to fulfillment of a debt or obligation. A **debt** is a specific sum of money owed or an obligation to pay, owed by one person to another. The term "person" in these definitions is meant in the strict legal sense, such that it includes not only individual beings, but also the business entities recognized as having a separate legal existence (corporations, limited partnerships, etc.).

How Debts Arise

There are basically four ways that debts arise:

1.   *By contract.* Basic business law tells us that a contract exists with the presence of offer, acceptance, and consideration. Most debts, whether business or consumer, arise by this type of agreement. Automobile loans, promissory notes and equipment leases all are examples of debts that exist due to a contractual relationship. Another common way that debts arise through contract is by way of the revolving credit card. When someone initially receives a credit card, one may neglect to read the terms and conditions that arrive along with the card. Perhaps this document is hidden among numerous product advertisements, or smells too much like strong perfume to read in its entirety. What the reader would discover is that, each time you sign a credit card receipt, you are agreeing to be bound by the terms and conditions, and any changes and alterations to them, that the company may issue. The debts on a credit card thus arise by way of a contract.

An important fact to remember – a verbal contract is still a contract, provided that all three elements (offer, acceptance, consideration) exist. For example, if Bud offers to mow your lawn for twenty dollars, you accept this proposal, and Bud actually completes the job, a debt will arise due to the verbal contract, with Bud as the creditor and you as the debtor.

No Contract

2.　　**By *quasicontract***. There are those circumstances where all elements of a contract do not exist, but the equitable powers of the law may deem that a debt arises in order to avoid the unjust enrichment of one of the parties. For example, an attorney is at home in the middle of a day, perhaps toying with the idea of working from a "virtual office." A crew of painters arrive, and begin painting the house. The attorney knows that the neighbors were planning to have their house painted, and it appears that a mistake is being made. However, the attorney chooses to do nothing to stop the painters. When the project is completed and the painters demand payment, the attorney informs them that it was a mistake and that payment will not be forthcoming. This may be a circumstance where the painters wish to test the equitable theory of quasicontract. Because the attorney was aware that the services were being performed, a reasonable court might determine that unjust enrichment occurred. The court would determine a fair sum of money to compensate the painters.

A slight change in the scenario may change the outcome. Suppose that no one is at home. The painters begin their work on the wrong house, and the resident arrives home, aghast at the hideous shade the house has been painted. The resident meets the presentation of the bill by the painters with a refusal to bear the cost of their mistake, and demands a return of the house to its former pleasant tone. The court in this circumstance may not find that the resident was unjustly enriched, and may instead require the painters to take some action to remedy the situation.

A party attempting to enforce a debt through quasicontract will be seeking an equitable remedy. When litigants resort to theories in equity, no black and white outcomes can be predicted. As much as students may want to know exactly what would happen under both of the above scenarios, it is still only a guess as to how a "reasonably prudent judge" would rule.

3.　　**By *tort***. The law of torts is the area of law involving private wrongs (as opposed to the public wrongs addressed by criminal law) other than breach of contract. Debts can arise due to the negligence or malfeasance of another, and the sum due from the tortfeasor debtor to the victim creditor may be determined by the court, by mediators, or even by agreement of the parties with the assistance of their insurance carriers. Some examples of torts from which debts may arise include medical and legal malpractice, personal injury, product liability, and defamation.

Consider the circumstances surrounding a minor automobile accident. Jane is driving down a neighborhood street when Chuck ignores a stop sign and runs into Jane's car. There is significant damage to Jane's car. Either by admission or through litigation, Chuck is determined to be at fault. A debt arises that Chuck owes to Jane in the amount determined necessary to compensate Jane for the damages to her car.

4.   *By statute.* The final category under which debts arise is the mechanism by which various governmental entities become the creditor, and citizens under various statutory schemes are the debtors. Just as citizens receive goods and services from governments, there are also statutory schemes that fund the provision of these services. The classic example is the Internal Revenue Code, under which each U.S. citizen determines how much is owed in taxes on income. The statutes also give the government creditor the tools to pursue the citizen debtor for nonpayment. There are also certain penalties assessed in various statutory schemes (such as fines for violation of environmental codes, housing codes, etc.) that will also give rise to the existence of a debtor-creditor relationship between a government and its citizens.

Suppose that the Springfield Nuclear Power Plant is caught dumping toxic waste into the river. The federal statutes regulating discharge of waste into waterways provides a penalty to be assessed for violation of the statute and, after the proper administrative procedures are followed, the fine that is assessed against the power plant is a debt owed to the federal government, arising by way of statute.

Liquidated vs. Unliquidated Debts

A concept worth noting while dissecting the existence of debt is the distinction between a liquidated and an unliquidated debt. A **liquidated**

debt is one in which the amount of money due can be calculated as a sum certain. This calculation may come from the face of an agreement, such as a promissory note. For example, if a debtor stopped making payments on an automobile loan, it would not be long before the bank or financing institution contacted the debtor with the news that the note will soon be accelerated (a concept that will be explored more thoroughly later). It will be a simple matter to look at the loan documents, and follow the mathematical formula for determining precisely how much is owed on the defaulted loan, and it will be a sum certain. A liquidated debt does not require a written contract – it can also be the sum of outstanding unpaid invoices for goods received. The requirement is that some method or documentation exists from which the sum certain can be determined.

Contrast this concept with its opposite, the **unliquidated debt**. It is one in which the amount due cannot be calculated as a sum certain, but instead a trier of fact must be engaged or an agreement reached as to the total amount due. Debts that arise by tort are classic unliquidated debts. No written agreement or formula exists to tell how much a broken leg is worth, or how much the reputation of a libel victim has been damaged. You may be able to look at the damage estimate provided after an automobile accident, but numerous and different estimates of the same damage can easily be obtained.

You will often see documents that contain a combination of liquidated and unliquidated debt. A promissory note may contain precise language for calculation of the sums due in case of default, but the note may also contain a provision for "reasonable attorney's fees." If enforcement of this note is required through litigation, it may be possible to prove up the liquidated debt through documents and affidavits. However, a live witness will have to testify about what amount of attorney's fees are reasonable for similar cases in that jurisdiction.

Secured Transactions

This is the first time in this text that the concept of a security interest will be discussed. Rest assured, it will not be the last. What is the difference between secured and unsecured debt? A **security interest**, as defined in the Uniform Commercial Code (UCC),[1] is "an interest in personal property or fixtures that secures payment or performance of an obligation." UCC Section 1-201(37). This interest is granted in the **security agreement**, signed by both the debtor and creditor. The property that is subject to the security interest is known as the **collateral**. State and federal laws recognize two basic types of creditors – secured and unsecured. The **secured creditor** is one who has an interest or security in collateral. For the secured creditor, there is the comfort of knowing that, if the debtor defaults, there is some property available to satisfy the debt.

The methods by which the secured creditor can obtain possession of its collateral are initially quicker and simpler than filing suit. For example, a bank that finances an automobile in which it retains a security interest can seek to repossess the car without judicial intervention, as long as there is no "breach of the peace." On the other hand, the unsecured creditor is forced to file a lawsuit, obtain a judgment against the debtor, and execute the judgment before there will even be an opportunity to satisfy its debt through seizure of personal property of the debtor.

If the debtor files bankruptcy, the differences become even more dramatic. For example, small businesses typically obtain their initial financing by borrowing money from a bank, which takes a security interest in virtually all of the property in which the debtor has an interest. If the business fails and files bankruptcy, this bank will have priority in its collateral. The unsecured creditors of this small business will have to take a place at the end of the line, awaiting distribution of the debtor's assets to the bank and any other secured creditors according to their priority. The unsecured creditors will then share pro rata in whatever pittance remains. The various laws regarding security interests will be discussed in greater detail in later chapters.

---

[1] The Uniform Commercial Code is a set of uniform laws covering all of the phases that ordinarily arise in a commercial transaction, from start to finish. The UCC has been adopted, with some alternative language or provisions, in all fifty states, as the principal laws governing the sale of and payment for goods.

What is a Lien?

A **lien** is a charge on property that must be satisfied before the property or its proceeds are available for the satisfaction of the debts of general creditors. These charges on property take many forms and are found in a multitude of transactions. The lienholder does not have the right to take action against the property until an act of default occurs, but the lien does prevent the debtor from disposing of the property without first satisfying the interests of any lienholders.

There are three basic types of liens:

1.   A **consensual lien**, as the name implies, is a lien that arises by the consent of the parties. It is granted by the debtor for the benefit of the creditor. Without a consensual lien in either real or personal property, the motivation is low for a bank, lending institution or financing organization to extend any significant amount of credit to a debtor. The classic example of a consensual lien is the security interest granted in personal property, such as the lien a bank or financing institution obtains when you borrow money to buy an automobile. In the automobile loan, the buyer signs a security agreement, in which the bank is granted a security interest in the automobile. Should the buyer fail to make the payments on time, the bank will have the right to obtain possession of its collateral – the car.

A lien on real property is generally created through a mortgage or a deed of trust, and will be governed by the code or statute of the state in which the real property is located. The typical deed of trust grants a lien on the described real property, outlines the rights, duties and obligations of the parties, names a trustee, and contains a power of sale clause. Through this power of sale, the trustee can conduct a nonjudicial foreclosure sale without resorting to the courts. As different collection methods are discussed later in this text, it will become apparent that this is a powerful tool for creditors. However, because this is not a book on real estate law, it will not dwell on the intricacies of drafting these documents or enforcing liens on real property.

2.   A **statutory lien** is a creature of statute and, as such, is heavily procedural. The purpose of a statutory lien is to provide protection for

parties who provide goods or services, or to assure payment of funds owed to governmental entities. Examples of the former are mechanics and materialmen's liens and artisan's liens. Those who may be eligible for such liens in order to ensure payment for goods and services must follow the procedures outlined in the relevant statute.

The most powerful tax lien is the federal tax lien outlined in Title 26 of the Internal Revenue Code:

> Section 6321. Lien for Taxes
> If any person liable to pay any tax neglects or refuses to pay the same after demand, the amount (including any interest, additional amount, addition to tax, or assessable penalty, together with any costs that may accrue in addition thereto) shall be a lien in favor of the United States upon all property and rights to property, whether real or personal, belonging to such person.

Upon determining that a tax is owed and unpaid, the Internal Revenue Service makes a tax assessment and provides notice to the taxpayer. A lien on the property of the debtor is created as of the date of the notice. However, for the lien to be effective as to third parties, the IRS must file its tax lien of record. For real estate, the lien must be filed in the deed records of the county where the property is located. To give notice of a lien on personal property, the filing should be made in accordance with the UCC laws as adopted in the state where the personal property is located.

Effectiveness of statutory liens against the debtor and other creditors will always be dependent upon adherence to the procedures outlined in the relevant statute. This makes sense, as these statutory liens do not have the element of consent between the debtor and the creditor. Protection is thus available for both parties – the statute exists to provide a remedy for creditors in certain situations, but contains a procedure giving notice and opportunity to cure for the debtor.

3.   A **judicial lien** is a lien that arises due to an order or judgment of a court. The most common of these remedies are the judgment liens, that arise when a judgment creditor takes the necessary actions to

enforce a valid judgment against the property of the defendant. There
are also some prejudgment actions that create liens upon property of
the debtor, allowing the creditor the protection of a charge on the
debtor's property while final judgment of the court is still pending.
These remedies are discussed at length in chapter four.

EXERCISE

Think about your own experiences with debts in regard to the four
ways that debts arise. How did your debts arise? When looking at the
four categories, can you think of any circumstances where you have
been a creditor? Are your debts liquidated or unliquidated? Finally,
have you ever had property subject to a lien? What was the property,
and what type of lien?

Chapter Two

A TYPICAL BUSINESS TRANSACTION

Like it or not, there is a vast difference between learning information from the safety and warmth of classrooms and textbooks, and the experience encountered when actually attempting to apply knowledge in the context of the work-for-pay world. Similarly, there is a great distance between the business world in which clients make their living and the atmosphere in which an attorney gives advice and counsel to that client. For example, a client may come to an attorney and say, "The Acme Company has not paid for the widgets we delivered, and I want to sue them." The attorney may immediately begin the process of sending the formal demand, drafting the lawsuit, and billing those billable hours. Why not get on the phone to the president of Acme and ask why the bills have not been paid? In commercial transactions, the best advice is sometimes in the form of business guidance rather than legal counsel.

Why is it important for paralegals to know "how business really works"? First, the best advice and counsel is given with an understanding of your client's issues. Second, we are all active members of the free market economy, as members of the legal profession, of the business community, and as consumers. It can only be a benefit to understand the companies that you work for, invest in, buy products from, and to which money is ultimately owed and paid. Before delving into an example transaction, it is important to note the difference in treatment between businesses and consumers.

What is a Consumer?

A **consumer** is a person who purchases goods and services for personal, family and household purposes. Consumer transactions are treated differently from business-to-business transactions due to the uneven playing field facing consumers. In the early law of sales, *caveat emptor* ("let the buyer beware") was the predominant theme. This was because the seller was usually the producer of the product, the buyer was face-to-face with the seller, and the product was available for examination at the time the sale was negotiated. Marketing and technology have changed this manner of doing business in virtually every circumstance. This dramatic change in the culture of sales has gradually led to the recognition that the consumer is disadvantage in many transactions. Numerous state and federal statutes now address the relationship between consumer debtors and business creditors. The following example will relate to a transaction between two businesses, as opposed to a consumer transaction.

The Credit Decision

Assume for the purposes of this example that you are the credit manager for an equipment manufacturing corporation. You are responsible for maintaining the integrity of your company's financed portfolio, and you have a fiduciary duty to stockholders to assure that appropriate standards are applied to all credit transactions. You are also under tremendous pressure from the sales and marketing divisions of your organization. Because their performance is measured by the number of units sold, and not whether the customer is worthy of the extension of credit, they demand very liberal credit approval. Financing is also a competitive business in its own right. Other institutions will be fighting you for the ability to collect the finance charges that accrue when equipment is purchased over time. Within the context of these opposing points of view, you must examine individual transactions to determine how much credit to extend and in what form.

What Type of Transaction is Proposed?

Although it is rare, you may have a customer who wants to pay **cash** and receive a bill of sale for the equipment. It may be that this business needs to make an investment in capital, and desires to have an asset that can be depreciated for tax purposes. The customer may have a financing institution that provides terms more favorable than you can deliver. There are also many organizations who specialize in leasing to businesses. They may extend the cash payment for the equipment and lease it back to your customer. (As noted above, this is a highly competitive business!)

The customer may want to enter into an installment purchase. In this type of transaction, title to the equipment passes to the purchaser, but payments are made over a period of time. The creditor collects a finance charge in compensation for the risk associated with payment over time. A security interest is usually granted to the creditor in the equipment being financed, so that the creditor can recover the product in case of default in payment.

The customer may also want to **rent or lease** the equipment. The utilization of the leasing structure has proliferated greatly in the past 20 years, and the variety and purpose of various lease agreements has been the subject of numerous cases and decisions. Consumers now have the additional options related to the lease of automobiles, and the lease agreements become more convoluted with each draft. So what is the deal with all these leases? Most of the time, it boils down to how both the buyer and the seller wish to view the asset being financed for tax purposes. Most of the time, buyer and seller can come up with a format that pleases both parties, and both walk away happy. In the instance of a default in payment, the issue of the terms contained within these lease agreements becomes critical. The status of the asset as property of the debtor or of the lessor is of great interest to other creditors who are looking for assets of the debtor that can be utilized in satisfaction of their debts.

An examination of a so-called lease transaction focuses on whether it is a true lease or a disguised installment purchase. In a **true lease agreement**, most frequently referred to as a rental agreement, the title to the property that is the subject of the agreement never passes to the customer. There is no purchase option at the end of the lease. The unit is returned to the seller. The risk of loss of the unit is mostly borne by the seller, and service is provided throughout the term of the agreement.

In other leases often described as **equity leases**, some of these questions remain ambiguous in the terms as they are drafted. The predominant feature is the purchase option at the end of the lease, so that a party who has been renting can exercise this option and gain title to the equipment at the point that the purchase option is exercised. In other words, as the lessor has made payments during the term of the agreement, equity has been accruing in the property.

Other creditors will claim that the accrual of equity constitutes an ownership interest in the property. For example, a debtor has been leasing equipment, and has completed 46 of 48 payments. The debtor files bankruptcy, and wants to return the equipment to the lessor, without making the final payments or exercising the purchase option. The lessor wants to pick up the equipment, since the lease agreement states that title remains with the lessor until performance of the purchase option.

However, it is the desire of other creditors that the equipment be sold, and the proceeds from that sale distributed to all of the creditors, according to any relevant priorities. The argument is that the debtor has paid for the equipment for almost four years, and would ultimately own the unit. If this were an installment purchase, the debtor would be building up an ownership interest in the equipment as each payment is made, and would only need to pay a very small sum to satisfy the seller.

True Lease or Disguised Installment Purchase?

The courts routinely examine lease transactions to determine whether they should be considered **disguised installment purchases** for the purposes of satisfaction of other creditors. Here are some of the criteria considered to be most compelling:

- Is the purchase option amount a nominal or meaningless sum, or is it rationally related to the value of the equipment at the end of the lease?

- Does the lessor record the transaction as a sale for its own accounting purposes, or does it continue to list the leased assets as owned equipment?

- Are services provided along with the lease, or is the lessee required to pay extra for maintenance?

- Does the lessor bear the risk of loss, or is it borne entirely by the lessee?

These and any other relevant factors are considered as each lease is examined on a case-by-case basis.

Information Available to Assist in the Credit Decision

Now that we have examined some of the complexities of the types of financed transactions that are available, it is time to get back to the job of making a credit decision. As a credit manager, you have many tools available to assist in your decision making. Most of the relevant information is gathered together into useful formats by **credit reporting agencies**. Now that the availability of on-line information has proliferated, there is no excuse for skipping the information-gathering aspect of credit approval. Most large companies subscribe to a service such as Dun & Bradstreet, which provides reporting on levels from the sublime to the useful. For consumer transactions, there are three major credit reporting agencies that also provide numerous levels of service.

It is important to get a potential customer to fill out a **credit application** of some sort. The way a business represents itself is just as important as the information held by a reporting service. By matching up the information, you can assess your customer's veracity. If a customer represents in a credit application that it is a corporation when it is a proprietorship, or that it has a net worth of a certain amount when the reporting service shows a lesser amount, there is more ammunition for proving a misrepresentation caused the extension of credit. The credit application can also include banking and other business references. If your business intends to seek information from references, the credit application needs to have a release of this information, signed by the customer, as this information is typically considered to be a confidential business record, not to be released without consent of the principal. See Appendix 1 for a sample application with appropriate release language.

The credit report, application and references may still give the credit manager a feeling that the customer is a credit risk, but not adequate reason to reject the application (especially in the face of pressure from the sales force!). But a credit manager can insist on some protections that will lessen the impact of a potential default. The most frequently used devices are **down payments** and **finance charge adjustments**. Receipt of some percentage of the principal up front assures that the seller will receive at least some part of the payment, and reduces the chances of fraud and other credit scams. Equipment sellers and lessors often adjust the percentage of the finance charge dependent upon the credit rating of the customer. The rationale is that, in case of default, at least additional points in charges were collected before the time the customer fails to pay.

Anyone who has shopped for an automobile will recognize the variation in down payments and finance charges based on their credit rating at that point in time. A recent graduate with no credit history may be asked to pay ten percent of the purchase price down and double-digit interest. An established professional who has paid off several car loans can purchase a more expensive car with no down payment and the most competitive interest rates.

Two other devices that may be utilized are personal guaranty agreements and letters of credit. The **personal guaranty** is an agreement from an individual or another business entity to be responsible for all of the debts of the customer. It is most frequently requested when the customer is a closely held corporation (a corporation in which substantially all of the stock is owned by a small number of people, or only one person) with little or no track record. The creditor may request the majority shareholder (often the 100% shareholder) to personally guarantee the debts of the corporation, due to the ease of formation and dissolution of this type of business entity. A sample personal guaranty is shown in Appendix 2.

A **letter of credit** is addressed from the buyer's bank to a seller, and authorizes drafts (payment by certified funds) to the seller up to a stipulated amount. Through either conditional or unconditional terms, it provides payment from the bank for the seller's benefit in instances of delinquency in payment by the buyer. This is a comfortable assurance for the seller, in that the bank is assuming the risk of credit extension to the customer, usually for the first year of a financed transaction. An example of a typical letter of credit can be found in Appendix 3.

The Collection Process Begins

Now that the difficult decision has been made to extend credit to the new customer, it is time to take on a new job. Imagine now that you are the manager of accounts receivable. It is your job to ensure that all of the different types of accounts are converted to cash. The target for your organization is known as "DSO" or "Days Sales Outstanding." This is typically the number of days between the time the invoice or notice of payment is sent to the customer, and the time the payment is actually received. Statistics gathered by creditor's organizations have consistently shown that age is the enemy of all collectors, i.e., the older an invoice becomes, the lower the likelihood of its collection.

In a customer-oriented business (as all businesses should be in this competitive era), it can be very damaging to the goodwill of an organization to begin with extreme collection tactics. This is why most accounts receivable organizations begin with what are known as "soft collections." Messages contained on the invoice ("Your account is thirty days past due. If your payment has been remitted, please disregard this notice"), clever notices (the elephant with the "did you forget?" note), and other passive correspondence are the main tools in this soft collection phase. Telephone calls made in this phase are usually customer-oriented and nonthreatening. An effective talk track is to call the customer and ask if the invoice was received and whether or not there are problems with the information and format of the bill. If all indications from the customer are that the invoice is correct and understandable, there is a comfortable segue into a question regarding payment, such as, "Were you aware that our invoices are due upon receipt?" If properly handled, many customers will leave the call thinking they have received excellent customer care, totally oblivious to the fact that it was a collection call.

A certain percentage of customers of any business will require a much tougher approach, known in the business as "hard collections." These efforts do not have to be rude or unpleasant, and should, wherever possible, show appropriate customer care. However, the focus in these types of calls and letters is to get a payment commitment for a particular date. This is the ideal time to start accumulating the information that will be vital to all steps in the collection process. During direct telephone contact with the debtor, the goal is to determine why the account is not being paid. Does the debtor have some legitimate dispute? Is there a cash flow problem caused by some event that may be rectified within an acceptable time frame? Has the business failed? Does the debtor acknowledge the debt, but need more time to make full payment? There is no collection technique as strong and powerful as talking to someone who owes money and trying to work through the issues. If the customer fails to perform by the established deadline, the information gained can be used in recommending further action.

Businesses vary in the amount of flexibility in payment terms extended during this collection phase. Some level of compromise should exist in every phase. Whether working on behalf of debtors or creditors, it is important to *negotiate, negotiate, negotiate* at every opportunity. In business, cash is king, and litigation is costly, time-consuming, and often has a negative result. Decision makers need to become experienced in determining that point where the "bird in the hand is worth two in the bush." Of course, there must be some type of structured limits on settlement authority, and a manager must have the power to compromise accounts. In casino parlance, the manager with the ability to give complimentary rooms and meals is said to "have the pencil." In dealing with receivables, each business should make sure there is someone who has the pencil and can enter into payment arrangements, make lump sum settlements, and evaluate other creative payment proposals presented by debtors.[1]

When negotiations fail, payment commitments are broken, and debtors are not responsive, it is time to send a **formal written demand** for payment with an appropriate deadline. If the basis of the debt is contractual, the contract needs to be accelerated, so that there is a

---

[1] I do not mean to take easy money away from my fellow collection attorneys, but I feel compelled to reveal that many accounts are settled by an attorney who is accepting a proposal made by the debtor months before the attorney was involved. Legal fees could have been saved, but no one had "the pencil."

figure that represents the total sum due under the terms of the contract. In the acceleration process, past due payments are totaled, interest or finance charges for future payments are removed, and the remaining principal balance is determined. The resulting liquidated sum will be stated in the formal demand letter.[2]

When no response is received to the formal demand, the receivables manager must make a business decision regarding further action. Some larger businesses, especially large retailers, have in-house collection organizations that take accounts that have gone through the softer collections and negotiations, and continue the process with a more vigorous attack. Other businesses contract with collection agencies who continue to apply pressure to the debtors. There is usually a carefully guarded monetary threshold below which litigation is not deemed to be cost-effective. Accounts above this line are sent directly to attorneys for legal action, or are farmed out through collection agencies to a network of attorneys in the various states where debtors may be located. There are several organizations that provide attorney referral services for companies who have collection-related matters that cross state boundaries, the most well-known being the Commercial Law League. Collections are big business. There are over 7,000 collection agencies in the U.S., and the Commercial Law League has thousands of members actively involved in the collection of bad debts. If the sum is large enough, and the debtor business appears to have assets that can ultimately be seized to satisfy the debt, most businesses will make the decision to engage an attorney and pursue collection of the debt.

The Demand Letter

The principal function of the initial letter to the debtor is to identify the claim and advise the debtor that an attorney has entered the picture. The letter also has the following important functions:

---

[2] The content and form of the letter from a legal perspective is not immediately relevant, as we are still discussing efforts made by a business prior to referral to an attorney. In most instances, a collection attorney will send another demand letter appropriate to the jurisdiction prior to filing suit.

- Preserving the rights of the creditor, such as the right to recover attorney's fees, under local statutes with specific requirements regarding an initial demand;

- Fulfilling other statutory requirements, such as the Federal Fair Debt Collection Practices Act requirements for consumer debts; and

- Opening a dialogue with the debtor, in hopes of reaching a settlement.

The point in drafting a demand letter is to get the attention of the debtor, and to include some magic factor that causes immediate payment of the claim. This must be done, however, within the bounds of ethical conduct. The following are some general considerations to keep in mind when drafting:

- Threatening to take legal action without authorization from the client to do so is both an ethical violation and a violation of most debt collection acts.

- Filing suit where the debt is barred by the statute of limitations is in violation of the Federal Fair Debt Collection Practices Act.

- Allowing a collection agency or client to use a law firm's letterhead to send "dunning" letters when accounts have not been referred to counsel is unethical.

- Demand letters seeking unearned interest constitute a violation of many state usury laws, and attorneys may be liable for statutory penalties related to charging excess interest, even though not parties to the transaction.

Appendix 4 contains examples of demand letters to be used for both commercial and consumer debt, for promissory notes, personal property leases, and to recover on bad checks. Remember, the challenge of drafting a demand letter is to create a document that urges the debtor to communicate and negotiate with the creditor. Do not rely too heavily on forms. Instead, draft a letter that is unique to the circumstances. To the extent possible, avoid legalese. The letter needs to be understandable for the debtor, but must also impart that "this is the last chance" urgency that compels contact with the creditor.

If the demand letter is successful and the debtor makes payment arrangements, always confirm the agreement in writing. This documents balances due and payment deadlines, which will be useful in case litigation is ultimately necessary. Further, it avoids the kind of confusion over due dates and amounts that allows the debtor to further delay the payment process. Here is some sample language:

1. Payment in full:
   "This letter is to confirm the agreement reached in our telephone conversation. You agreed that the balance due on this account in the sum of $$$$ will be paid by (Due Date). Please make your check payable to (Creditor) and forward it to this office for appropriate credit. If payment is not received by that date, our client will have no alternative except to proceed with legal action."

2. Installments:
   "This letter is to confirm the agreement reached in our telephone conversation. You agree to pay the total sum due of $$$$ in payments of $$$$ per month for (No. of Months). The first payment is due on the ## day of the month and on the same day each month until the total sum is paid. Please make your check payable to (Creditor) and forward it to this office for appropriate credit.

   We will not be contacting you to remind you each time a payment is due, or if a payment has been missed. If payment is not received by that date, our client will have no alternative except to proceed with legal action."

Larger sums and more complex agreements, especially those involving collateral, should be documented in a more formal manner, with signatures of the parties obtained. However, either of the above types of letters can be drafted with an "Agreed and Accepted" signature line, and a request that the debtor sign and return the original letter. Debtors need to be aware that there are tax consequences to settling a debt for less than the original balance due. If a creditor forgives a debt, the amount unpaid is considered as income. A creditor that forbears $600 or more in debt must send the debtor and the IRS a Form 1099 report of income at the end of the tax year, and the debtor must pay tax on the sum as income.

EXERCISE

It is popular these days for providers of equipment of all types, from cellular phones to automobiles, to encourage customers to lease instead of purchase. Look for a newspaper ad, a brochure or some other written materials provided by an equipment seller that describe a lease promotion. Examine the terms provided. Determine the monthly payments, the finance charge, the purchase option, and any other costs that may be included in the lease. Does it appear to be a true lease, or a disguised installment purchase?

Assume now that you work for the finance department for the company you selected. Eddie Punchclock entered into the lease in question, and made no payments for six months. Draft a demand letter to Eddie, informing him that the lease will be accelerated if he does not bring it current. Review the forms, but be creative! Use your own style to persuade the debtor to make payment arrangements.

Chapter Three

LAWS THAT LIMIT
COLLECTION ACTIVITY

The common law did not contain effective deterrents to unconscionable debt collection activities. A debtor who was a victim of unreasonable debt collection activities would have to file suit for causes of action such as defamation, intentional infliction of emotional distress, or invasion of privacy. These types of actions were difficult to prove and prohibitively expensive, and provided little protection from coercive tactics of debt collectors. Much of the negative stereotype of debt collectors lingers in spite of the fact that state and federal laws now limit the activities of collectors and provide remedies for consumers abused during the debt collection process. This chapter discusses the federal debt collection statute and some recent case law interpreting the statute, plus a brief review of some state laws regarding debt collection.

The Federal Act — Who Does It Cover?

The **Fair Debt Collection Practices Act** (15 U.S.C. section 1692 *et seq.*) was enacted in 1977 to prevent abuses against consumer debtors by collection agencies. (For text of this Act see Appendix 5.) At the time of enactment, Congress articulated three particular purposes for the Fair Debt Collection Practices Act (the Act):

1. to preserve the debtor's privacy and dignity;

2. to protect the debtor from improper coercive collection methods used by collection agencies; and

3. to establish a regulatory regime that did not disadvantage legitimate debt collectors.

Almost 20 years later, some significant cases have finally begun to establish the effectiveness of the Act as recourse for abused consumer debtors.

The federal Act applies only to the collection of **consumer debts**, those incurred by an individual primarily for personal, family or household purposes. Under the Act, a **debt collector** is any person, other than the creditor, who regularly collects debts owed to others. The original 1977 Act had a specific exemption for any attorney collecting a debt on behalf of a client. The presumption was that the Act was to focus primarily on the actions of collection agencies. However, under a 1986 amendment to the Act, the definition was broadened to include attorneys who collect debts on a regular basis. This was to some degree a reflection of the number of lawyers who were becoming more involved in debt collection, either within their private practices or within the business structure of their own collection agencies.

Questions soon arose as to how much of an attorney's activities would be covered by the provisions of the Act. There was immediate debate regarding whether the concept of "regularly engaged in collection activities" extended to attorneys who file consumer debt collection litigation on behalf of creditors. The staff of the Federal Trade Commission and some other trade groups argued that the Act applied to collection letters and phone calls of an attorney, but not to legal notices such as formal demand letters or other activities associated with collection related litigation.

In April of 1995, the U.S. Supreme Court unanimously held in *Heintz v. Jenkins*, 113 S.Ct. 1489 (1995), that all of the provisions of the Fair Debt Collection Practices Act apply to lawyers who regularly, *through litigation*, attempt to collect consumer debts. Heintz, an attorney, brought suit on behalf of a bank, seeking to recover the deficiency balance on an automobile loan after the car had been repossessed and sold. As part of an effort to settle the suit, Heintz sent a letter to the attorney for Plaintiff Darlene Jenkins listing the amounts owed, including $4,713.00 for insurance on the car, pursuant to the term of the note providing that the bank will purchase insurance should Jenkins fail to do so. Jenkins then brought suit against Heintz individually under the Act, because the bank's claim included a charge for *loan default* insurance, and not just the *property damage* insurance authorized by the loan documents. Jenkins claimed this was a false misrepresentation of the amount of the debt and an attempt to collect an amount not authorized by the agreement creating the debt, both specific violations of the Act.

The United States District Court dismissed Jenkins' suit for failure to state a claim, holding that the Act does not apply to lawyers engaging in litigation. The Court of Appeals reversed this judgment, interpreting the Act to apply to litigating attorneys. The Supreme Court agreed that the Act applied to the litigating activities of attorneys, citing what it called "two rather strong reasons." First, the Court stated that a lawyer who regularly tries to obtain payment of consumer debts through legal proceedings is engaged in activities that clearly fit within the plain English definition of "debt collector" as it appears in the Act. Second, the Court noted the 1986 repeal of the attorney exemption from the Act in its entirety, without "creating a narrower, litigation-related exemption to fill the void." (at 1491) The Court reasoned that Congress must have intended for lawyers to be subject to the Act whenever their activities fall under the "debt collector" definition.

The question that remains outstanding after *Heintz* is the extent to which an attorney must be involved in this type of case to be considered as "regularly" engaged in consumer debt collection activities. The Federal Trade Commission (the FTC) had previously issued the opinion that any person who collects debts only in "isolated instances" would be excluded from the Act, but in *Heintz,* the Supreme Court did not find any of the FTC's commentary to be binding. How many consumer debt cases must an attorney handle to move from "isolated instances" to "regularly engaged"? As this will clearly be a matter for case-by-case interpretation, the best and safest course of action is for all attorneys and paralegals to obey the provisions of the Act, whether handling one case or one thousand.

What Are the Provisions of the Act?

The Fair Debt Collection Practices Act is basically an act regarding the regulation of communications, both with the consumer debtor and with third parties when making inquiries about the consumer debtor. When it comes to **communicating with the debtor**, the Act prohibits the debt collector from engaging in a number of activities:

- The debt collector may not communicate with the debtor at any unusual time or place, or at any time or place known to be inconvenient. Absent knowledge to the contrary, there is a presumption that a convenient time frame is from 8:00 a.m. to 9:00 p.m. in the time zone of the consumer's location.

- The debt collector cannot communicate with the consumer at work if this is known to be prohibited by the consumer's employer.

- The debt collector may not communicate directly with a consumer known to be represented by an attorney, unless the attorney has failed to respond within a reasonable time or has given permission for direct contact with the debtor.

- The debt collector may not engage in "any conduct the natural consequence of which is to harass, oppress or abuse any person in connection with the collection of a debt." (Section 1692d) This includes the use or threat of violence, the use of obscene or profane language, the publication of a list of consumers who allegedly refuse to pay their debts, the advertisement for sale of any debt to coerce payment of the debt, annoying and abusive uses of continuous telephone calls, and placing calls without meaningful disclosure of the caller's identity.

- The debt collector may not use any false, deceptive, or misleading representations in connection with debt collection. This includes representing or implying that a person is an attorney or a government representative, implying that the debtor has committed a crime, threatening to take any action that cannot legally be taken or that is not intended to be taken, or communicating or threatening to communicate false credit information.

- The debt collector may not use unfair or unconscionable means to collect a debt, such as collecting any amount not authorized by the agreement creating a debt, communicating with a debtor by postcard, and using a business name or envelope that indicates the communication is from a debt collector.

The debt collector's initial communication with the consumer triggers the **validation of debt procedure** under the Act. Within five days of the initial communication:

- The collector must send a written notice to the consumer containing the amount of the debt, the name of the creditor, and a statement that unless the consumer disputes the validity of the debt within 30 days of receipt of the notice, the debt will be assumed to be valid by the debt collector.

- The notice must state that if the consumer notifies the debt collector in writing within 30 days that the debt is disputed, the collector will obtain verification of the debt and mail it to the debtor.

- A statement must be included notifying the consumer that, upon written request within the 30-day period, the name and address of the original creditor will be provided to the consumer, if it is different from the current creditor.

If a consumer debtor notifies a debt collector of refusal to pay a debt, or wishes the debt collector to cease further communications, the debt collector must cease further communications except to advise the consumer that collection efforts are being terminated, notify the consumer of remedies that may be invoked, or notify the consumer if the collector or creditor intends to invoke some specific remedy.

In addition to this validation process, it is important to note that the Act contains what current practice considers to be a consumer debtor "Miranda Warning." The Act states that it is false or misleading to fail to clearly disclose in *all communications* made to collect a debt or to obtain information about a consumer, that the debt collector is attempting to collect a debt and that any information obtained will be used for that purpose. Most practitioners interpret this to mean that language notifying the debtor of this fact must be in all letters and contained in all verbal contacts.

As for **communications with third parties** regarding the debt, the Act prohibits the debt collector from communicating about the debt with any person other than the consumer, the consumer's attorney, a credit reporting agency (if otherwise permitted by law), the creditor or creditor's attorney, or the debt collector's attorney, unless the debtor has given prior consent in writing. There are certain exceptions where third-party communications are allowed for the purpose of gathering information about the debtor. For example, the debt collector may contact telephone companies, but only for the purpose of obtaining "location information" such as address, phone number or place of employment. During this contact, the debt collector identifies the employer only where expressly requested, and may not state to the third party that the consumer owes a debt.

What Are the Penalties?

A debt collector who violates the Act is liable for actual damages, additional damages up to $1,000 ($500,000 for class actions), plus attorneys fees and court costs. As for whether the Act has proved to be effective in protecting consumers, a large base of case law is developing, especially regarding what constitutes a "deceptive" statement under the Act. Of hundreds of cases involving deceptive statements in collection letters, nearly all have decisions favorable to the consumer advancing the claim. See National Consumer Law Center, Fair Debt Collection Appx. H.2.4. (Boston: NCLC 1991 and Supp.). Collection agencies and their trade organizations have already begun to monitor activity under the Act, and to try to assure that member agencies comply with all provisions of the Act.

State Debt Collection Acts

A debt collector must assure compliance with the appropriate statutes in all states in which collection activity takes place. Many state acts contain more detailed requirements for collection agencies, including statutory schemes for registration or certification. State acts also vary in their applicability to commercial and consumer transactions, as well as inclusion and exclusion of attorneys. All of the state acts bear the similarity of prohibiting certain abusive and coercive tactics in the collection of debts, as well as many of the same types of misrepresentations prohibited by the federal Act. (See Appendix 6 for text of the following Acts.)

California Debt Collection Act

The Robbins-Rosenthal Fair Debt Collection Practices Act is found under Title 1.60C, Section 1788 *et seq.* (the California Act). One unique aspect of the California Act is that it lists not only the purpose of prohibiting unfair and deceptive practices by creditors, but also requires debtors to "act fairly in entering into and honoring such debts." Section 1788(b). Other features of the California Act:

- Applies to consumer debts only.

- Specifically excludes attorneys from definition of "debt collector."

- Contains very specific "laundry lists" of prohibited activities related to threats, phone calls, communications with employers or family members, misrepresentations, and collection costs.

- Provides a misdemeanor criminal penalty in instances of use by a debt collector, creditor, or an attorney of any communication that simulates legal or judicial process.

- Prohibits debtors from applying for credit when lacking the ability or intent to pay the obligation, and from using a credit card after it has been terminated.

- Limits liability to individual actions (no class actions), actual damages, and additional liability as a penalty only in cases of willful and knowing violations, not to exceed $1,000.

Texas Debt Collection Act

The Texas Debt Collection Act (Texas Revised Civil Statutes, Article 5069-11.01 *et seq.*) was enacted in 1973 to regulate the practices of debt collectors in Texas, almost five years before enactment of the federal Act. The definitions are broad – debt collector includes any person engaging directly or indirectly in debt collection. A straightforward list of forbidden acts expressly prohibits use of violence, threats or coercion; use of profane or obscene language; harassing or abusive conduct; and engaging in fraudulent, deceptive or misleading representations in attempting to collect debts.

Debt collectors that violate the Texas Act are subject to civil penalties
that may include liability for actual damages, attorney's fees and costs,
and a court-issued injunction. A unique facet of the Texas Act is that a
violation is also considered a "deceptive trade practice" governed by
the Texas Deceptive Trade Practices Act (Tex. Bus. & C. Code Section
17.41 *et seq.*) and therefore gives rise to treble damages in addition to
the actual damages. In addition, the Attorney General of Texas may
seek to restrain or enjoin any person believed to be in violation of the
Texas Act. Texas law also provides that violators are guilty of a
misdemeanor, punishable by a fine from $100 to $500 for each
violation.

Florida Debt Collection Acts

The Florida statutes relating to debt collection provide an interesting
contrast to the California and Texas acts. The Florida legislature
addresses both commercial and consumer collections, and utilizes the
tools of registration and regulation in conjunction with the more
traditional "laundry list" of prohibited acts. Commercial interests are
protected under Florida Statutes Section 559.541 *et seq.*, which
requires agencies engaging in commercial collections to register with
the Department of Banking and Finance, and to post a bond. Failure to
do so may impose a criminal penalty ranging from second degree
misdemeanor to third degree felony.

Consumer protection under Florida Statutes Section 559.55 *et seq*
includes a requirement of registration of collection agencies engaged in
collection of consumer debt (but excludes original creditors, members
of the Florida Bar, financial institutions, licensed real estate brokers,
and consumer finance companies from registration). In addition to a
relatively typical listing of prohibited actions, the Florida statute also
requires a thirty day notice to a consumer if the right to bill and collect
a debt is assigned to a third party. A detailed administrative process is
also outlined, by which the Division of Consumer Services receives,
classifies, and identifies complaints from consumers, and forwards the
complaints to the Department of Banking and Finance for investigation.
The Department issues warnings, reprimands, and suspensions or
revocations of registration as appropriate. In addition to this rather
stringent regulatory scheme, the individual consumer may still bring a

civil action for actual damages, and grants the court discretion to award punitive damages as it sees fit.

The variance between the state acts sends a clear warning to all engaged in debt collection. It is not enough to be well-versed in the provisions of the federal Act. Check the statutes and regulations in each state where collection activity will take place, in order to avoid potential liabilities.

Self-Help Repossession

Earlier you were introduced to the concept of a security interest in collateral, granted in order to secure payment or performance of an obligation. The secured creditor may engage in all of the collection activities described up to this point and, if unsuccessful, decide it is time to obtain possession of the collateral in order to satisfy the debt. Article 9 of the UCC authorizes a secured creditor to repossess collateral without resort to the judicial process. This action, generally referred to as **"self-help" repossession**, is available after a debtor has defaulted under a security agreement as long as the creditor does not **"breach the peace."** UCC Section 9.503.

Default is the only prerequisite to repossession, so the creditor is not required to give the debtor any notice of intent to repossess the collateral. Default is usually established by the debtor's nonpayment under the terms of the agreement, but in some instances may not be so apparent. For example, if the creditor has previously given the debtor extensions of time or has been actively engaged in negotiations with the debtor, the creditor must be careful not to repossess collateral prior to the expiration of any extension agreements. The UCC also grants the right to repossess collateral upon default "unless otherwise agreed." A creditor planning to repossess collateral should carefully review all loan and security documents to confirm that there are no contractual limitations or restrictions on the right to repossess the collateral.

Self-help does not involve state action, so the 14th Amendment to the federal constitution ("no state shall deprive any person of life, liberty or property without due process of law"), does not restrain self help repossession. There is no need for lawyers, courts, or judges. The only restriction is the UCC requirement that the creditor seize the collateral without breach of the peace. What constitutes a **"breach of the peace"** is not defined by the UCC and, therefore, is a question of fact that turns on the circumstances of each case. There is a large body of case law from which to extract certain general principles, especially related to automobile repossession.

As a general rule, there is no breach of peace where repossession is accomplished without the use of force or the threat of force. Third parties in possession of a debtor's vehicle may allow the property to be repossessed, and there is no breach of the peace. Seizure of vehicles with keys left in them, or through use of duplicate keys, is acceptable. Repossession of automobiles from driveways or public streets has been widely upheld as lawful. This also includes removal of cars from apartment parking lots and parking lots at the debtor's place of employment. Courts have also held that an automobile may be repossessed from any place accessible to the public. For example, a creditor may repossess a car from the debtor's open garage, driveway, or an unenclosed carport. However, a creditor cannot break the lock on a garage door or even open a closed garage in attempting to repossess an automobile.

Although confrontation in and of itself may not constitute a breach of the peace, it is likely to invite a breach. Creditors have been held liable where the creditor seized the door of the car and refused to let go, where the debtor was abducted along with the automobile, where the creditor forced the debtor off the road, engaged in physical contact with the debtor, or used a dangerous weapon. Violating any criminal laws during the course of repossession, such as trespass, assault and battery is considered wrongful. Even though the presence of a law enforcement official would appear to reduce the threat of violence during a repossession, the use of state authority is always considered a breach of peace. Courts react negatively to the presence of public officials at a private seizure of property because of the appearance that the force of law is behind this self-help remedy.

The use of subterfuge or trickery is more questionable. The use of stealth has been upheld in some circumstances, such as where the creditor persuades the debtor to turn over the car under the pretext of a test drive. However, trickery that involves misrepresentations, such as in statements about identity or motive, may not only constitute breach of the peace but violate some state debt collection acts.

Once the car has been repossessed, the creditor resells the car in a public or private sale. Any sale must be conducted in a "commercially reasonable manner." This does not mean the creditor must get the highest possible price, but that the sale should be held according to standard custom in a particular business or in an established market. The difference between the accelerated balance of the automobile loan and the amount received at the sale is the "deficiency balance." This is the amount of money, plus any expenses of repossession, that constitutes the damages in the suit filed by the creditor against the debtor.

Breach of the peace during repossession subjects a creditor to tort liability for **wrongful repossession**. The debtor is generally entitled to actual damages, measured by the debtor's equity in the collateral, and punitive damages in appropriate circumstances. A creditor can always choose to avoid the risk of breaching the peace by filing a lawsuit and seeking a judicial remedy. Although there are some potential liabilities associated with judicial remedies, they are less problematic than those associated with self-help. In difficult or risky situations, the use of judicial remedies may be the most effective course of action.

EXERCISE

Assume that you are a collector, trying to collect a debt from a consumer. Write a "talk track" for your first telephone conversation with the debtor. Make sure that your questions and comments are in compliance with both the federal Act, plus any acts of your state. Now it's time to play the part of the debtor. Go back through your script, and create as many potential responses as you can from a difficult debtor. Does this change your questions? Do all those tough responses make it harder to comply with the Act?

Chapter Four

PREJUDGMENT REMEDIES

Prejudgment Remedies

Creditors who cannot negotiate voluntary payment from the debtor face the prospect of a litigation process that is often too slow and too costly for their purposes. The probability of prevailing in the lawsuit may be high, but the reality is that the debtor may not have the funds or assets left to satisfy the judgment by the time judgment is obtained. The only answer for the creditor is to use one of the processes that allows seizure of the property of the debtor after suit is filed, but prior to final judgment. Do not mistake the existence of these remedies as an arsenal of weapons ready to be launched at the debtor without restriction. Numerous procedural safeguards exist for protecting the interests of the debtor.

The Concept of Procedural Due Process

The 14th Amendment to the United States Constitution provides that no "state shall deprive any person of life, liberty, or property without due process of law." Any creditor's remedy that involves state action (i.e., the instigation of litigation), is required to meet certain procedural safeguards, in order to avoid wrongful seizure of a debtor's property. These safeguards have not always been outlined and defined to the extent found in current case law and statutes. Beginning in the late 1960s, courts and legislatures began to scrutinize prejudgment remedies utilized by creditors to remove property from debtors.

In *Sniadach v. Family Finance Corp.*, 395 U.S. 337, 89 S. Ct. 1820 (1969) the Supreme Court found the Wisconsin statute providing for prejudgment garnishment of wages unconstitutional. The Wisconsin procedure, which was virtually identical to the garnishment laws of almost all other states at the time, allowed a creditor to freeze a debtor's bank account at the inception of a suit to collect a debt. The debtor received no prior notice, had no opportunity for a hearing before the account was frozen, and lost the use of the funds unless a bond was posted, guaranteeing payment of the judgment. Although this procedure had withstood prior constitutional attacks, the Court held that the procedure violated "the fundamental principles of due process." Justice William O. Douglas emphasized the hardship that resulted from wage garnishment, and suggested that notice and a hearing were required, except in "extraordinary situations."

The due process rights first recognized in *Sniadach* relative to wage garnishment were extended to property other than wages in *Fuentes v. Shevin,* 407 U.S. 67, 92 S. Ct. 1983 (1972). *Fuentes* involved the prejudgment replevin of consumer goods,[1] and reiterated the requirement for notice to the debtor and an opportunity to be heard absent "extraordinary situations." But what circumstances are considered "extraordinary" by the Supreme Court? In *Sniadach,* the Court mentioned circumstances "requiring special protection to a state or *creditor* interest," leaving the implication that there were some circumstances where protection of a creditor's interests could be balanced against due process requirements. *Fuentes* did nothing to explain or expand this concept of "extraordinary situations."

In *Mitchell v. W.T. Grant Co.,* 416 U.S. 600, 94 S. Ct. 1895 (1974), a creditor sued in Louisiana to collect the purchase price of property sold to the debtor. The creditor also had a lien on the property, and sought issuance of a writ of sequestration (a type of replevin). In asking for the writ, the creditor alleged reason to believe that the debtor would dispose of the goods during the pendency of the lawsuit if the writ was not granted. The Court in *Mitchell* held that a creditor with a preexisting interest in the property to be seized and reason to believe the property is threatened if the debtor continues in possession is entitled to seize the property without prior notice and hearing. However, the Louisiana statute that was upheld as constitutional by the Court in *Mitchell* contained procedural safeguards that were absent in the statutes examined in *Fuentes.* The Louisiana statute required the creditor to allege specific facts supporting its claim, rather than conclusory allegations. Further, the statute gave the debtor the right to an immediate post-seizure hearing.

---

[1] This prejudgment remedy is described in more detail on page 41.

The *Mitchell* decision provided an example of the "extraordinary situation" that was previously undefined, but the Court also created confusion about the basic constitutional questions. Had *Sniadach* and *Fuentes* been overruled? Does *Mitchell* apply only where the creditor has an interest in the property being seized? Some answers were provided in *North Georgia Finishing, Inc. v. Di-Chem, Inc.*, 419 U.S. 601, 95 S. Ct. 719 (1975). The Supreme Court declared Georgia's prejudgment garnishment statute unconstitutional, but suggested it would have been acceptable if adequate procedural safeguards had been present to protect the debtor's interests. This was a significant ruling, because the creditor had no preexisting interest in the property that was seized by the creditor.

The decisions in these landmark cases regarding procedural due process have generated much scholarly debate. State legislatures have revised and updated many statutes in an attempt to ensure that their statutes conform to the constitutional interpretations suggested by the Supreme Court. Prejudgment garnishment of wages has been eliminated or restricted by most states. After *Mitchell* and *North Georgia*, it is safe to presume that the following provisions apply to prejudgment remedies:

- The 14th Amendment limits seizure of property from debtors without "due process," since the enforcement of the remedy involves state action.

- In most situations where a creditor exercises a prejudgment remedy, due process requires that a debtor be given adequate notice and an opportunity for a hearing before a judge prior to seizure of debtor's property.

- A pre-seizure notice and hearing are not necessary when the creditor has a preexisting interest in the property to be seized and there are facts to suggest that the debtor might dispose of or harm the property.

- Prior notice and hearing are not required of a prejudgment remedy even if the creditor has no interest in the property, if there is a belief substantiated by facts that the debtor might destroy, injure or dispose of property that could be used to satisfy a creditor's judgment.

As with all constitutional issues, the application of prejudgment remedies is always a balancing act. Any state statute contains procedures that are designed to balance the conflicting interests between the debtor's right to continued possession of the property and the creditors interest in immediate seizure of the property. Strict adherence to the procedures outlined in applicable jurisdictions protects creditors from the liabilities that may ensue due to a wrongful seizure of a debtor's property.

Purpose of Prejudgment Remedies

The wheels of justice turn slowly. Collecting a claim through the judicial process is often time consuming, and there is no guarantee that the debtor will still have property sufficient to satisfy a judgment by the time it is obtained. The purpose of formal prejudgment remedies is to allow a creditor to exert some type of control, or freeze, on the debtor's assets until final judgment is rendered. This protects the creditor from debtors who may destroy, move, conceal or dispose of assets while litigation is pending. As previously explained, these prejudgment remedies follow specific statutory processes designed to adequately preserve the constitutional rights of debtors while balancing the creditor's need to protect its ability to satisfy a judgment.

Attachment

Attachment is the seizure of the debtor's property by a sheriff or constable in order to secure payment of a creditor's claim after a judgment is obtained. Historically, the prime use of attachment in the common law was to force the appearance of a defendant who had failed to respond to the initial summons. The writ of attachment commanded the sheriff to attach the property of debtors to compel their appearance. If the debtor appeared, the court exerted its jurisdiction, and the property was returned. If the debtor failed to appear, the property was forfeited. In the 17th century, this process changed so that the debtor might appear, but the property was held to satisfy the judgment. The remedy changed from a means to compel the appearance of the debtor to a powerful collection tool for creditors.

Attachment is now a purely statutory remedy, subject to the protections of due process. Because this remedy provides for seizure of any **nonexempt property** of the debtor, it is not generally available in every kind of action. Under the broadest state statutes, attachment is available for actions involving the recovery of money, including both tort and contract actions. For example, the statutes of the state of New York allow attachment:

> "... in any action, except a matrimonial action, where the plaintiff has demanded and would be entitled, in whole or in part, or in the alternative, to a money judgment against one or more defendants..." N.Y. Attachment, New York CPLR, Article 62, Section 6201.

More restrictive statutes, such as that of the State of California, limit attachment to liquidated contract claims only, with the rationale that the total amount of the claim is a fixed or readily ascertainable amount.(Code of Civil Procedure, State of California, Title 6.5, Attachment, Section 483.010).

Further limitations on the use of attachment are not uncommon. In addition to restricting the type of case, most states also confine the remedy to a list of particular circumstances, known as **grounds for attachment.**

Typical grounds for attachment as listed in the Texas statute, for example, are that the defendant:

- Is not a resident of Texas;

- Is about to move from Texas permanently, and has refused to pay or secure the debt to the plaintiff;

- Is in hiding;

- Has hidden or is about to hide the property;

- Is about to remove the property from Texas without leaving an amount sufficient to pay the defendant's debts;

- Is about to remove all or part of the property from the county in which the suit is brought with the intent to defraud the creditors;

- Has disposed of or is about to dispose of all or part of the property with the intent to defraud the creditors;

- Is about to convert all or part of the property into money for the purpose of placing it beyond the reach of the creditors; or

- Owes the plaintiff for property obtained by the defendant under false pretenses.

Tex. Civ. Prac. & Rem. Code Section 61.002.

Although attachment procedures vary from state to state, certain basic steps are required in each **attachment process**:

The underlying litigation must commence. A plaintiff can invoke the attachment process from the initial filing of the lawsuit, or make a separate application at any time during the pendency of the suit. The underlying suit must also be of a type where attachment is an available remedy.

An affidavit is required. The plaintiff files a motion or application for issuance of a writ of attachment, but it must be supported by affidavits that document the specific grounds justifying the remedy. It is not adequate for a plaintiff to merely allege the grounds for attachment. The sworn affidavit must state specific facts that give rise to one or more of the grounds that support attachment.

A bond is required. The creditor must post a bond indemnifying the debtor for damages due to wrongful attachment. This bond is typically twice the amount of the plaintiff's claim or double the value of the property being attached. If the defendant prevails in the underlying action or the attachment is found to be wrongful, the plaintiff is required to pay damages and costs not exceeding the amount of the bond.

The writ is issued by the court. The application, affidavits and bond are submitted to the court. Since *Sniadach* and its progeny, most states require some sort of hearing before a judge, even if it is *ex parte* (a hearing or meeting with the judge in which only one party is represented). About half of the states require notice and an opportunity for a hearing prior to issuance of an attachment. Others allow the judge to issue the writ *ex parte* where "irreparable harm" or some other required statutory plateau is met. No state will issue a writ based solely on the ministerial actions of a clerk, without a hearing before a judge. Remember, attachment is perceived as a harsh remedy. Study the applicable state statute closely, because the principles of strict construction will always apply.

The writ is delivered and the property is seized. The writ is delivered to the sheriff, constable, or other equivalent official. The sheriff takes control of, or "levies," on the available personal property of the debtor. If no personal property subject to execution is located, the sheriff returns the writ *"nulla bona"* or "no good."[2] Personal property seized by a sheriff is typically inventoried and listed on the return, then held until resolution of the lawsuit.

Protections for the Debtor

The debtor has several potential responses to attachment. First, a hearing can be requested to challenge either the availability of the attachment remedy overall, or the violation of any specific procedure in the statute. Second, every state allows a debtor to regain possession of the seized property by filing a bond, usually either in the amount pled for in the lawsuit, or an estimated value of the seized property. Finally, if the debt collection action ends with a judgment for the defendant, the debtor can recover the attached property, costs associated with the

---

[2] I always recommend that an attorney or paralegal familiar with a case either discuss the property to be seized with the sheriff prior to levy, or actually go with the sheriff. It is foolish to spend your client's money and time on an attachment unless you know exactly what property you are attempting to seize. You know what you are looking for – help the sheriff find it for you.

attachment, and any damages suffered because of the action. In many jurisdictions, punitive damages can be recovered if the creditor's actions are found to be malicious or grossly negligent.

Pros and Cons of Attachment

When any legal remedy is contemplated, clients must be informed of both the positive and negative aspects of pursuing the proposed course of conduct. For a creditor, prejudgment attachment has the following advantages:

- During the pendency of the lawsuit, the debtor cannot sell or otherwise dispose of the property.

- The attachment lien is effective against subsequent purchasers of the property, should the debtor attempt to sell property seized in an attachment.

- Most states have priority rules of distribution of assets between creditors, as opposed to the pro rata distribution used in the Bankruptcy Code. Most of the rules of lien priority are "first in time" rules, such that an attachment lien will entitle the creditor to a lien on the property that is superior to judgment liens obtained by other creditors at a later date.

- The threat of removal of property that is crucial to the debtor's business creates excellent opportunity to negotiate and settle from a position of relative strength over the debtor.

In spite of what may appear to be some excellent advantages, attachment is far from being a trouble-free remedy. Attachment is an expensive remedy for clients to pursue. It requires strict adherence to procedure, which means research of the statute and careful drafting of documents, including specific affidavits. In addition, due process dictates the involvement of a judge or magistrate in some type of hearing. The involvement and supervision of an experienced attorney will be necessary at every stage. There will be bonds to post, expenses of the sheriff to pay, storage costs for the property, etc. Even the decision to begin a prejudgment procedure requires extensive research into the type, value and location of personal property subject to seizure, often in the hands of a recalcitrant debtor who is making every effort possible to stop discovery of the existence of the property. Then there is always the potential liability for wrongful attachment, described earlier. The client may expend the time and money for an attachment, and be foiled immediately by the surprise bankruptcy filing of the debtor, or other creditors may elect an involuntary bankruptcy proceeding before any benefit can inure to the client.

Prejudgment Replevin

Replevin (also known as "sequestration" and "claim and delivery") is a remedy employed to recover possession of any personal property to which the creditor has title or a right to possession. The procedures are very similar to attachment, except that replevin is not quite as restrictive in its procedural requirements. This is because the party initiating the replevin action is seeking possession of property in which it has an interest. Replevin is the prejudgment remedy for secured creditors seeking return of collateral, usually after self-help remedies have failed. Replevin is also frequently used by parties who lease or rent property that is being wrongfully held in violation or after breach of a lease agreement. Because unsecured creditors do not have an interest in specific property of the debtor, they must resort to attachment as a prejudgment remedy.

Replevin compares to attachment in the following ways:

- The plaintiff in the underlying lawsuit must be seeking possession of personal property in which the plaintiff has an interest. This means that the property and the right to possession must be the subject of the lawsuit.

- The plaintiff in a replevin action typically must show by affidavit the nature of the interest in the property, a description of the property, its value and location, and the reason plaintiff is entitled to immediate possession of the property. [3]

- As with attachment, states are split regarding allowance of replevin of property without notice and an opportunity to be heard. In the states that allow *ex parte* seizure, the statutes typically require a showing that there is immediate danger of harm to, or loss of, the property in question. The standards are not as stringent as with attachment, which involves a debtor and creditor who both have an interest in the property.

- The plaintiff must post a bond and the defendant is given an opportunity to recover the property by posting its own bond.

- If the court authorizes the writ of replevin, the sheriff seizes the property and delivers it directly into the possession of the creditor. As custodian of the property, the creditor is obligated to protect and preserve it until the final judgment determines the rights of the parties relative to the property.

- The creditor must ultimately obtain judgment in the underlying lawsuit. If the plaintiff does not prevail, the property is restored to the debtor, who is entitled to damages and costs.

As stated previously, the typical replevin action is initiated by a secured creditor. The previous chapter discussed the methods available to obtain return of collateral without resort to judicial means, as long as there is no "breach of peace." What if this "self-help" remedy fails? For example, a seller of manufacturing equipment sells a widget machine to The Widget King, Inc. (TWK). All methods of collection have been attempted, but TWK still refuses to pay. The seller attempts repossession of the widget machine, but employees of TWK refuse to allow the movers onto the premises to remove the equipment, and the situation almost becomes hostile. The seller is afraid that the equipment will be damaged if it is not recovered. It requires continuous

---

[3] As a prerequisite to prejudgment replevin, some states may require proof that demand was made to relinquish the property, and that the defendant failed to comply.

maintenance by trained technicians, and the brief foray into TWK's premises confirms the seller's fear that the unit is not being properly serviced. What can the seller do now?

First, the seller files suit against TWK, seeking both payment of the sums owed under the contract and recovery of the widget machine. The seller also presents a motion requesting replevin, supported by an affidavit stating the nature of its interest in the property (in this case, a security interest granted in the machine, in writing, at the time it was financed by the seller), a description of the property, and the reason seller is entitled to possession of the property. It is important to check the appropriate state statute, as further sworn proof may be required. Assuming seller is in a state that requires a showing of immediate harm to the property if it is not recovered, an affidavit can be prepared that outlines the service requirements on this equipment, and expressing facts leading to the conclusion that maintenance is not being performed. The attorney for the seller presents the motion and affidavit to the judge, and, if the proof is adequate and the statutory requirements are all met, a writ will be issued to the sheriff or constable. This time, the sheriff will make the trip to The Widget King with the writ in hand, and the employees will have to release the widget machine, or face the possibility of a contempt proceeding!

Garnishment

Garnishment is a collection remedy directed toward property of the debtor that is in the hands of a third party. Instead of paying money owed to the debtor or transferring property to the debtor, the third party (known as the garnishee) is required to hold the property pending outcome of the lawsuit, or in some instances to turn the property over to the creditor.

In many states, prejudgment garnishment is incorporated within the attachment procedure, with the rules adjusted to protect the interests of the third party. In other states, garnishment is treated as a second action, with the garnishing creditor as plaintiff and the third-party garnishee as defendant. Garnishment is also a postjudgment remedy, but with fewer procedural steps. Judgment has been obtained, so due process of law has been satisfied.

The third party served with a notice of garnishment must answer the writ in one of the following ways:

- The garnishee acknowledges that it has property of the debtor, or in which the debtor has some interest. The garnishee lists the property, and either "freezes" the debtor's access to the property, or tenders the property to the creditor.

- The garnishee denies that it has property of the debtor, or indicates that it had property of the debtor, but that the property was delivered to the debtor prior to service of the writ.

- The garnishee states that it has property of the debtor, but claims a superior interest in the property to that of the creditor bringing the action, such as a prior lien on the property.

There are two common instances where money belonging to a debtor is in the hands of third parties:

1. money on deposit with banking institutions; and
2. unpaid wages in the hands of employers.

Money on deposit with banks is frequently a target of garnishment actions, and employees and counsel for banking institutions are accustomed to garnishment procedures.[4] Wages are viewed as essential to a debtor's survival, and garnishment of wages is restricted to varying degrees and in a number of ways. Some states do not allow prejudgment garnishment of wages, but will allow postjudgment garnishment. Other states, such as Texas, will only allow garnishment

---

[4] An excellent garnishment story came to me from the Law Offices of Muller, Muller, Richmond, Harms, Myers & Sgroi, servicing the State of Michigan. The firm thought it had good bank account information on a debtor, and were eager to freeze the account with a postjudgment garnishment. The bank sent back its written garnishment disclosure indicating the account was open, but contained no funds. The debtor received the same disclosure in the mail, ran to the bank, and demanded an audit of his account, insisting that he had money on deposit and the bank must have made a mistake. The bank discovered its error, promptly filed an amended disclosure, and impounded the funds. The debtor had unwittingly helped the plaintiff collect against him!

of wages for the payment of child support. California allows garnishment of wages both pre-and postjudgment. Even where wage garnishment is allowed, the portion of an individual's wages that can be garnished is limited by the Consumer Credit Protection Act, 15 U.S.C. Section 1671 *et seq*. Under the Federal Wage Garnishment Law, the amount of pay subject to garnishment is based on an employee's disposable earnings – the amount left after all legally required deductions. The amount garnished may not exceed the lesser of:

- 25% of the disposable earnings; or

- the amount by which an employee's disposable earnings are greater than 30 times the federal minimum wage.

If a state wage garnishment law differs from the federal law, the law resulting in the smaller garnishment must be observed.

EXERCISE

Your client is owed a large sum of money by Fastandloose Corporation, and all efforts to collect have been ignored. Here is the information you currently have:

- The local newspaper reports that Fastandloose sold half of their assets to a company in New Jersey.

- Your client says that he heard from a friend that the principal of Fastandloose transferred assets of the company to an uncle.

- Your client sold Fastandloose a large piece of equipment, and has a security interest in that unit. The bills are unpaid.

- Fastandloose wrote a check on its account at First National Bank, but it bounced. You have the bank address and the account number.

Analyze the various prejudgment remedies. Which ones are available to your client? What are the risks you may encounter? What other information from your client would help reduce these risks?

POSTJUDGMENT COLLECTION

Obtaining a Judgment

The prejudgment remedies considered in the previous chapter are effective in limited instances. The debtor may be pressured into payment or settlement, or property may be seized to guarantee payment after judgment. The typical action for collection of a debt is not going to use these extreme and sometimes expensive measures. Instead, the desire is to obtain a judgment as quickly and economically as possible. When deciding whether to sue a debtor, the creditor must consider a number of factors:

- Is the underlying debt large enough to justify the time and expense of litigation?

- Will there be property of the debtor sufficient to satisfy the judgment if one is obtained?

- Are there any valid defenses or potential counterclaims? Have you found all of the skeletons that your client may be keeping in the closet?

- Do you have the appropriate documentation and witnesses readily available to prove the claim?

- What is the standing of your debtor in the business community? Will filing suit have a negative impact on other business relationships?

- What is the likelihood of prevailing if the case must go to trial? Does the relative size of the client as compared to the debtor make a sympathetic "David versus Goliath" scenario for the debtor to play out before a jury?

Even if a creditor knows that a debtor is unable to pay a judgment, it may be prudent to proceed. The judgment establishes priority over other creditors, and can be recorded in the event that the debtor ultimately has property subject to execution. There are also many debtors who like to try to "wait out" the collection process. These debtors hope that the creditor will decide that their case is not worth the time and energy and, once suit is filed, will negotiate some form of payment.

Another frequent result after a creditor files a collection suit is entry of a **default judgment.** A creditor is entitled to a default judgment if, after the debtor is properly served, the debtor fails to file an answer or otherwise make an appearance in the lawsuit. After waiting the requisite period of time, the creditor typically files a certificate of last known address of the debtor, presents the court with a proposed default judgment, and proves attorney's fees as required, either through affidavit or live testimony.

Even after the debtor makes an appearance in a lawsuit, the creditor can attempt to expedite the process through use of **summary judgment.** The court will dispose of a matter by summary judgment if affidavits and arguments presented establish that there is no genuine issue of material fact, and that the plaintiff is entitled to judgment as a matter of law. Since collection suits usually involve liquidated debts, it is often easy to meet the standard of proof for summary judgment through affidavits of records custodians, authenticating the business records underlying the account, showing the amount due, and subtracting any payments, offsets or credits. The court can also grant a partial summary judgment, leaving contested issues for trial before the judge or jury.

An attempt at summary judgment will at least focus attention on the disputed issues, and this will make the discovery process less time-consuming than in other types of litigation. However, it is important to remember throughout the pretrial and discovery process that the ultimate purpose of litigating a collection case is to put money in the client's pockets. The creditor should include interrogatories and requests for production that focus on the property of the debtor as well

Get Home Equity loan, pay off Cards
Deduction on income tax
Deduct House taxes on income tax
Chapter 5: Postjudgment Remedies *Deduct intrest on House loan* 49

as on the disputed issues. Interrogatories should request information on
specific types of property, for example:

- Do you own any automobiles? If so, describe each automobile
  by year, make and model, and give an estimate of the fair
  market value of each.

- Do you own a boat or boats? If so, describe each boat by year,
  make and model, and give an estimate of the fair market value
  of each.

The questions can continue in this manner for every feasible type
property, with particular emphasis on things of value, such as furs,
guns, collections of any type, etc. When the judgment is ultimately
obtained, it is best to be prepared to take immediate steps to collect
from the debtor, and a preliminary knowledge of the property available
is the best preparation.

Exempt Assets

Not all of a debtor's assets are available to creditors through the
judicial process. Certain assets are beyond the reach of creditors. State
laws and the Bankruptcy Code recognize these property exemptions.
The purpose of personal property exemptions is to protect some of an
individual debtor's property so that seizure by creditors does not leave
the debtor destitute. State statutes and constitutions vary widely and
usually have some historical basis for the type or amount of personal
property that is exempt.

Personal property exemptions can be categorized by type of property
(furniture, tools of trade, etc.), value of property, or types of property
with an overall value limit. Most states also address certain particular
types of property, such as insurance policies, retirement funds, and
current wages.

Almost all states provide a **homestead exemption** for real property,
with the purpose of protecting the family home from seizure by
creditors. Homestead laws protect real property only and are,
therefore, not applicable to renters or apartment dwellers. The state

homestead statutes may require residence in the home, or may have limits as to the value of the property. The more liberal statutes may have limitations on the size of the property, but no cap as to value. In a few states, a formal declaration of property as a homestead is required before it can be classified as exempt.

Mortgages and security interests are not affected by personal or homestead exemptions. A financing institution that loans money for the purchase of a home or an automobile is able to repossess or foreclose when payments become delinquent, even where these types of property are exempt. The federal tax lien, that most powerful of collection tools, reaches beyond all exemption statutes. Exempt personal property and homesteads can be levied upon to satisfy unpaid taxes. Some states may also have particular situations (taxes, child support, etc.), where exempt property is available for satisfaction of these debts.

The Bankruptcy Code has its own property exemptions, but states are allowed to either require their own exemption scheme, or let the debtor choose between the federal exemptions and those of their own state. For example, Article 10-A, Section 282 of New York Debtor and Creditor Law, states that an individual debtor filing bankruptcy in New York may exempt only the property excluded from collection of money judgments against the debtor, plus certain other listed property. (See Appendix 7-1 for the New York exemption lists.) The federal property exemption list is therefore not available to debtors filing bankruptcy in New York. The majority of states require their own exemption schemes. However, Texas allows bankrupt debtors to select either the Texas property exemptions (see Texas exemptions in Appendix 7-2) or the federal list. The Texas debtor can choose the exemption scheme most favorable in a personal bankruptcy, which is almost without exception the extensive property exemptions found in the Texas Property Code.

The federal property exemptions, listed in the Bankruptcy Code under Section 522(d), are as follows:

- The debtor's aggregate interest in real property or personal property that the debtor or a dependent of the debtor uses as a residence, in a cooperative, or in a burial plot, not to exceed $15,000 in value.

- The debtor's interest in one motor vehicle, not to exceed $2,400.

- The debtor's interest in household furnishings, household goods, wearing apparel, appliances, books, animals, crops, or musical instruments that are primarily for personal, family or household use, not to exceed $400 in value for any one particular item or $8,000 in total aggregate value.

- The debtor's interest in jewelry held for personal, family or household use, not to exceed $1,000 in value.

- The debtor's interest in any property, not to exceed in value $800, plus up to $7,500 of any unused amount of the first listed exemption (a sort of makeup call for debtors who do not own their place of residence, so that they can claim any other personal property as exempt).

- The debtor's interest in any implements, professional books, or tools of the trade of the debtor, not to exceed $1,500.

- Any unmatured life insurance contract owned by the debtor, other than a credit life insurance policy.

- The debtor's interest in any accrued dividend, interest under, or loan value of unmatured life insurance contract owned by the debtor under which the insured is the debtor, not to exceed $8,000 in value.

- Professionally prescribed health aids for the debtor or a dependent of the debtor.

- The debtor's right to receive Social Security, unemployment compensation, local public assistance, veterans' benefits, disability benefits, alimony, child support, or payments from various types of pension plans.

- The debtor's right to receive, or property traceable to, an award under a crime victim's reparation law, a payment on account of wrongful death, payment under a life insurance policy, payment on account of personal bodily injury (not to exceed $15,000), or a payment in compensation for loss of future earnings of the debtor.

For comparison, see the California property exemptions, listed in Appendix 7-3. The federal and California exemption schemes have only minor differences, such that it is realistic for a bankrupt debtor in California to actually contrast the two lists, and select the more favorable exemptions.

Also see Florida exemption list in Appendix 7-4.

Collecting a Judgment

When the creditor obtains a judgment and the debtor still refuses to pay, the creditor may now turn to the state to enforce its judgment against the nonexempt property of the debtor. In most states, a judgment is statutorily endorsed with lien status, either automatically or after certain formal acts have been performed. This **judgment lien** is a general lien only, not a specific lien on any of the debtor's property. With this general lien in place, the judgment creditor can take the appropriate actions that attach the lien to specific property. For real property, the lien ordinarily attaches when it is docketed or otherwise indexed or recorded in the deed records where the debtor's property is located. The enforcement of a judgment lien against personal property is typically accomplished through execution or levy, where a writ is requested instructing the sheriff or constable to physically seize the nonexempt property of the debtor, sell the property, and give the proceeds to the creditor for satisfaction of the judgment.

Judgments do not exist in perpetuity. After a period of years, judgments expire or become unenforceable. Ten years is a typical period of time found in state statutes for judgments to continue to be enforceable. Some states allow an application to be made during this time frame that will continue the life of the judgment for another statutory period. There are also state statutes that require periodic attempts at enforcement of the judgment. It is important to be aware of the procedures that keep a judgment lien in effect and enforceable. A debtor may not currently have assets to satisfy a judgment, but may obtain property in the future subject to execution. Law firms usually have "tickler" systems that extend to the ten-year period, with reminders to take the appropriate action to avoid dormancy of an uncollected judgment.[1]

For protection and enforcement of a judgment lien on real property:

- Determine the location of any real property of the debtor. File the appropriate documents to record the creditor's judgment in the deed records of the county where the property is located.

- Determine the length of time that the judgment will remain active, and record the date in a tickler system, with adequate lead time to take the actions necessary to renew the judgment.

- Research the process in your jurisdiction for foreclosure on real property. Examine the possibility of foreclosure of the judgment lien on known real property. Remember to examine any homestead restrictions that may apply, and to search for any priority liens, such as purchase money mortgages.

The process for collection of a judgment through levy on personal property begins with the request for a writ of execution. The writ instructs the sheriff to levy on nonexempt personal property of the debtor. The application is made to the clerk of the court and is merely a ministerial act. The judgment has been obtained, so the due process requirements necessary in prejudgment remedies were satisfied by completion of the judicial procedure. After issuance of the writ, the sheriff takes the property into custody pending an execution sale. After levy, the sheriff files a return describing the property taken into

---

[1] Lest readers think that the chances are remote for collection of a judgment after earlier attempts have failed, I get at least one call a year from title companies or attorneys for debtors. They are attempting to clear a title clouded by a judgment filed by my company five to ten years ago. I am always surprised when I receive payment for these older judgments.

possession. If the sheriff found no nonexempt personal property, the writ is returned *nulla bona*, or "no good." After sale of any seized property, the fees and costs of levy, storage and sale are retained by the sheriff, and the remainder of the funds are paid to the judgment creditor.

Foreign State Judgments

Under common law, collecting a judgment through property located in another state required bringing a new action in that state. **The Uniform Enforcement of Foreign Judgments Act (UEFJA)** has simplified the process for states that have adopted it. The act allows a judgment creditor to abstract its foreign judgment without having to file a new action and secure a new judgment. The UEFJA provides that a foreign judgment filed in accordance with the act, has the "same effect and is subject to the same procedures, defenses, and proceedings for reopening, vacating, staying, enforcing, or satisfying a judgment as a judgment of the court in which it is filed."

The following is the basic process for establishing a judgment in a state that has adopted the UEFJA:

- The judgment creditor files a certified copy of the foreign state judgment with the clerk of the court, along with an affidavit showing the name and last known address of the judgment debtor.

- The clerk mails the notice of the filing of the foreign state judgment to the judgment debtor at the address given.

- If the judgment debtor shows the court that an appeal from the foreign judgment is pending or that a stay of execution has been granted, the court must stay enforcement of the judgment until the appeal is concluded, the time for appeal expires, or the stay of execution expires or is vacated.

- If no response is received to the filing of the foreign state judgment, it is recorded as a judgment of the court in which it is filed, and postjudgment collection procedures may commence.

Postjudgment Discovery

A creditor whose attempts at execution have ended with return of a *nulla bona* writ, may not be convinced that no property exists to satisfy the judgment. Judgment creditors may also wish to dispute the claim of certain properties as exempt. Most states have some type of supplementary proceedings available in aid of execution on judgments. Statutes in aid of judgment or execution usually provide for some or all of the following types of relief:

- Discovery aimed at the debtor and third parties, including postjudgment interrogatories and depositions.

- Court orders to facilitate satisfaction of the judgment, including orders to turn over specific property, orders preventing transfer of property to third parties, and appointment of a receiver to manage property of the debtor.

- Contempt orders aimed at debtors or third parties who have refused to cooperate with discovery requests or who have failed to appear for postjudgment proceedings.

Postjudgment Garnishment

As a matter of procedure, postjudgment garnishment is very similar to prejudgment garnishment. Generally, the clerk of the court issues the writ, and the judgment creditor ensures that the writ is served on the garnishee and the debtor. After service of the writ of garnishment, the garnishee may not make any payments or deliver any property to the debtor. Instead, property or payments are transferred to the sheriff or the judgment creditor. Service of the writ on the garnishee creates a judgment lien on property in the hands of the garnishee at the time of service. In some states, the lien will extend to property that comes into the hands of the third party after service of the writ.

Example: Seller has obtained a judgment against The Widget King, Inc. (TWK) and knows that the proceeds for the sale of a factory will be in the hands of a title company within the week, but does not know exactly when the closing will occur. Of course, the first thing the seller does is check the procedures of the state statutes regarding postjudgment garnishment, to assure that the garnishment will cover property that comes into the hands of the garnishee after service. Then, seller takes a certified copy of the judgment to the clerk of the court, and requests a writ of garnishment directed toward the title company, requiring the title company to turn over to seller any funds, up to the amount of the judgment, costs, and interest (both pre- and postjudgment, at the legal rates). If all proper procedures have been followed, and the funds are actually delivered to the title company, the result should be favorable for the widget seller.

Fraudulent Transfers

When trying to collect on a valid judgment, creditors are often frustrated by the attempts of debtors to evade payment by transferring assets to other parties. For example, a debtor, realizing that judgment is about to be rendered, may attempt to transfer property to a spouse, another relative, or to a shell corporation. The debtor hopes that the creditor will be unable to locate the property, or that it will become too difficult to pursue these hidden assets. When the debtor transfers property with the intent to prevent a creditor from collecting a valid debt, thus perpetrating a fraud upon the creditor, it is known as a **fraudulent transfer**.

The Uniform Fraudulent Transfer Act (TUFTA) has been adopted by approximately 30 states. Appendix 8 contains TUFTA as adopted in Florida. Other states may have their own form of statute related to fraudulent transfers. TUFTA makes two different types of transfers fraudulent:

- a transfer made by a debtor with the actual intent to hinder, delay, or defraud its creditors; and

- a transfer made by a debtor for less than a reasonably equivalent value at a time when the debtor was in a precarious financial position.

Fraud by its nature is difficult to prove by direct evidence. Those who are committing subterfuge do not openly express their intent, and

TUFTA requires proof that the debtor intended to hinder, delay or defraud its creditors. Because of this, the courts have recognized categories of circumstantial evidence that can be used to show the debtor's fraudulent intent, known as the "**badges of fraud**." Although one badge of fraud may satisfy a court that a transfer was intended to defraud creditors, it only stands to reason that the more "badges of fraud" shown to exist, the more likely a transfer will be found to be fraudulent. The following badges of fraud are found at TUFTA, Section 24.005 (b):

- The transfer is general without excepting things of necessity; that is, the debtor transferred all assets without retaining anything to live on.

- The debtor continues in possession of and uses the property transferred as its own.

- The transfer was made in secret.

- The transfer was made while suit against the debtor was pending.

- An agreement allowing the debtor to utilize the property, such as a trust, is present.

- The existence of a clause in the agreement that states "this was an honest deal" or other self-serving recitals.

- The insolvency of the debtor at the time of the transfer.

- Disparate value between what the debtor transferred and what the debtor received.

- The relationship between the debtor and the transferee.

- There exists no business justification for the transfer.

These "badges of fraud" are utilized as circumstantial evidence by the creditor to show the intent of the debtor to defraud. TUFTA also has a provision for what is known as "**constructive fraud,**" where intent of the debtor is irrelevant. TUFTA labels as fraudulent every transfer made:

1. without a reasonably equivalent value in exchange for the property transferred; and

2. while the debtor was insolvent, was rendered insolvent, or was left with an unreasonably small amount of assets to continue in business.

TUFTA, Section 24.005.

TUFTA provides first for a comparison between the value of the object transferred and the value received by the debtor in exchange. If the value is significantly disparate, a "reasonably equivalent value" has not been received. The second requirement is that the debtor be in a precarious financial position at the time of the transfer, as gauged by the debtor's insolvency. TUFTA provides for a comparison of the debtor's assets and liabilities (Section 24.003) and if liabilities are greater than assets, the debtor is deemed to be insolvent.

A fraudulent transfer must be attacked by a creditor in order to be overturned, and thus is a voidable transfer, and not void. The creditor has a choice of remedies:

• Bring an action to set the transfer aside (i.e., rescission); or

• Ignore the transfer, in order to levy upon and sell the property fraudulently transferred.

EXERCISE

Match the personal property exemptions in your state with the federal exemptions listed in this chapter. Which are more favorable? Are there circumstances you can think of where one would be more favorable than the other?

Matilda Bridge owes a large sum of money to Centre Banque after her business, the Gingham Goose, fails. Just before default is declared on her note, Matilda transfers a piece of real property to her uncle, Grady Niblo. How can you prove that the transfer to Uncle Grady is a fraudulent conveyance? What if you represent Matilda? How do you defend the conveyance?

Chapter Six

SECURED TRANSACTIONS UNDER THE
UNIFORM COMMERCIAL CODE

As previously discussed, creditors typically secure the debtor's performance of an obligation by way of a **security interest**, through **liens** on **collateral**. This **consensual lien** is outlined in a **security agreement**, where the security interest is granted by the **debtor**, in favor of the secured party or **creditor**. Security interests are governed by Article 9 of the UCC, which has now been adopted in some fashion by each state. Although there may be some differences in formats, numbering and language, the basic concepts of Article 9 can be found inside of each state's statute.

What is it that makes this seemingly simple concept so difficult? First, the security interest must come into being through a concept known as **"attachment."** Additionally, there is a notice process known as **"perfection,"** and this process differs depending on **classification of collateral** into different types. The timing of attachment and perfection will determine the **priority** of various creditors, not just other secured creditors, but also judicial and statutory lienholders. Finally, there are some special priority rules that can move a creditor's security interest above those of other creditors. All of these concepts are found within the various versions of Article 9 of the UCC.

Article 9 covers any transaction that is intended to create a security interest in personal property or fixtures. Therefore, Article 9 does not apply to realty, or to statutory or judicial liens.

Attachment

Attachment of a security interest means that a security interest has become enforceable against the debtor.[1] Attachment is also a necessary condition before a secured party may perfect its security interest. Section 9.203 of the UCC sets forth the three requirements for attachment:

- There must be a pledge or writing signed by the debtor that reasonably identifies the collateral;

- The debtor must have rights in the collateral; and

- The secured party (creditor) must give value, usually by advancing money or credit or legally binding itself to do so.

All three conditions must exist simultaneously, or the security interest does not attach. Without attachment, the security interest has no legal effect and the creditor may not exercise the rights of a secured party.

Pledge or Writing Requirement

The first requirement for attachment of a security interest is phrased with the alternative "or," such that a pledge *or* a writing will suffice. A **pledge** is an oral grant of a security interest coupled with the transfer of the collateral to the creditor. The most basic form of pledge is a "pawn." The debtor receives a cash loan, and leaves an item of personal property, such as a diamond ring, as collateral. If the loan is not repaid within the agreed time period, the creditor is entitled to sell the ring in satisfaction of the debt. The creditor has a pledge if the security interest depends upon possession of personal property, obtained and held primarily to secure the loan.

A **writing** is a contract, usually called a **security agreement**, where the debtor grants the security interest by specific written terms. Although

---

[1] Be careful not to confuse attachment of a security interest with the prejudgment remedy of attachment. These are two different legal concepts that, unfortunately, bear the same name.

both parties customarily sign a security agreement, the UCC requires only the debtor's signature as an element of attachment.

Description of Collateral

A description of the collateral is sufficient, whether or not it is specific, if it reasonably identifies the personal property in question. When the term "reasonable" is used in a statute, it is bound to be an area where triers of fact must analyze each particular situation, and interpretation of case law becomes the measure for statutory interpretation. In this instance, courts tend to liberally construe the reasonable specificity requirements. Although the burden of proof is on the secured party, most courts allow extrinsic evidence to augment the description contained in the security agreement. For example, a jeweler borrows money from a bank, and the security agreement lists as collateral "40 diamond rings." The jeweler defaults on the loan, and at the time of default has 100 diamond rings in his possession. Of course, the bank wants to claim as its security the most valuable of the rings. The jeweler can introduce extrinsic evidence regarding which rings were intended as security, such as a listing provided to the banker at the time of the initial loan, containing a more specific description of the 40 rings.

As in the above example, the issue of collateral description typically arises when a debtor defaults in payment and the creditor seeks to enforce its security interest against the collateral. At this point, the debtor and creditor may disagree about what property was intended as collateral. The creditor is usually looking for a broad interpretation that encompasses as much property as possible, while the debtor favors a narrow reading that limits the available collateral. Since great degrees of specificity are not required and the liberal interpretations allow use of extrinsic evidence, the only real limitations placed by the courts have to do with whether the collateral description is actually or potentially misleading.

Debtor's Rights in the Collateral

A security interest cannot attach unless the debtor has rights in the collateral. The law will not tolerate granting liens in property in which the debtor does not have an ownership interest. This interest does not have to be a 100% ownership. If the debtor has any legally cognizable interest in the property, then the debtor has rights in the collateral. For example, a debtor may be purchasing a large piece of manufacturing equipment over time. A bank may have a lien on the property, but the debtor has equity in the equipment through its payments. The debtor can grant a security interest in equity in the equipment, subject to the prior lien.

Mere possession by the debtor is not sufficient to create rights in the collateral. In circumstances such as bailments and consignments, a debtor may have rightful possession to the property, but no interest in the property.

Value Given by Creditor

A security interest cannot attach until value is given by the secured creditor. In the case of a security agreement, value is given when credit is actually extended by the creditor or the loan funded. In a conditional sales contract, where the creditor agrees to sell certain goods to the debtor and retains a security interest in those goods, value is given when the secured party sells or agrees to sell the goods.

To put it all together, attachment of a security interest occurs at the moment that all of the above elements exist simultaneously. If the debtor and creditor have a written security agreement granting creditor a security interest in all widgets in the warehouse, debtor actually owns the widgets, but creditor has never funded the loan, then creditor does not have a security interest in the widgets. The creditor has not given value, and attachment does not occur.

Collateral

Collateral is the term used to describe personal property that is subject to a security interest. Many decisions related to Article 9 secured transactions turn on the type of collateral involved. In the discussions regarding perfection and priority, classification of the collateral is relevant.

Classification of Collateral

There are three general categories of collateral: **tangibles, intangibles, and quasi-tangibles.** There are also numerous subcategories as well. Collateral fits into these categories based either on the nature of the collateral or the particular use for the property.

Where collateral may fit into more than one category, the **primary use test** determines the proper classification. In the primary use test, the uses of the property are analyzed, and the property is classified by the primary use. For example, if a computer is used for a home business, but is also used for game playing and household finances, the primary use would determine whether it was classified as "equipment" or "consumer goods." It is only necessary to tip the scales in one direction to determine the primary use.

Types of Collateral

Tangibles.

Tangibles are goods. Under the UCC, goods include all things that are movable at the time the security interest attaches or that are fixtures. All of the physical possessions typically viewed as goods (furniture, cars, clothing, equipment, automobiles, etc.) that we can see, touch, feel and move are tangibles. There are four subcategories:

- *Inventory.* Goods held for disposition by a business, for sale or lease, including raw materials and work in progress, are considered to be inventory. UCC Section 9-109(4). The principal test is whether the goods are held for sale rather than for use.

- *Equipment.* Those goods used primarily in the business are considered to be equipment. UCC Section 9-109(2). The property utilized to produce the output of the business, never sold as an end product or as part of the inventory, belongs in the equipment category. This is also the residual category for tangibles – goods are equipment if they do not fit into another category of goods.

• **Consumer goods.** Goods are consumer goods if they are used or bought primarily for personal, family or household purposes. UCC Section 9-109 (1).

• **Farm Products.** Goods are farm products if they are:

   1. crops, livestock or supplies used or produced in farming operations or
   2. products of crops or livestock in their unmanufactured state, and
   3. in the possession of a debtor engaged in farming operations.

UCC Section 9-109(3). Once a farm product is processed, it loses its classification as a farm product, and moves to another subcategory. For example, tomatoes growing and then harvested on a farm are farm products. If the tomatoes are canned and shipped to a restaurant, they become inventory. If purchased by a family for consumption, the tomatoes become consumer goods.

Intangibles.

Intangibles are a type of collateral with no physical form, but with well-recognized rights. Every inventor knows that there are ideas and concepts that do not have physical form, yet these ideas have value. Great cash rewards may come to the person who retains the right to capitalize on the idea. Section 9-106 defines two subcategories:

• **Accounts.** An account is "any right to payment for goods sold or leased or for services rendered which is not evidenced by an instrument or chattel paper, whether or not it has been earned by performance." This is the classification for the ordinary business account receivable. The account may be documented by a written invoice, but the writing is not of legal significance. The intangible is the right to receive payment.

• **General Intangibles.** If a type of collateral cannot fit neatly into any other category, chances are it is a general intangible. Even the definition within Section 9-106 is one of exclusion: "'General intangibles' means any personal property (including things in action) other than goods, accounts, chattel paper, documents, instruments, investment property, rights to proceeds of written letters of credit, and money." Examples are copyrights, trademarks, and other types of intellectual property, as well as the good will of a business (the intangible value of the name, reputation, and customers of a going concern).

Quasi-Tangibles

The final general category of collateral is **quasi-tangibles**. As the name implies, this classification of collateral is for those objects that are hybrids of the tangible and intangible. Quasi-tangibles are all characterized by having specific legal rights embodied in some type of written document. This document not only evidences the legal right, but also carries its own legal significance. There are three subcategories:

- *Instruments.* This definition includes negotiable instruments, as well as any other documents evidencing a right to payment in money that are transferred by delivery in the ordinary course of business. Common examples are checks and certificates of deposit. This category does not include security agreements or leases, as the drafters of the UCC made the close call of classifying the transferable rights contained in these documents as "chattel paper."

- *Documents.* Although the name of this category has a broad usage in the English language, its use in the UCC actually is of a limited and specific type of document, defined under Section 1-201(15) as a "document of title." This is a document that, in the ordinary course of business or financing, is treated as adequately evidencing that the person in possession of the document is entitled to receive, hold, and dispose of both the document and the goods covered by the document. The classic examples are bills of lading and warehouse receipts. The drafters left the definition broad, in order to encompass any other documents that may come into use, recognizing that documents more often reach a destination prior to the goods covered by the documents.

- ***Chattel Paper.*** Chattel paper is a writing or a group of writings that contains both a monetary obligation and a security interest in, or a lease of, specific goods. Since parties seeking to obtain financing will often wish to pledge a security interest obtained as a creditor in another transaction, it is necessary to have a classification for the group of documents including the right to an interest in property or to payments under a lease. "Chattel paper" can therefore include a security agreement and any other documents transferring the rights contained under the agreement. For example, a finance company has a security agreement that grants a security interest in a recreational vehicle. The finance company receives a monthly payment under the agreement. The finance company wants to borrow money to expand its facility, and pledges the security agreement to its bank. Should the finance company default, the bank will be entitled to receive the monthly payments, and will take over the security interest in the recreational vehicle.

Perfection of a Security Interest

A creditor who has fulfilled the three elements of attachment (as discussed earlier) has a security interest in collateral that is enforceable against the debtor. What if the debtor has granted a security interest in the same collateral to more than one creditor? Although an enforceable lien exists against the debtor, the creditor is not fully protected from the actions of third parties claiming an interest in the property unless the lien is **perfected**. The purpose of perfecting a security interest is to provide public **notice** to parties contemplating doing business with the debtor that other parties may have a security interest in personal property of the debtor. Further, perfection establishes **priority** in the collateral among competing interests, including those holding statutory, liens, judicial liens, and any other consensual lienholders.

There are three methods for perfection of a security interest under Article 9 of the UCC:

- File a financing statement form (i.e., UCC-1), covering the collateral;

- Secured party or secured party's agent possesses the collateral; or

- Automatic perfection as a matter of law, such as in the limited instance of purchase money security interests in consumer goods.

The method of perfection to be used is determined by the nature of the collateral that is the subject of the security interest.

Perfection by Filing

Most types of collateral either may or must be perfected by filing as described in Article 9. Filing is not effective as to money or instruments, due to their negotiable nature. The secured party has the responsibility for filing, which includes assuring that the form contains the necessary information and is filed in the correct place. Filing is not necessary or effective to perfect a security interest in property subject to federal or state statutes regarding registration of title, such as aircraft, automobiles, trailers, boats, and the like.

Content of Filing. Section 9-402 of the UCC outlines the formal content requirements for the financing statement, including a sample form UCC-1 contained in subsection (3). The filing must contain:

- Names and addresses of the debtor and the secured party;
- A reasonable description of the collateral; and
- The debtor's signature.

Minor errors in the financing statement that are not seriously misleading are disregarded. Section 9-403 (8). For example, a debtor has a corporate name, such as Widgets, Inc., but does business as "The Widget Factory." The secured creditor files a UCC-1 under the trade name, instead of the actual corporate identification. In similar cases, courts have held that this type error is not "seriously misleading," since the reasonably prudent creditor will search the UCC records under both names. As stated in the Official Comment, this is, "...in line with the policy of this article to simplify formal requisites and filing requirements and is designed to discourage the fanatical and impossibly refined reading of such statutory requirements in which courts have occasionally indulged themselves."

A financing statement may be amended, but requires the signature of both the debtor and the secured party, to preclude the parties from adversely affecting each other's interests. Section 9-403 (4).

Location of Filing. Section 9-401 contains three alternative filing locations for states to incorporate within their own statutory schemes. Each state is then able to select the alternative that is most workable, based on its particular needs. The alternatives are as follows:

- The first alternative provides for security interests in fixtures, timber, minerals and the like to be filed in the office where a mortgage on the real estate is filed or recorded, and in all other cases in a centralized location, such as the office of the secretary of state.

- The second alternative is identical, except that it has a separate provision for collateral related to farming operations to be filed in a designated office in the county where the farming operation is located.

- The third alternative mirrors the second, but has an additional provision allowing for businesses located only within one county to file within an office of that county.

As an example, the state of Maryland requires filing of all UCC-1 forms with the State Department of Assessments and Taxation, except for security interests in crops, minerals, oil and gas, timber and fixtures. These listed interests are perfected by filing with the Clerk of the court in the county where the collateral is located.

Even if a filing is in the wrong place, it is still good against those who have knowledge of its contents. However, it would not be effective to establish priority over a subsequent filing in the correct location.

Time and Length of Filing. A secured party may file a financing statement at any time. A financing statement may be filed before a security agreement is made or before a security interest attaches. In this instance, perfection occurs at the time the security interest attaches. A financing statement may also be filed at any time after attachment.

However, the secured creditor who waits to file runs the risk that subsequent creditors will gain priority in the same collateral.

The initial filing is effective for five years. The secured party may file a continuation statement to extend the initial five-year period, in five-year increments. The continuation statement must be signed by the secured party (the debtor signature is not required), identify the original statement by file number, and state that the original financing statement is still effective.

After the secured obligation is paid, the debtor is entitled to filing of a termination statement, giving notice that the secured party no longer claims a security interest in the collateral. The creditor is not required to file the termination statement unless, after payment is complete, the debtor makes a written demand for filing of the termination statement. In that instance, the secured party must comply with the demand.

Perfection by Possession

Possession was historically the earliest mechanism for perfection of a security interest, since possession by the secured party provided effective notice that some interest was claimed in the collateral. A security interest in any item of tangible collateral may be perfected by possession of that collateral. A security interest in quasi-tangibles can be perfected only by possession, since it is collateral that is represented by a writing, and thus easily possessed. Purely intangible collateral cannot be possessed, and perfection must be by filing.

Perfection by possession occurs when the secured party or its agent takes actual custody of the collateral, and is effective as long as the creditor possesses the collateral. There is no "relation back" as with filing, so that possession before attachment will not preestablish an effective date. A creditor may take possession of a certificate of deposit as collateral for a future loan, but until the security agreement is signed and the loan is actually funded, perfection by possession does not occur.

Rights and Duties Related to Collateral. A secured party must use reasonable care in the custody and preservation of collateral in its possession. Section 9-207 of the UCC outlines the various rights and duties regarding collateral once it is in the possession of the secured party. Unless the parties agree otherwise, the following standards are applied:

- Reasonable expenses incurred relative to the collateral are chargeable to the debtor and are secured by the collateral.

- The debtor bears the risk of loss or damage due to any deficiency in insurance coverage.

- The secured party may hold any profits from the collateral as additional security.

- The secured party must keep the collateral identifiable, but fungible goods may be commingled. ("Fungible goods" are those of a nature that one unit or part may be exchanged or substituted for another equivalent unit, such as with food, where one orange is the same as another orange.)

- The secured party may repledge the collateral, as long as the terms do not impair the debtor's rights.

- A secured party may operate collateral for the purpose of preserving the collateral or its value.

The secured party is liable for damages for failure to meet any of the obligations listed above, but will not lose the security interest.

Automatic Perfection

Consumers are frequently purchasing goods on credit, and granting a security interest to the creditor in the goods purchased. For example, if someone purchases a washer and dryer from a department store on credit, chances are that hidden within the terms and conditions of the credit agreement is the granting by the consumer of a security interest in the goods actually being purchased. This is known as a **purchase money security interest** and entitles the creditor to take possession of the purchased property in case of default.

If creditors extending credit to consumers were required to file a UCC-1 on each of these transactions, it would involve excessive costs and massive filings with little or no benefit to those utilizing the records. This is why a purchase money security interest in consumer goods is automatically perfected under the UCC, such that filing and /or possession are not necessary. In the case of this type of consumer transactions, attachment and perfection are deemed to occur simultaneously.

Perfection Table

The information regarding types of collateral and the methods for perfection is summarized in the following chart:

TYPE OF COLLATERAL	HOW TO PERFECT
Tangibles	
Equipment Goods used in business other than inventory.	Possession or Filing
Inventory Goods debtor holds for sale, resale or lease (including packaging, raw materials and work-in-process).	Possession or Filing
Farm Products Crops, livestock, and supplies used in farming operations, while in the debtor's hands.	Possession or Filing
Consumer Goods Goods held primarily for personal, household, or family use.	Automatically perfected as of date of attachment
Intangibles	
Accounts Right to payment for goods or services	Filing Only
General Intangibles Intellectual property rights, good will, company name, customer lists, mailing lists, etc.	Filing Only
Quasi-Tangibles	
Instruments	Possession Only

TYPE OF COLLATERAL	HOW TO PERFECT
Checks, certificates of deposit, etc.	
Documents Warehouse receipts, bills of lading.	Possession Only
Chattel Paper Writing or a group of writings containing a monetary obligation and a security interest in or a lease of specific goods.	Possession Only

Priorities

The topic of priority among security interests and various other liens represents an excellent segue into a discussion of bankruptcy, in that priorities are of no concern where debtors fulfill their obligations to creditors. The only time to care about priorities is when default occurs, at which time the creditors begin to work themselves into a frenzy, like sharks, hoping to grab some piece of property of the debtor. One can also visualize creditors circling like vultures over the debtor. Either metaphor will suffice. At any rate, the best feeding is left for the creditors who take the appropriate actions to establish their position relative to the property of the debtor.

Who may be in competition with the perfected secured creditor regarding the same property? Here is a list of some potential competitors:

- Other secured parties under the UCC;

- Judicial lien creditors (by judgment, attachment, garnishment or the like);

- Statutory lienholders by operation of law (mechanic's and materialmen's liens, artisan's liens, and other statutory protections for providers of good and services);

- Statutory liens and priorities of governmental units (federal and state tax liens, etc.);

- Subsequent purchasers of the collateral; and

- General or unsecured creditors.

There is a remarkable amount of case law regarding the priority among creditors claiming security interests in the same property under the various state versions of Article 9 of the UCC. However, there are only three **basic priority rules** that will be at the core of each priority dispute:

remember

Rule One. In a priority contest between two or more perfected secured parties, the first to file or perfect has priority in the collateral. UCC Section 9-312(5)(a). For example, Widgets R Us, Inc. (Widgets) is borrowing money for an expansion, and seeks loans from Banc One and Banc Two. Widgets gets a loan from Banc One, secured by its equipment and inventory. Banc One files a UCC-1 one week after the security agreement is signed, on February 20, 1997. Widgets also gets a loan from Banc Two, secured by all of the property of Widgets, tangible, intangible or quasi-tangible. A UCC-1 is filed immediately, on February 19, 1997. Who has the priority in the equipment and inventory? Banc Two, because, although it was not the first to enter into the security agreement, it was the first to perfect its security interest by filing the UCC-1.

Rule Two. In a priority contest between a perfected secured party and an unperfected secured party, the perfected secured party always has priority in the collateral. UCC Section 9-312(5)(a). In the prior example, assume that Banc One never filed a UCC-1. It would not matter that Banc One had the original loan and security agreement. Banc Two, and any other creditors who filed a UCC-1 relative to the inventory and equipment, will prevail.

Rule Three. In a priority contest between two or more unperfected secured parties (where secured parties have attachment only), the first secured party to attach has priority in the collateral. UCC Section 9-312(5)(b). Assume that Banc One and Banc Two did not file UCC-1 financing statements. Banc One is now the prevailing party, because it had attachment of its security interest before the loan of Banc Two was completed.

The UCC attempts to establish perfection of a security interest as the ultimate priority, but recognizes that a perfected creditor may still become subordinated to some other competing interest. One special priority is that granted to the holder of a **purchase money security interest**. As discussed previously, a purchase money security interest is a security interest in specific collateral, securing an obligation created so that the debtor can actually purchase the specific collateral. A familiar example is the typical automobile purchase. The car is selected from the dealer and a price is agreed upon. The customer borrows the money to finance the purchase and grants a lien in the automobile to the financing entity. A security interest is created in the specific collateral (the car) to secure the obligation created (the car loan) so that the debtor can actually purchase the collateral (the car).

There are two types of purchase money security interests:

- A **vendor** purchase money security interest, where the seller takes a security interest in collateral that it sells to the debtor, to secure the obligation related to the purchase. For example, an office furniture company that also finances purchases made by its customers will take a vendor purchase money security interest in the furniture it finances.

- A **lender** purchase money security interest, where the creditor gives value to the debtor for the specific purpose of acquiring the collateral from a seller, and takes a security interest in the property that is actually purchased. This is frequently encountered with automobile loans, where the car is selected from a dealer, but the financing is provided by a bank, which takes a security interest in the car.

A creditor asserting a purchase money security interest has the ability, by following particular procedures, to protect itself from creditors who may ultimately try to include this collateral within certain "blanket" interests. Consider the matter of the **after-acquired property clause**, contained within many collateral descriptions. A lending institution, providing the primary financing for a business, will want to encompass as much collateral as possible within its security agreement. This creditor will include a **blanket description** of the collateral that attempts to incorporate every bit of personal property the debtor currently has or may ever acquire. The description, included in both the security agreement and the UCC-1 filing, would look something like this:

> Creditor claims a security interest in all equipment, furniture, fixtures, and all personal property, tangible, intangible or quasi-tangible, in which the debtor currently has an interest, or *in which the debtor may acquire an interest in the future.* (emphasis added.)

The clause contained in this collateral description, encompassing personal property of any type obtained by the debtor in the future, is known as an after-acquired property clause. Clearly, a party extending credit to a debtor specifically for the purchase of a particular item must have some mechanism to remove this collateral from the blanket interest that may be claimed by this prior creditor. Otherwise, this creditor begins the transaction with an interest subordinated to the earlier creditor. The UCC provides a process that gives super-priority to the purchase money security interest in two instances:

Security in Inventory. The after-acquired property clause is frequently used when inventory is collateral, since old inventory typically is depleted and is replaced by new inventory. Inventory would be poor collateral if the security interest did not cover incoming inventory. However, if the original secured creditor had a complete lock on after-acquired inventory, the debtor who is attempting to finance new inventory would have little chance. To establish a super-priority status, the holder of a purchase money security interest in inventory must

- perfect before or at the time the debtor obtains possession of the inventory; and

- give appropriate notice to all holders of a security interest in the same types of inventory who have filed financing statements *before* the purchase money security interest is filed.

The notice must be in writing, must state that the person giving notice has or expects to acquire a purchase money security interest, and must describe the inventory by item or type. By following these requirements, outlined in UCC Section 9-312(3), the new creditor perfects with a super-priority.

Collateral Other than Inventory. There is no time limit under which a party must file a UCC-1 financing statement to perfect a security interest. Of course, by not acting quickly, a secured creditor runs the risk of losing position over subsequent creditors. The super-priority status for purchase money security interests in collateral other than inventory is granted to creditors who file within a specified number of days after the debtor takes possession of the collateral. The UCC provides for filing within ten days, but most state statutes are more generous.[2] No notice to other secured parties is required.

There is one remaining type of lien that may take priority over a perfected security interest in the same property. It is in the instance of a particular type of statutory lien known as a **possessory statutory lien**. This lien is incorporated within state law, and is generally granted to carpenters, mechanics, and artisans as a mechanism to guarantee payment for work performed. As long as these lienholders retain possession of the item on which the work was performed, they will have priority over conflicting security interests in the same collateral to the extent of the value for the services and materials provided. UCC Section 9-310. Philosophically speaking, the perfected secured party should ultimately gain the benefit of the work or services performed to enhance the collateral, once the possessory lien is satisfied.

It should now be clear that the UCC and state laws for creditor protection put a premium on swift action. In most instances, the "first in time" rule applies, and the creditor who acts quickly has first crack at the debtor's property. However, the existing priorities are frozen at the point that the debtor initiates a bankruptcy proceeding. Further, the Bankruptcy Code emphasizes equality of treatment of creditors rather than rewarding a stampede for the cash. Creditors do not lose their hard-fought position regarding collateral, but are unable to improve their position relative to other creditors after the debtor files.

---

[2] For example, Texas allows 20 days, while Florida allows 21 days.

EXERCISE

Walter Woogie's Sports Palace is a popular restaurant and bar. Walter would like to borrow more money for an expansion. There are many types of property Walter can use as collateral. Classify each one of these:

- the glasses, plates, and utensils
- the oven *inventory*
- the beer and liquor *inventory*
- unpaid tabs of regular customers *Acct receivable*
- the cash register *inventory*
- Walter's customer list *intangible*
- the big-screen television (Walter keeps this at home, except in football season)

You work for the bank that is lending money to Walter. Fill out a UCC-1 form that encompasses all of Walter's collateral.

Qualified
most pension plans are exempt.

Chapter Seven

BANKRUPTCY BASICS

Introduction

It is by no means the intent of this text to provide a comprehensive treatise on bankruptcy law. Numerous books have been written on the subject, with in-depth analysis of this complex and specialized area of the law. However, it is helpful to have a road map of the basic structure of this complex federal law, since bankruptcy is frequently the final stopping point in the debtor-creditor journey. This chapter outlines some of the fundamental principles and procedures. For a more exhaustive treatment of the subject, please consult one of the sources contained in the bibliography.

Bankruptcy Overview

The best way to begin an understanding of bankruptcy is to outline the differences between bankruptcy law and the state debtor-creditor laws:

- Bankruptcy is **federal law**, currently incorporated in Title 11 of the United States Code (in future references, the Code). Although state laws will often be upheld in a bankruptcy proceeding, the federal bankruptcy system brings in a complete legal structure with jurisdiction over all aspects of the debtor's affairs.

- As mentioned previously, the Code does not emphasize speed of action by the creditor. Instead, it emphasizes *protecting all creditors* equally and guarding their interests. All creditors within a particular class are treated the same, and a creditor will rarely be able to improve its position during a bankruptcy proceeding.

- At the same time, the Code provides relief for the debtor in a way that state laws do not – through a **discharge of debts**. One of the primary purposes of bankruptcy is to relieve the honest debtor of burdensome debts, and to provide the debtor with a "fresh start."

A Brief History

The first English bankruptcy statutes were directed at merchants who failed to pay their bills, and were so punitive that one delegate to the Constitutional Convention in Philadelphia was reluctant to give Congress the power to enact bankruptcy laws. In spite of this concern, Article 1, Section 8 of the Constitution states:

> The Congress shall have the power to establish uniform Laws on the subject of Bankruptcies throughout the United States.

Early endeavors at bankruptcy legislation were basically unsuccessful. These first attempts were purely debt collection and distribution methodologies, and the concept of discharge of debts was not recognized until 1841. That enactment lasted only 18 months. Increasing interstate commerce and the conflicts created by diverse state laws finally gave birth to the most durable version, the Bankruptcy Act of 1898. This act was superseded by the principal source of modern bankruptcy law, the Bankruptcy Reform Act of 1978, now known as the Bankruptcy Code. With its amendments, the 1978 Act is the Code contained in Title 11 today.

Structure of the Code

The Code is divided into the following Chapters:

1. Chapters related to the **proceedings in general**, applicable to all bankruptcy cases:

   Chapter 1 General Provisions, Definitions and Rules of Construction
   Chapter 3 Case Administration
   Chapter 5 Creditors, the Debtor and the Estate

2. Chapters outlining the different kinds of **bankruptcy cases:**

Judgements expire 10 years

Chapter 7 Liquidation
Chapter 9 Adjustment of the Debts of a Municipality
Chapter 11 Reorganization
Chapter 12 Adjustment of Debts of a Family Farmer with Regular Annual Income
Chapter 13 Adjustment of the Debts of an Individual with Regular Income

3. Other statutes relevant to bankruptcy law:

> **The Bankruptcy Rules**. The Code deals with substantive laws of bankruptcy, with procedures described only in broad terms. The Bankruptcy Rules (28 U.S.C.A. Section 2075) govern procedures in the Bankruptcy Courts. The Rules are divided into ten parts, each of which governs a different stage of the bankruptcy process.

> **Other Federal Statutes**. Title 28 has a number of provisions relating to bankruptcy. For example, Chapter 6 deals with the appointment, duties and functions of bankruptcy judges, Chapter 39 provides for the U.S. Trustee system, Chapter 85 governs bankruptcy jurisdiction, and Chapter 87 deals with matters of venue.

The structure of the Code is far from perfect. A debtor must choose only one of the Chapters under which to file, but is subject to the administrative provisions contained in Chapters 1, 3 and 5. This means that much time is spent by novices (and often by intermediates, and experts) referring back and forth between the chapters and sections, trying to interpret how the administrative rules relate to the particular chapter selected. This book will therefore stick to basic interpretation, and not provide deep analysis of various code sections. Further, the discussion is limited to the most frequently utilized chapters: Chapters 7, 11 and 13.

1978 Bankruptcy goods

Choosing a Chapter

The debtor seeking relief under the Bankruptcy Code must initially choose between two types of relief available: **liquidation** and **reorganization**. This relief is available through the following chapters:

Chapter 7. The most common type of bankruptcy case, Chapter 7 involves the liquidation of the debtor's assets by a trustee, with the proceeds divided among the creditors according to their priority. A debtor under Chapter 7 must be a "person," including individuals, partnerships and corporations, but not including governmental entities or sole proprietorships. In liquidations involving individuals, the debtor gets a "fresh start" by receiving a discharge of most debts. Liquidation for a business entity usually results in termination of the business.

Chapter 11. This is used by business debtors (usually corporations) to avoid liquidation and continue the business. Chapter 11 is designed to help the debtor rehabilitate a business by extending, reducing, or otherwise adjusting debts, through adoption of a court approved plan of reorganization. Any person eligible under Chapter 7 may also file under Chapter 11, except stock and commodities brokers. Companies in Chapter 11 typically remain in possession of their assets and continue to operate the business throughout the proceeding.

Chapter 13. Individuals with regular income who want to adjust their debts rather than liquidate their assets may utilize Chapter 13 to formulate a plan for approval by the court. Unlike Chapter 7, the Chapter 13 debtor does not receive a discharge of all debts, but instead submits a plan for repayment of some portion of their debts over a four- or five-year period. Only an individual whose debts do not exceed $750,000 of secured debt and $250,000 of unsecured debt may file a Chapter 13.

The following issues may also be determinative of the chapter selected by the debtor:

- Does the debtor wish to be discharged from the debts, or does the debtor, for some reason, want or need to pay the creditors?

- Does the debtor wish to maintain control of the assets of the business, or is liquidation of the business the ultimate goal?

- Is the debtor able to bear the cost of a reorganization, and is reorganization a viable alternative for the business?

A thorough interview of the clients and careful consideration of the factors involved in their particular circumstance should lead to the appropriate chapter selection.

Commencement of the Case

A bankruptcy case begins with the filing of a petition with the bankruptcy court. Typically, the debtor files the petition, and it is known as a **"voluntary"** filing. A debtor can be forced into bankruptcy by creditors filing an **involuntary petition**. Three creditors with unsecured claims totaling at least $10,000 must join in the petition. If the debtor has fewer than 12 unsecured creditors, only one creditor with a claim of at least $10,000 is necessary. [Section 303 (b)] The filing must be under either Chapter 7 or 11. In an involuntary case, the debtor has the right to file an answer and controvert the petition. If the debtor does not answer the petition promptly, the court will enter an order for relief against the debtor. If the debtor does answer in a timely manner, the petitioning creditors must establish one of the following:

1. the debtor is not generally paying its present *bona fide* debts as they become due or

2. within 120 days of the petition date, a receiver, assignee, or custodian has taken possession of substantially all of the debtor's property. [Section 303 (h)]

If the debtor establishes that the grounds for involuntary relief have not been satisfied, the court may grant a judgment in favor of the debtor for its costs and attorney's fees. Section 303 (i)

The court may dismiss a bankruptcy case "for cause," including a delay by the debtor that is prejudicial to the creditors, failure to pay filing fees or trustee fees, or failure to comply with orders of the court. There are also various instances where a Chapter 11 case can be converted to a Chapter 7, and vice versa. For example, the court can convert a Chapter 11 to a Chapter 7 for cause, such as the debtor's inability to effectuate a plan, unreasonable delay by the debtor, or the absence of a reasonable likelihood of rehabilitation.

The Automatic Stay

One of the most fundamental aspects of the Bankruptcy Code is the **automatic stay** that commences upon filing under any chapter. The purpose of the stay is to freeze all collection activities against the debtor or the bankruptcy estate (consisting of all of the debtor's property). Through the automatic stay, the estate is preserved in an effort to allow all creditors to share in the estate or, in the case of Chapters 11 and 13, to give the debtor time to formulate a plan. The automatic stay is triggered by the filing of the petition, and dates from the time of filing, not from the time that the creditors receive notice of the petition.

The following acts, as outlined in Section 362 of the Code, are within the scope of the automatic stay:

- All judicial actions that were or could have been commenced before the filing of the petition.

- Enforcement of prebankruptcy judgments against the debtor.

- Any act to take possession of property of the debtor, including self-help remedies available to secured lenders.

- Any exercise of a right to setoff by a creditor.

- Any act to create, perfect or enforce a lien.

The following are the most common of the acts that are not stayed by bankruptcy filing:

- State and federal court criminal proceedings.

- Collection of alimony, maintenance or support payments.

- Perfection of certain interests in property, such as perfection of an existing mechanic's and materialmen's lien, or of a purchase money security interest within ten days of the transaction.

- Termination of contracts by their own terms after filing.

- Proceedings arising from purely post-petition events.

- The commencement or continuation of an action by a governmental unit to enforce its police or regulatory powers.

Motion to Lift the Automatic Stay

Creditors may file a motion with the court to obtain relief from the automatic stay. [Section 362(d)] This is probably the most contentious area of bankruptcy practice. Relief from the stay can take the form of termination, annulment, modification or conditioning of the stay. There are two standards for relief from the stay. One standard for relief is "for cause," including a lack of adequate protection for the creditor. The second standard, applied to property of the debtor, is that the debtor lacks equity in the property, and the property is not necessary to an effective reorganization.

Cause for relief from the automatic stay may include:

- Lack of insurance to protect the collateral.

- Failure to make postpetition payments required by the court or an applicable provision of the Code.

- Use of the bankruptcy filing for delay or other bad faith purposes.

- Failure to allow inspection of the collateral while it is in postpetition use.

The debtor bears the burden of proof on all elements regarding cause for relief from the automatic stay.

When requesting relief from the automatic stay, the secured creditor's first desire may be return of the collateral. The purpose of adequate protection is to protect a creditor's interest in collateral that might be harmed as a result of the delays inherent in the bankruptcy process. The court may determine that other actions may provide the protection requested by the creditor, short of returning the equipment. Some examples of court-ordered protections:

- A cash payment or periodic cash payments.

- An additional or replacement lien to the extent that the use, sale or lease of the property results in a decrease in its value.

- Additional insurance payments to protect the property.

- Granting of other relief that will provide the creditor with the "indubitable equivalent" of the creditor's interest in the property.

As for the second standard for relief, that the debtor lacks equity in the collateral and the property is not necessary to an effective reorganization, the creditor moving to lift the stay will bear the burden of proof regarding the debtor's equity position. The debtor will bear the burden regarding the need for the property in reorganization. In Chapter 7, since there is no reorganization, the creditor who shows no equity in the collateral is granted relief from the automatic stay.

The Chapter 7 Bankruptcy

A Chapter 7 case begins with the filing of a petition, whether voluntary or involuntary. The commencement of the Chapter 7 case creates an "**estate**" consisting of all of the debtor's legal and equitable interest in property at that time. Promptly after entry of the order for relief, an interim trustee is appointed. Although the creditors have the ability to elect a trustee at the creditor's meeting, the typical practice is for the interim trustee to continue to serve without objection.

The **trustee** acts as the representative of the bankruptcy estate, and performs the following functions:

- Collects, sells, and reduces to cash the assets of the estate.

- Continues temporarily to operate the debtor's business if necessary to preserve the value of the business assets.

- Examines the debtor under oath at the meeting of creditors.

- Files inventories, makes periodic reports to the court on the financial condition of the estate, and keeps records of cash receipts and disbursements.

- Files a final accounting when the case is closed.

- Investigates the debtor's financial affairs and opposes the debtor's discharge, if advisable.

- Examines Proofs of Claim filed by creditors, and objects to improper claims.

- Upon request of interested parties, furnishes information related to the bankruptcy.

Chapter 7 cases are classified as asset cases or no-asset cases. A **no-asset case** exists when the trustee determines that the debtor has no nonexempt assets that can be liquidated to pay dividends to the creditors. This designation will typically appear on the Notification to Creditors, stating that this is a no-asset case, and no Proof of Claim should be filed. If the trustee later determines that nonexempt assets do exist, the creditors are notified and given an opportunity to file a claim.

The trustee is able to make a basic determination regarding the assets from the documents the debtor is required to file along with the Chapter 7 Petition. The Voluntary Petition is typically accompanied by the following documents (See Appendix 9 for forms). Additional timeframes may be allowed for particular items:

- **Statement of Financial Affairs.** A form with 15 questions to be answered by all debtors, plus additional questions if the Chapter 7 relates to operation of a business.

- **Schedules.** Forms much like the schedules filed with an income tax return, the schedules are designated by letters (i.e., Schedule A: Real Property, Schedule B: Personal Property, etc.) and provide a comprehensive overview of the debtor's property, income and the claims of creditors against the estate.

- **Summary of Schedules.** A summary sheet showing which schedules are attached, and providing totals relative to assets and liabilities as listed on the schedules.

- **Statement of Attorney for Petitioner**. A statement of the compensation paid or agreed to be paid to the attorney representing the debtor.

- **Statement of Intention Regarding Property Subject to Liens.** This form, for consumer debtors only, requires the debtor to state an intent regarding property such as automobiles. The debtor may choose to return the collateral to the secured lender, or reaffirm the debt and retain possession of the property. The debtor has 30 days from petition date to file this document.

- **List of Creditors**. More commonly known as the "matrix," it contains the names and addresses of all creditors, in a format prescribed by the court.

After the petition is filed, the court issues a notice, directed to all creditors, the debtor, his attorney, and any other parties in interest. Among other information, it contains the date of the filing, the date, time and place set for the creditor's meeting, and the last date for objections to the debtor's discharge. As stated earlier, this notice will also indicate if the Chapter 7 is a "no-asset" case. In an asset case the notice will notify creditors of the last date to file proofs of claim.

The **meeting of creditors** is almost uniformly referred to as the "Section 341(a) Meeting." For a Code section so frequently cited, the content is amazingly simple:

> Within a reasonable time after the order for relief in a case under this title, the United States Trustee shall convene and preside at a meeting of creditors. Section 341(a)

At the meeting, the debtor is placed under oath by the trustee, and is questioned regarding the content of the schedules. Any creditors attending the meeting are also entitled to question the debtor regarding matters relating to the bankruptcy estate. The trustee sees that all information is available regarding the property of the estate, as it is the trustee's duty to administer this property. The trustee determines which property is subject to the claims of secured parties, determines which property may be abandoned as burdensome or of no value to the estate, and examines the property claimed by the debtor as exempt.

The individual debtor under Chapter 7 has the right to declare certain property as exempt, in order to fuel the "fresh start." As described in Chapter Five, the Code provides a list of property exemptions, but also allows states to opt out and require debtors to select state exemptions only. Some states allow debtors to select either the federal list or the state exemption scheme. It is essential for the attorney and legal assistant in those states to compare the two sets of exemptions and select the list that is most favorable to the debtor.

The trustee or any creditor may file objections to the list of exemptions claimed by the debtor. The objection must be filed within 30 days of the creditor's meeting, and the objecting party has the burden of proof.

In a Chapter 7 case, all creditors who believe they have a claim against the estate must timely file a **Proof of Claim,** a form containing the amount, type, and other supporting information for all debts. Failure to do so will result in disallowance of the claim, and will bar the creditor from sharing in distributions from the estate. Unless otherwise ordered by the court, the Proof of Claim must be filed within 90 days of the first date set for the meeting of creditors. Since the first meeting date is contained in the initial notice to creditors, the filing date should be calculated and calendared immediately upon receipt of the notice. The Proof of Claim form requests basic information regarding the creditor and its claim, including the basis for the claim and the classification (secured, unsecured, etc.). Any supporting documents, such as contracts or invoices, are attached to the form.

If there is property of the estate to distribute, the trustee will follow the priorities established under the Code, in Section 507. Secured claimants are generally entitled to return of the collateral or to the value of the collateral securing the claim. After satisfaction of secured claims, there are certain types of unsecured claims that are classified as **priority claims.** Proceeds of the liquidation are paid in the following order:

1. Administrative expenses of the case, including necessary costs and expenses of preserving the estate;

2. Claims arising out of authorized postpetition transactions in involuntary cases;

3. Certain employee claims for wages accrued within 90 days of the bankruptcy filing, up to $4,000 per claimant;

4. Certain contributions to employee benefit plans within prescribed statutory limits;

5. Certain farmer and fishermen claims up to $4,000 for each claimant;

6. Deposits in connection with consumer transactions, up to $1,800 per claimant (such as apartment security deposits);

7. Claims for debts to a spouse, former spouse or child of the debtor, for alimony, maintenance or support;

8. Certain tax claims;

9. Certain FDIC claims.

After payment of any claims that fit in these statutory categories, any remainder is paid as follows:

1. Allowed prepetition claims timely filed;

2. Allowed prepetition unsecured claims that were filed late;

3. Fines and punitive damages; and

4. Post-petition interest on prepetition claims.

This concept of paying claims in a prescribed order is known as the **"absolute priority rule"** and applies in Chapter 11 and 13 cases as well. Unsecured claims are paid in the priority established in the Code, and no claim in a lower class of priority is paid prior to payment in full of all claims in a higher class of priority.

The debtor's primary purpose for filing under Chapter 7 is the **discharge of debts**. Prior to the discharge hearing, the debtor must obtain any reaffirmation agreements regarding property the debtor wishes to retain or debts intended to pay in full. A **reaffirmation agreement** is an agreement between the debtor and one of the creditors wherein the debtor agrees to pay an otherwise dischargeable debt. As a general rule, this type of agreement is void, but the Code recognizes the agreement if the following requirements are met:

1. The agreement must be entered into before the granting of the discharge;

2. The debtor must have 30 days after approval of the agreement to rescind it;

3. The debtor must attend the discharge hearing and be informed of the reaffirmation requirements by the court; and

4. If the debtor is seeking to reaffirm a consumer debt that is not secured by real property, the court must find that the agreement will not impose an undue hardship on the debtor and will be in the debtor's best interest, and was made in good faith.

Under the Code, the court must grant the individual debtor a discharge of prepetition debts unless one of the grounds for denial of a discharge is met. Those grounds include the following:

1. The debtor is not an individual;

2. The debtor transferred or concealed property within one year of bankruptcy with the intent to hinder, delay or defraud creditors;

3. The debtor failed to keep adequate financial records;

4. The debtor committed some act of misconduct during the pendency of the case, including perjury, false statements, false oaths, or failure to obey a court order;

5. The debtor has failed to satisfactorily explain any loss or deficiency of assets; and

6. The debtor has been granted a previous discharge within six years of the filing date of the current case.

If there is no objection to the discharge, the debtor will appear before the court to receive the discharge. This hearing gives the court an opportunity to explain the nature of the discharge and to administer the warnings regarding any reaffirmation agreements. There are certain debts excepted from discharge as a matter of public policy. These **exceptions from discharge** include the following:

•   Taxes entitled to priority;

- Taxes connected to fraudulent returns, late returns, or failure to file;

- Withholding taxes and other taxes collected from third parties;

- Debts incurred by fraud or false financial statements;

- Debts that are not scheduled in time for the creditor to timely file a Proof of Claim;

- Debts arising from fraud or defalcation while acting in a fiduciary capacity;

- Debts arising from embezzlement or larceny;

- Alimony, separate maintenance, or child support;

- Claims resulting from willful and malicious injury to another entity or to the property of another entity;

- Student loans, provided the nondischargeability of debt will not impose an undue hardship on the debtor and his or her dependents;

- Certain governmental fines and penalties;

- Claims resulting from death or personal injury caused by the debtor's unlawful operation of a motor vehicle (such as driving while intoxicated);

- Certain claims owed to federally insured financial institutions that have failed, or to the FDIC.

For most debtors, entry of the discharge ends their concern with the Chapter 7 case, and the "fresh start" commences. Since most Chapter 7 cases are "no-asset" cases, with no property to liquidate, and no distribution to the creditors, they are closed as soon as the discharge is entered. If there are assets, the case remains open until the trustee has liquidated the assets and distributed the cash.

Reorganization Under Chapter 11

Chapter 11 provides a means by which a business can reorganize its debts, keep its assets, and continue to operate. There is not an initial appointment of a trustee, as in the Chapter 7. Instead, the debtor becomes the **"debtor-in-possession"** with the right to engage in ordinary business transactions without court supervision. Unless the creditors request the appointment of a trustee to run the debtor's business, the debtor retains complete control of the operation of the business.

Under Chapter 11, a debtor attempts to reorganize its business for the benefit of the debtor, its creditors, and any other interest holders. Formulation of a plan of reorganization is the primary tool through which the Chapter 11 business gets its "fresh start." A **plan of reorganization** sets forth the means for satisfying the holders of claims against, and interests in, a debtor. Generally, a **claim against a debtor** arises from a normal debtor/creditor transaction, such as a promissory note or an open account. An **interest in the debtor** is held by a party that has an ownership interest in the debtor, such as a general partner in a partnership case or a stockholder in a corporate case.

The debtor has the exclusive right to file a plan of reorganization during the first 120 days after filing, plus any extensions the court may grant as requested. After the exclusivity period, other individual creditors or creditor groups may propose their own competing plans. The Code requires a plan proponent to fully disclose to creditors and interest holders sufficient information about the debtor, its assets and the plan. This **disclosure statement** must be approved by the court before acceptance of that plan can be solicited, and must contain information adequate to enable holders of claims against or interests in the plan to make an informed judgment with respect to acceptance or rejection of the plan.

The Code provides that claimants and interest holders are to be grouped into **classes of claimants** under a plan and that they will vote to accept or reject a plan by class. While bankruptcy courts continually disagree on the proper method to be used in classifying claimants, a general rule of thumb is that creditors with similar legal rights are placed together in the same class. For example, all creditors entitled to priority under the Code might be placed in one class, while all creditors holding general unsecured claims might be placed in a class. Generally, every secured claimant is placed in a class by itself, since each secured party usually has a lien on distinct property and therefore has distinct legal rights.

The Code does not require each holder of a claim to vote in favor of the plan in order for the court to confirm the plan. Instead, the plan must be accepted by each class of claimants. In order for the plan to be accepted by a class of creditors, those holding at least two-thirds in dollar amount and more than one-half in number actually voting on the plan in the class must vote for the plan. As if this were not confusing enough, the court may confirm the plan even though fewer than all classes of claims and interests vote to accept the plan. In that case, the plan must be accepted by at least one **"impaired" class** of claims, without including any acceptance of the plan by an insider. A claim is considered impaired if the plan does not call for repayment in full or if legal rights are altered in some other way. An interest that is adversely affected under the plan is also considered to be impaired.

Finally, even if all impaired classes of claims or interests under the plan do not vote to accept the plan, the debtor may request the court to confirm the plan pursuant to the **"cramdown" provisions** of the Code. Those provisions permit the plan to be confirmed if the court determines that the plan is feasible, does not discriminate unfairly between the classes, and is fair and equitable in its treatment of the impaired, dissenting classes of claims or interests.

After the creditors are provided with the Disclosure Statement, the Proposed Plan of Reorganization, and a ballot for voting on the plan, a **confirmation hearing** is set. At the confirmation hearing, the court determines whether the requirements of the Code have been met that will allow entry of a Confirmation Order. Among those requirements is that a creditor must receive through the plan at least what they would receive in a Chapter 7 liquidation.

Another important tool available to the Chapter 11 creditor is the
ability to assume or reject **executory contracts** and **unexpired leases**.
Generally, an **executory contract** is a contract under which both
parties have unfulfilled future obligations other than the mere payment
of money. Therefore, a promissory note is not an executory contract,
but an employment contract may be executory. Since a reorganization
continues a business, the debtor in possession will want to evaluate all
real and personal property leases, plus any other executory contracts,
and decide which leases it wants to continue or "assume." The debtor
will also want to eliminate unnecessary and burdensome contracts that
may have contributed to its financial distress. The debtor will then
"reject" the contract.

During the postpetiton time frame, while the decision-making process
regarding these contracts may still be ongoing, the debtor in possession
must continue to make postpetition payments under the contracts and
leases. If the debtor elects to assume a contract, it is required to **"cure
the default"** in the contract by providing payment of any past due
prepetition debt on the effective date of the plan. If a contract or lease
is rejected, any related property is returned to the creditor, and a proof
of claim is filed for the remaining balance.

The Chapter 13 Case

The purpose of the Chapter 13 plan is the adjustment of debts of
individuals with regular income. The regular income requirement
provides the mechanism for funding the plan. In a Chapter 13, a trustee
is appointed in every case, but does not take possession of the property
of the estate. The plan proposing the adjustment of debt must be
promptly filed, and creditors do not vote on this plan.

The Chapter 13 trustee is entrusted with the duty to pay creditors a
portion of the debtor's future earnings or income pursuant to the terms
and conditions of the plan. The debtor sends a monthly check to the
trustee, and the trustee divides the proceeds among the creditors in
accordance with the plan.

There is only a single financial requirement for treatment of unsecured creditors under the Chapter 13 plan. The Code requires the court to determine whether an unsecured creditor would receive less under a Chapter 13 plan than it would under a Chapter 7 liquidation. If the court so determines, the Chapter 13 plan cannot be confirmed. The term of the plan for repayment of debts cannot exceed three years, or five years with prior court approval.

Unlike the limited Chapter 11 discharge that arises at the time the plan is confirmed, the Chapter 13 debtor is not discharged until full performance of the plan is completed. If the inability to perform is traced to reasons beyond the debtor's control, the debtor may receive a "hardship" discharge, as long as the debtor has performed sufficiently to ensure that the creditors have received more under the partially performed plan than they would have under a liquidation.

The Role of the Bankruptcy Paralegal

Bankruptcy is an area of practice well-suited to utilization of paralegals. It involves a large amount of information gathering from the client, review of documents, preparation of forms, and recognition of problem areas for review with the attorney. Once an attorney has assumed representation of a Chapter 7 debtor, the majority of the initial work is delegated to the paralegal. The tasks usually include:

- Presenting a comprehensive questionnaire to the client, and interview of the client after completion of the questionnaire.

- Gathering and reviewing relevant documents for preparation of the petition and schedules.

- Identifying potential problem areas, such as nondischargeable debts, recent loans, etc., and reviewing with the attorney.

- Preparing the petition, schedules, and other relevant forms.

- Reviewing the completed petition and forms with the client, and obtaining the appropriate signatures.

- Educating and preparing the client for the creditor's meeting.

- Receiving post-filing telephone calls from creditors and other parties in interest regarding the bankruptcy.

- Keeping a "tickler system" of all relevant filing dates throughout the bankruptcy and keep the attorney and client informed of these deadlines.

- Preparing any necessary documents, such as reaffirmation agreements, in anticipation of the discharge hearing.

- Reviewing bankruptcy mailing and pleadings, and addressing any relevant requirements.

This list is by no means comprehensive, but it does give a flavor for the many important and varied tasks performed by bankruptcy paralegals. More than many other specialties, this is an area where a successful practice requires a diligent team effort for attorneys and paralegals.

EXERCISE

The Rocky Mountain Rock Crushing Company files a petition under Chapter 11. The Ajax Equipment Company has a purchase money security interest in a rock-crushing machine valued at $200,000. Only two payments were made. Expert testimony is available that the equipment depreciates at a rate of $2,000 per month. What theories can you think of to support the motion to lift the automatic stay on behalf of Ajax? If you represent Rocky Mountain, how will you defend this action?

BIBLIOGRAPHY

Baird, Douglas B., Theodore Eisenberg and Thomas H. Jackson, *Commercial and Debtor-Creditor Law: Selected Statutes*, Westbury, New York: The Foundation Press, Inc., 1996.

Baird, Douglas B., *The Elements of Bankruptcy*, Westbury, New York: The Foundation Press, Inc., 1993.

Blum, Brian A., *Bankruptcy and Debtor/Creditor*, Boston, MA: Little, Brown and Company, 1993.

Epstein, David G., *Bankruptcy and Other Debtor-Creditor Laws, 5th Ed.*, St. Paul, Minn.: West Publishing Co., 1995.

Nickles, Steve H. and David G. Epstein, *Creditors' Rights and Bankruptcy*, St. Paul, Minn.: West Publishing Co., 1989.

Stone, Bradford, *Uniform Commercial Code in a Nutshell, 2nd Ed.*, St. Paul, Minn.: West Publishing Co., 1984.

Williams, Jack F. and Pamela Salsburg Williams, *Creditors' Rights and Bankruptcy*, New York, N.Y.: Matthew Bender, 1992.

Williams, Rosemary, *Bankruptcy Practice Handbook*, Deerfield, IL: Clark, Boardman, Callaghan, 1991.

GLOSSARY

Abandonment The relinquishing of property without necessarily designating who shall take possession of it. Related to the homestead exemption on real property, it is the conduct of the debtor that results in loss of the exemption after moving away from the place with the intent never to occupy it again as a home. Also, a bankruptcy term describing a trustee's release of property from the bankrupt estate.

Adequate protection Protection afforded by Bankruptcy Code for holders of secured claims. Lack of adequate protection of the creditor's interest in the collateral is the basis for relief from the automatic stay under section 362(d)(1), and for creditor protection from sale or use of the collateral under sections 363 and 364.

Account "Any right to payment for goods sold or leased or for services rendered which is not evidenced by an instrument or chattel paper, whether or not it has been earned by performance." UCC Section 9.106

Adversary Proceeding A trial of a disputed issue held within a proceeding in the bankruptcy court.

Affidavit A written statement of facts, sworn to and signed before a person authorized by law to administer oaths.

After-acquired property clause A clause included in security agreements and UCC-1 financing statements that incorporates a security interest in collateral acquired after the date of the initial transaction.

Attachment **1)** The seizure and taking into custody of the debtor's property by a sheriff or constable, in order to secure the debt or claim of a creditor; **2)** Under the Uniform Commercial Code, the simultaneous existence of all elements that render a security interest in property enforceable against a debtor.

Automatic Stay Triggered by the filing of a bankruptcy petition, a device under Section 362 of the Bankruptcy Code under which all collection activity against the debtor is frozen, and the bankruptcy estate is preserved to facilitate a more orderly liquidation or reorganization.

Badges of fraud Circumstances or facts accompanying a transfer of property by a debtor that the courts recognize as reliable indicators of fraudulent intent.

Bankruptcy Inability to pay debts as they become due, or the state of being subject to the laws of the Bankruptcy Code.

Bankruptcy estate All of the debtor's legal or equitable interest in property at the time of filing a bankruptcy petition, regardless of location of property or possession by other than the debtor.

Bankruptcy petition The document filed in order to commence a bankruptcy proceeding.

Breach of the peace A disturbance of public peace, which can be brought about by attempts to repossess property or satisfy a debt. The UCC allows "self help" repossession of collateral by secured parties as long as there is no breach of the peace.

Chattel paper A writing or a group of writings that contains both a monetary obligation and a security interest in, or a lease of, specific goods. Chattel paper can therefore include a security agreement and any other documents transferring the rights contained under the agreement.

Collateral The property that is subject to a security interest.

Conditional sales contract Contract in which the creditor agrees to sell certain goods to the debtor and retains a security interest in those goods, and value is given when the secured party sells or agrees to sell the goods.

Confirmation Order The final order of the Bankruptcy Court related to confirmation of a plan of reorganization under Chapter 11.

Consensual lien A lien granted by the debtor to the creditor through mutual consent, usually contained in a security agreement.

Consumer A person who purchases goods and services for personal, family and household purposes. Consumer transactions are treated differently from business to business transactions due to the uneven playing field facing consumers.

Consumer debt A debt incurred by an individual primarily for personal, family or household purposes.

Creditor A person who has a legal right to fulfillment of a debt or obligation.

Cure of default The opportunity provided to a debtor to pay a past due obligation and any related expenses in order to bring contracts or accounts current and preserve rights in related collateral.

Debt A specific sum of money owed or an obligation to pay, owed by one person to another.

Debtor A person who owes a debt that is due or will become due. Under the Bankruptcy Code a debtor is the person or entity which either files a voluntary bankruptcy petition, or is subject to an order for relief entered after the filing of an involuntary bankruptcy petition.

Debtor-in-possession A debtor in a Chapter 11 case that continues in possession and control of the property of the estate, in lieu of the appointment of a trustee.

Default The failure of a debtor to perform an obligation, typically by late payment or nonpayment of debts as they become due.

Default judgment A judgment obtained after the defendant fails to timely file an answer or otherwise make an appearance in the lawsuit.

Deficiency balance The difference between the amount owed on an obligation and the sum received from sale of collateral, plus any costs of sale. This is the balance that the creditor can seek to recover from the debtor.

Discharge of debtor In the context of bankruptcy, the release of the debtor from all debts as the culmination of the bankruptcy proceedings, and barring the collection of pre-bankruptcy claims against the debtor.

Discovery The process by which parties to litigation obtain information and facts relevant to the lawsuit, typically through depositions, interrogatories, admissions, document production requests, etc.

Document A sub-category of quasi-tangible collateral limited to a specific types of document, defined under Section 1-201(15) as a "document of title." In the ordinary course of business or financing, a document is treated as adequately evidencing that the person in possession of the document is entitled to receive, hold, and dispose of both the document and the goods covered by the document. The classic examples are bills of lading and warehouse receipts.

Equipment Goods that are used primarily in a business but are not inventory.

Equity Within the debtor/creditor context, the debtor's ownership interest in collateral as payments are credited against the principal balance owed.

Execution The legal process of enforcing a judgment by seizing and selling the property of the judgment debtor.

Executory contract A contract under which both parties have unfulfilled future obligations other than the payment of money. Under Chapter 11 of the Bankruptcy Code, this type of contract can be assumed or rejected by the debtor-in-possession.

Exempt assets Property of a debtor that is not subject to seizure by creditors under state or federal laws for satisfaction of creditor's claims against the debtor.

Ex parte A proceeding in which the court takes action on the application of only one side of a controversy, without notice or participation of the other party.

Fair market value The amount a piece of property would bring if sold on the open market in a good faith, arm's length transaction between a willing buyer and a willing seller.

Farm products A classification of tangible collateral consisting of crops, livestock, supplies, etc. used or produced in farming operations, but only if they remain in the possession of a debtor engaged in farm operations.

Financing statement A statement filed by a secured creditor in accordance with the UCC as adopted in each state, in order to perfect a security interest in collateral and establish priority as against other creditors.

Fixtures Items of personal property that have become so affixed to real property that the law utilizes a different treatment than detached personal property.

Foreclosure Procedure for sale of property by a creditor upon default by the debtor, in order to satisfy the outstanding debt on the property. Includes the process for sale of real property by the mortgagor upon default in payment by the mortgagee.

Fraudulent transfer A transfer of property of a debtor made with the intent to defraud creditors, and is voidable by certain creditors.

Garnishment A procedure for obtaining property of a debtor that is in the possession or control of third parties.

General intangibles A subcategory of collateral defined in the UCC as "Any personal property...other than goods, accounts, chattel paper, documents, instruments, and money." Section 9.106

Guarantor A third party who guarantees performance of an obligation by the principal debtor. Differs from a co-signer in that a creditor must first seek payment from the underlying debtor before resort to collection from the guarantor.

Homestead exemption Varying state and federal protections of a debtor's home from execution and foreclosure by creditors.

Insolvent A person or entity that cannot pay debts as they become due, or whose liabilities exceed assets at a fair valuation.

Instruments A subcategory of quasi-tangible collateral which includes negotiable instruments, as well as any other documents evidencing a right to payment in money that are transferred by delivery in the ordinary course of business. Common examples are checks and certificates of deposit.

Intangibles A type of collateral with no physical form, but with well recognized rights, categorized as either general intangibles or accounts.

Inventory A type of tangible collateral consisting of goods held for sale or lease or furnished under contracts of service, as well as raw materials, work in progress, or materials used or consumed in a business.

Judicial lien A lien obtained by judgment, levy, or other legal or equitable process, and issued by order from the court.

Lien A charge on property that must be satisfied before the property or its proceeds are available for the satisfaction of the debts of general creditors.

Liquidated debt One in which the amount of money due can be calculated as a sum certain.

Liquidation Bankruptcy proceeding in which all of debtor's non-exempt assets are collected by the Chapter 7 trustee, reduced to cash, and the proceeds distributed to various creditors in accordance with the priority rules outlined in the Bankruptcy Code.

Nonexempt assets Assets that are not protected from seizure by creditors for the satisfaction of debts under either state or federal law.

Nulla bona A sheriff's return of a writ indicating that no property of the judgment debtor has been found that is subject to execution and seizure for sale and satisfaction of the judgment.

Objection to discharge An attempt by a creditor to prevent the discharge of debts of a debtor under the Bankruptcy Code.

Objection to the dischargeability of a particular debt In bankruptcy an attempt by a creditor to exclude a debt from the scope of an order of discharge

Perfection A method to provide public notice to parties contemplating doing business with the debtor that an enforceable lien exists against certain property. Perfection also establishes priority in the collateral among competing interests, including those holding statutory liens, judicial liens, and other consensual lienholders.

Personal property Property other than real property.

Plan of Reorganization Document filed by a Chapter 11 debtor, outlining the amounts and distribution proposed for the various classes of creditors to receive.

Pledge An oral grant of a security interest coupled with the transfer of the collateral to the creditor.

Primary use test Test for classification of collateral that is used by the debtor for multiple purposes, focusing on the primary use of the collateral.

Priority claim Claim that receives more favorable treatment under the Bankruptcy Code than other unsecured claims.

Proof of Claim Filing required of creditor in bankruptcy, outlining the basis of the claim, the amount due, and any features that may be relevant to the status or priority of the claim.

Purchase money security interest A security interest in specific collateral, securing an obligation created so that the debtor can actually purchase the specific collateral.

Quasicontract A circumstance where all elements of a contract do not exist, but the equitable powers of the law may deem that a debt arises in order to avoid the unjust enrichment of one of the parties.

Quasi-tangible A type of collateral characterized by having specific legal rights embodied in some type of written document. This document not only evidences the legal right, but also carries its own legal significance. Three sub-categories are instruments, documents, and chattel paper.

Reaffirmation agreement An agreement between the debtor and a creditor under Chapter 7 of the Bankruptcy Code under which the debtor agrees to pay an otherwise dischargeable debt.

Reorganization A type of bankruptcy, contained in Chapter 11 of the Bankruptcy Code, in which the debtor business is allowed to propose a plan for reduction of burdensome debts, repayment of creditors, and continuation of the business through implementation and performance of the plan of reorganization.

Replevin An action in which a creditor can seek removal of specific property from the possession of a debtor, pending judgment in the final action.

Secured creditor is one who has an interest or security in collateral.

Security agreement An agreement, signed by both the debtor and creditor, that creates a consensual security interest in property.

Security interest "an interest in personal property or fixtures that secures payment or performance of an obligation." UCC Section 1-201(37).

Self-help repossession Removal of collateral by the secured creditor without engaging in a formal legal process.

Statutory lien Lien that is created by following particular processes and procedures outlined in a state or federal statute.

Summary judgment Judgment reached without trial on factual issues, in that the court has determined, based on the arguments of the parties, that there are no genuine issues of material fact, and one party is entitled to judgment as a matter of law. *No trail*

Tangibles A classification of personal property that consists of goods such as inventory, equipment, consumer goods, and farm products.

Tort The area of law involving private wrongs (as opposed to the public wrongs addressed by criminal law) other than breach of contract.

Trustee A person who holds property for the benefit of another. Under the Bankruptcy Code, the trustee is appointed to administer collect, and liquidate the debtor's estate, and to assure the proper distribution of any proceeds to the creditors according to their priority.

Uniform Commercial Code A comprehensive set of statutes governing virtually all aspects of commercial transactions, adopted in some form by all states. The nine articles govern matters such as sales, bank deposits and collections, and secured transactions (Article 9).

Unliquidated debt One in which the amount due cannot be calculated as a sum certain, but instead a trier of fact must be engaged or an agreement reached as to the total amount due.

Unsecured creditor A creditor having no collateral or security agreement to assure payment of its claim.

Writ An order issued by a court requiring or authorizing the performance of a certain act.

APPENDICES

Appendix 1. Credit Application with Release Language

Appendix 2. Personal Guaranty

Appendix 3. Irrevocable Letter of Credit

Appendix 4. Sample Demand Letters (9)

Appendix 5. Federal Fair Debt Collection Practices Act

Appendix 6. State Debt Collection Acts (3)

Appendix 7. Personal Property Exemption Statutes (4)

Appendix 8. Florida Fraudulent Transfer Act

Appendix 9. Bankruptcy Forms (11)

CREDIT INFORMATION FORM

Customer Credit Information

Full Legal Name _____

Date Started _____ Number of Employees_____

Street Address_____

City_____ State____ Zip Code_____

Nature of Business_____

Contact Name_____ Phone No._____

[] Corporation   [] Partnership   [] Proprietorship

Has Business ever filed a bankruptcy petition or had one filed against it?____ If

yes, please state the court and case number_____

Are you a current or previous customer?____

If yes, list account numbers_____

Bank References

Bank Name _____

Name of Officer _____

Address _____

City/State/Zip _____

Account # and Type _____

Loan Account #_____

Bank Name _____

Name of Officer _____

Address _____

City/State/Zip _____

Account # and Type _____

Loan Account #_____

Information on Principals

Name_____

Social Security # _____

Address_____

City/State/Zip _____

Name_____

Social Security # _____

Address_____

City/State/Zip _____

Bank Credit Information Release Authorization

To: The Bank References shown above:

Please accept this authorization to disclose the customary information you would normally release to a potential creditor including:

- Length of time account has been active
- Average monthly balances
- Details of lending relationship
- Number of return items

Customer affirms that the information provided above is true and correct to the best of its knowledge and agrees that all of its obligations will immediately become due and payable, without demand or notice, if any information provided on this application or any other financial information provided proves to be untrue. Customer also agrees that a credit investigation will be conducted, and consents to contact with the named banks.

_____

Customer Signature

Title_____

PERSONAL GUARANTY

THIS CONTINUING GUARANTY ("Guaranty") is entered into between [Name of Creditor] ("Creditor") and [Name of Guarantor] ("Guarantor"). This Guaranty relates to extension of credit by Creditor to [Name of Debtor] ("Customer").

WHEREAS, Customer is seeking to obtain credit from Creditor; and

WHEREAS, Creditor requires security for payment of the current indebtedness and all future indebtedness of Customer to Creditor; and

WHEREAS, Guarantor is willing to furnish the required security in the form of a personal guaranty of payment of the current and future indebtedness of Customer.

NOW, therefore, in consideration of the extension of credit by Creditor to Customer, Guarantor agrees as follows:

1. Guarantor unconditionally guarantees to Creditor payment at maturity or by acceleration of all indebtedness which Customer owes to Creditor, now and in the future. Guarantor shall also pay to Creditor reasonable attorney's fees and all costs and expenses incurred in collecting payments from Customer or enforcing this Guaranty.

2. The Guaranty shall be revolving and continuous, and shall include all indebtedness and obligations of Customer to Creditor which now exist or are incurred in the future by Customer, until Creditor receives written revocation from Guarantor. The written revocation shall not impair or terminate Guarantor's liability with respect to any indebtedness or obligations incurred by Customer prior to Creditor's receipt of said revocation.

3. Guarantor waives the giving of any notices and the making of any demands. Guarantor agrees that Creditor may change the form of any indebtedness, extend indebtedness, change the time of deliveries or payments, or otherwise modify the terms of sale or lease to Customer, all without in any manner affecting Guarantor's liability hereunder. Guarantor agrees that in the event of default by Customer, Guarantor's liability shall not be

the event of default by Customer, Guarantor's liability shall not be conditioned upon Creditor instituting suit or foreclosing upon any lien or security interest in satisfaction of the obligations of Customer.

4. This Guaranty shall continue until all obligations of Customer are fully satisfied, and shall bind the heirs, executors, administrators and assigns of the Guarantor.

Signed this _____ day of _____, 199_.

_____
[Signature of Guarantor]

_____
Print Name of Guarantor

Address _____
Telephone _____
Social Security Number _____

IRREVOCABLE STANDBY
LETTER OF CREDIT

Anytown Bank and Trust, N.A.
P.O. Box 2000
Anywhere, USA 10009

Irrevocable Standby Letter of Credit

Date and Place of Issue:
September 1, 1998
Anywhere, USA

Account Party:
ABC Company, Inc.
P.O. Box 1006
Anywhere, USA 10009

Advising Bank:
Anytown Bank and Trust, N.A.
P. O. Box 2000
Anywhere, USA 10009

Number:_____

Beneficiary:
Big Corporation
1001 Big Square
New York, New York

Amount:
$40,000 U.S. Dollars

Date of Expiration:_____
at our counters in Anywhere, USA

To Whom It May Concern:

We hereby issue this irrevocable standby letter of credit in your favor in the amount of _____Forty Thousand and No/100_____ which is available by negotiation of your draft(s) at _____ Anywhere, USA _____ sight drawn on us. Bearing the clause: Drawn under standby letter of credit No. _____ dated _____ on Anytown Bank and Trust, N.A., Anywhere, USA and with presentation of the following required documents:

Written notification from Big Corporation that there has existed an unremedied monetary default for more than 30 days in the lease agreement between ABC Company, Inc. and Big Corporation.

Written notification from Big Corporation that there has existed an unremedied monetary default for more than 30 days in the lease agreement between ABC Company, Inc. and Big Corporation.

We hereby engage with drawers and/or bona fide holders that drafts drawn and negotiated in conformity with the terms of this credit will be honored on presentation at our counters and that drafts accepted within the terms of this credit will be honored at maturity.

Yours very truly,

Anytown Bank and Trust, N.A.

_____

Lloyd Smith, President

DEMAND LETTER FOR
A COMMERCIAL DEBT

Mr. Art Vandalay, President
Discount Widget Company
1000 Main Street
Arlen, Texas 77777

Re: Indebtedness to: [client name]
Current balance: $_____

Dear Mr. Vandalay:

The above debt has been referred to this law firm for collection. In order to resolve this matter without further action, immediately forward your check for the full amount indicated above to this office.

If you believe you do not owe this balance, please advise [contact person] of this office. If you are financially unable to pay this debt in full, indicate the terms you would like our client to consider. Please be advised, however, that any proposal you make will not necessarily delay our client's action to collect this debt. No offer will be binding unless accepted and confirmed in writing by our client or this office.

If this debt is not satisfactorily resolved in thirty (30) days, our client's alternative will be to file suit against you. If litigation is necessary, attorney's fees and court costs will be requested in addition to the principal sum due.

Your immediate attention is expected.

Very truly yours,

Rich Lather, Esq.
Attorney at Law

DEMAND LETTER FOR A
CONSUMER DEBT
(WITH FDCPA WARNING)

Ms. Susan Bishop
1000 Elm Street
Arlen, Texas 77777

Re: Indebtedness to: [client name]
        Current balance: $_____

Dear Ms. Bishop:

The above debt has been referred to this law firm for collection. In order to resolve this matter without further action, immediately forward your check for the full amount indicated above to this office.

If you believe you do not owe this balance, please advise [contact person] of this office. If you are financially unable to pay this debt in full, indicate the terms you would like our client to consider. Please be advised, however, that any proposal you make will not necessarily delay our client's action to collect this debt. No offer will be binding unless accepted and confirmed in writing by our client or this office.

Unless you dispute the validity of the debt, or any portion thereof, within 30 days after receipt of this notice, the debt will be assumed to be valid by this office. If you notify this office in writing within 30 days that this debt or any portion thereof is disputed, we will provide verification of the debt to you. Also, upon your written request within 30 days after receipt of this letter we will provide you with the name and address of the original creditor, if different from the above-referenced creditor.

You are advised that any information obtained from you will be used in attempts to collect this debt.

If this debt is not resolved in thirty (30) days, our client's alternative will be to file suit against you. If litigation is necessary, attorney's fees and court costs will be requested in addition to the principal sum due.

Very truly yours,

Rich Lather, Esq.
Attorney at Law

NOTICE OF INTENT TO
ACCELERATE
PROMISSORY NOTE

[Certified Mail, Return Receipt Requested]

Mr. Art Vandalay
Discount Widget Company
1000 Main Street
Arlen, Texas 77777

Re: Promissory Note dated _____, in the original
principal amount of $_____ executed by _____
(the "Note")

Dear Mr. Vandalay:

The undersigned represents _____ in connection with
the above-referenced Note. You are in default in your payment obligations
under the Note. The monthly payment due for_____,19__, and all
subsequent payments remain unpaid. As of the date of this letter, the arrearage
for monthly payments is the sum of $_____. You are also
liable for late charges in the sum of $_____. Your total liability
as of the date of this letter is $_____, which is the total of the listed
amounts.

The full amount of your indebtedness must be paid within ten (10) days of the
date of this notice, along with additional monthly payments that may accrue in
the interim. If full payment is not received at the offices of
_____ on or before _____, 19__, before 4:45 p.m.,
the Note will be accelerated, and the entire amount of unpaid principal and
accrued interest will automatically be due.

Any payment made must be by cashier's check or certified funds.

Very truly yours,

Rich Lather, Attorney at Law
cc: Ms. Ima Fool (Guarantor)

DEMAND FOR RETURN
OF COLLATERAL

[Certified Mail, Return Receipt Requested]

Mr. Art Vandalay
1313 Mockingbird Lane
Arlen, Texas 77777

Re: Promissory Note dated _____, in the original principal
amount of $_____ executed by _____ (the
"Note") secured by [describe collateral]

Dear Mr. Vandalay:

The undersigned represents _____ in connection with the
above-referenced Note. You are in default in your payment obligations under
the Note. The monthly payment due for _____, 19__, and all
subsequent payments remain unpaid. As of the date of this letter, the
arrearage for monthly payments is the sum of $_____. You are also
liable for late charges in the sum of $_____. Your total
liability as of the date of this letter is $_____, which is the
total of the above amounts.

The full amount of your indebtedness must be paid within ten (10) days of the
date of this notice, along with additional monthly payments that may accrue in
the interim. If full payment is not received at the offices of _____
on or before _____ 19__, before 4:45 p.m., the Note will be
accelerated, and the entire amount of unpaid principal and accrued interest will
be automatically due.

Any payment made must be by cashier's check or certified funds.

Unless within thirty (30) days after receipt of this notice you dispute the
validity of the indebtedness referred to above in whole or in part, we will
assume that this indebtedness is valid in all respects. If we are notified in
writing within the thirty (30) day period that all or any portion of this
indebtedness is disputed, we shall obtain verification of the indebtedness and
mail a copy of such verification to you. Finally you are advised that any

mail a copy of such verification to you. Finally you are advised that any information obtained from you will be used for the purposes of the collection of this debt.

Very truly yours,

Rich Lather
Attorney at Law

c: Ms. Ima Fool
 (Guarantor)

NOTICE OF ACCELERATION
OF PROMISSORY NOTE

CERTIFIED MAIL - RETURN RECEIPT REQUESTED

Mr. Art Vandalay
Discount Widget Company
1000 Main Street
Arlen, Texas 77777

Re: Promissory Note dated _____ in the original principal amount of
$_____ executed by _____ payable to the order of
_____ (the Note)

Dear Mr. Vandalay:

Please refer to my letter to you dated _____ on behalf of _____
concerning default in your payment obligation on the above-referenced Note.

The default described by such letter has not been cured as required. You are
hereby advised that the Note has been accelerated, and the entire indebtedness
evidenced by the Note is immediately due and payable.

For information concerning the amount required to pay the Note in full, contact
_____ at _____.

Very truly yours,

Rich Lather, Esq.
Attorney at Law

c: Ms. Ima Fool (Guarantor)

NOTICE OF DEFAULT IN
PERSONAL PROPERTY LEASE

Mr. Art Vandalay
Discount Widget Company
1000 Main Street
Arlen, Texas 77777

Re: Lease Agreement with _____ dated
_____ concerning [describe equipment]

Dear Mr. Vandalay:

This firm has been retained by [name of lessor] in connection with your default on the above-referenced Lease Agreement. Please be advised that your monthly payment for the month of _____,19__, and all subsequent monthly payments have not been paid. The total of such payments is $_____. You have also incurred late payments at the rate of $_____ per payment, for an additional $_____. The total indebtedness on the Lease Agreement as of this date is $_____. Please consider this as a formal demand for cure of the default in the Lease Agreement.

If payment is not received by lessor within ten (10) days of the date of this letter, the lease shall terminate automatically without any further notice to you. In such instance, you will be subject to the liabilities for early termination and default as set forth in the Lease Agreement, and all remedies provided at law.

Should you wish to discuss this matter, please contact _____ of this office immediately.

Sincerely,

Rich Lather, Esq.
Attorney at Law

DEMAND FOR REPLACEMENT
OF BAD CHECK

CERTIFIED MAIL - RETURN RECEIPT REQUESTED

Mr. Art Vandalay
Discount Widget Company
1000 Main Street
Arlen, Texas 77777

Re: Indebtedness to _____, evidenced by check number
_____ in the sum of $_____.

Dear Mr. Vandalay:

I represent _____. My client has forwarded to me the
original of the above-listed check, dated _____ and signed by you.
This check has been returned to my client, dishonored due to insufficient funds
in the account. Formal demand is made upon you to immediately replace the
check with cash or certified funds. Upon your tender of good funds, the check
will be returned to you.

Please note that although the imprint on the check indicates that the transaction
underlying the payment involved Discount Widget Company, the signature on
the check is yours, and indicates no representative capacity. Consequently, this
instrument represents your personal obligation to pay the indebtedness in
question.

If you fail to make payment as demanded in this letter, or fail to make suitable
arrangements concerning this indebtedness, a civil lawsuit may be instituted
against you. If litigation is necessary, attorney's fees and court costs will be
requested in addition to the principal sum due.

Please contact me at once concerning this very serious matter.

Sincerely,

Rich Lather
Attorney at Law

NOTICE OF PERSONAL
PROPERTY FORECLOSURE
(PRIVATE SALE)

CERTIFIED MAIL - RETURN RECEIPT REQUESTED

Mr. Art Vandalay
Discount Widget Company
1000 Main Street
Arlen, Texas 77777

Re: Promissory Note dated _____ in the original principal
amount of $_____, executed by _____, payable to
_____, and secured by _____.

Dear Mr. Vandalay:

Your default in payment of the Promissory Note has previously resulted in an acceleration of the indebtedness due. (secured creditor) has now instructed me to notify you of its intent to proceed with foreclosure by private sale of that certain personal property identified as: (description of collateral) .

The private sale will take place on or after (date) at (time) .

You may redeem the property subject to sale by tendering the full amount of the indebtedness, accrued interest, attorneys' fees, and the expenses incurred in taking, holding, and preparing the collateral for disposition. The tender of such sums must be made prior to the scheduled sale, in good, immediately collectable funds, such as a cashier's check or certified funds.

In the event you do not fully satisfy the debt and redeem the property subject to sale, proceeds from the sale will be applied to the entire indebtedness (including fees and expenses) due at the time of sale. Should sale proceeds not be sufficient to satisfy the indebtedness, you will be liable for any deficiency.

Sincerely,

Rich Lather
Attorney at Law

NOTICE OF PERSONAL
PROPERTY FORECLOSURE
(PUBLIC SALE)

CERTIFIED MAIL - RETURN RECEIPT REQUESTED

Mr. Art Vandalay
Discount Widget Company
1000 Main Street
Arlen, Texas 77777

Re: Promissory Note dated _____ in the original principal
amount of $_____, executed by _____, payable to
_____, and secured by _____.

Dear Mr. Vandalay:

Your default in payment of the Promissory Note has previously resulted in an
acceleration of the indebtedness due.[Secured creditor] has now instructed me
to notify you of its intent to proceed with foreclosure by public sale of that
certain personal property identified as: [description of collateral] .

Enclosed is a copy of the Notice of Public Sale which will be posted at the
_____ County Courthouse, within 48 hours of the date of this letter.
Pursuant to the terms of the Security Agreement, a sale of such personal
property will take place on [date], at _____ a.m. Central Standard
Time at [sale location].

You may redeem the property subject to sale by tendering the full amount of
the indebtedness, accrued interest, attorneys' fees, and the expenses incurred
in taking, holding, and preparing the collateral for disposition. The tender of
such sums must be made prior to the scheduled sale, in good, immediately
collectable funds, such as a cashier's check or certified funds.

In the event that you do not fully satisfy the debt, and redeem the property
subject to sale, proceeds from the sale will be applied to the entire
indebtedness (including fees and expenses) due at the time of sale. Should sale
proceeds not be sufficient to satisfy the indebtedness, you will be liable for any
deficiency.

NOTICE OF PUBLIC SALE

Notice is hereby given that [name of client] (Secured Party), of [address] intends to sell at public sale, for cash, the property described in the attached Exhibit "A" (the Collateral).

The Collateral was obtained from [name of debtor] (Debtor) of [address], under the terms of the security agreements which granted security interests in the Collateral to Secured Party in order to secure payment of the debt. The indebtedness owing by Debtor to Secured Party is in default. The Collateral is going to be sold at public sale to reduce the indebtedness owed by Debtor to Secured Party.

The public sale will take place at [location] on [date], at [time] o'clock _.m. Secured Party reserves the right to bid at the sale for credit on the indebtedness of Debtor to Secured Party and become the purchaser of all or part of the Collateral and furthermore reserves the right to require a minimum bid from any and all potential bidders and further reserves the right to reject all bids and adjourn the sale to such other time or times as Secured Party may deem proper. All sales tax and transfer fees relating to the sale of the Collateral shall be the sole responsibility of any successful bidder. Sale of the Collateral is without recourse or warranty against Secured Party. The Collateral is being sold on an "AS-IS" and "WHERE-IS" basis, and Secured Party disclaims any implied warranty with respect to such Collateral.

All questions and inquiries concerning the Collateral and the sale, or requests to inspect the Collateral, may be addressed to [creditor contact], [address].

[CREDITOR]

By:
[Attorney Name]
[Address]

15 U.S.C. 1692
THE FEDERAL FAIR DEBT
COLLECTION PRACTICES ACT

§ 1692. Congressional findings and declaration of purpose

(a) Abusive practices

There is abundant evidence of the use of abusive, deceptive, and unfair debt collection practices by many debt collectors. Abusive debt collection practices contribute to the number of personal bankruptcies, to marital instability, to the loss of jobs, and to invasions of individual privacy.

(b) Inadequacy of laws

Existing laws and procedures for redressing these injuries are inadequate to protect consumers.

(c) Available non-abusive collection methods

Means other than misrepresentation or other abusive debt collection practices are available for the effective collection of debts.

(d) Interstate commerce

Abusive debt collection practices are carried on to a substantial extent in interstate commerce and through means and instrumentalities of such commerce. Even where abusive debt collection practices are purely intrastate in character, they nevertheless directly affect interstate commerce.

(e) Purposes

It is the purpose of this subchapter to eliminate abusive debt collection practices by debt collectors, to insure that those debt collectors who refrain from using abusive debt collection practices are not competitively disadvantaged, and to promote consistent State action to protect consumers against debt collection abuses.

§ 1692a. Definitions

As used in this subchapter -

(1) The term "Commission" means the Federal Trade Commission.

(2) The term "communication" means the conveying of information regarding a debt directly or indirectly to any person through any medium.

(3) The term "consumer" means any natural person obligated or allegedly obligated to pay any debt.

(4) The term "creditor" means any person who offers or extends credit creating a debt or to whom a debt is owed, but such term does not include any person to the extent that he receives an assignment or transfer of a debt in default solely for the purpose of facilitating collection of such debt for another.

(5) The term "debt" means any obligation or alleged obligation of a consumer to pay money arising out of a transaction in which the money, property, insurance, or services which are the subject of the transaction are primarily for personal, family, or household purposes, whether or not such obligation has been reduced to judgment.

(6) The term "debt collector" means any person who uses any instrumentality of interstate commerce or the mails in any business the principal purpose of which is the collection of any debts, or who regularly collects or attempts to collect, directly or indirectly, debts owed or due or asserted to be owed or due another. Notwithstanding the exclusion provided by clause (F) of the last sentence of this paragraph, the term includes any creditor who, in the process of collecting his own debts, uses any name other than his own which would indicate that a third person is collecting or attempting to collect such debts. For the purpose of section 1692f(6) of this title, such term also includes any person who uses any instrumentality of interstate commerce or the mails in any business the principal purpose of which is the enforcement of security interests. The term does not include -

(A) any officer or employee of a creditor while, in the name of the creditor, collecting debts for such creditor;

(B) any person while acting as a debt collector for another person, both of whom are related by common ownership or affiliated by corporate control, if the person acting as a debt collector does so only for persons to whom it is so related or affiliated and if the principal business of such person is not the collection of debts;

(C) any officer or employee of the United States or any State to the extent that collecting or attempting to collect any debt is in the performance of his official duties;

(D) any person while serving or attempting to serve legal process on any other person in connection with the judicial enforcement of any debt;

(E) any nonprofit organization which, at the request of consumers, performs bona fide consumer credit counseling and assists consumers in the liquidation of their debts by receiving payments from such consumers and distributing such amounts to creditors; and

(F) any person collecting or attempting to collect any debt owed or due or asserted to be owed or due another to the extent such activity

(i) is incidental to a bona fide fiduciary obligation or a bona fide escrow arrangement;

(ii)concerns a debt which was originated by such person;

(iii) concerns a debt which was not in default at the time it was obtained by such person; or

(iv) concerns a debt obtained by such person as a secured party in a commercial credit transaction involving the creditor.

(7) The term "location information" means a consumer's place of abode and his telephone number at such place, or his place of employment.

(8) The term "State" means any State, territory, or possession of the United States, the District of Columbia, the Commonwealth of Puerto Rico, or any political subdivision of any of the foregoing.

§ 1692c. Communication in connection with debt collection

(a) Communication with the consumer generally

Without the prior consent of the consumer given directly to the debt collector or the express permission of a court of competent jurisdiction, a debt collector may not communicate with a consumer in connection with the collection of any debt -

(1) at any unusual time or place or a time or place known or which should be known to be inconvenient to the consumer. In the absence of knowledge of circumstances to the contrary, a debt collector shall assume that the convenient time for communicating with a consumer is after 8 o'clock antemeridian and before 9 o'clock postmeridian, local time at the consumer's location;

(2) if the debt collector knows the consumer is represented by an attorney with respect to such debt and has knowledge of, or can readily ascertain, such attorney's name and address, unless the attorney fails to respond within a reasonable period of time to a communication from the debt collector or unless the attorney consents to direct communication with the consumer; or

(3) at the consumer's place of employment if the debt collector knows or has reason to know that the consumer's employer prohibits the consumer from receiving such communication.

(b) Communication with third parties

Except as provided in section 1692b of this title, without the prior consent of the consumer given directly to the debt collector, or the express permission of a court of competent jurisdiction, or as reasonably necessary to effectuate a postjudgment judicial remedy, a debt collector may not communicate, in connection with the collection of any debt, with any person other than the consumer, his attorney, a consumer reporting agency if otherwise permitted by law, the creditor, the attorney of the creditor, or the attorney of the debt collector.

(c) Ceasing communication

If a consumer notifies a debt collector in writing that the consumer refuses to pay a debt or that the consumer wishes the debt collector to cease further communication with the consumer, the debt collector shall not communicate further with the consumer with respect to such debt, except -
    (1) to advise the consumer that the debt collector's further efforts are being terminated;
    (2) to notify the consumer that the debt collector or creditor may invoke specified remedies which are ordinarily invoked by such debt collector or creditor; or
    (3) where applicable, to notify the consumer that the debt collector or creditor intends to invoke a specified remedy. If such notice from the consumer is made by mail, notification shall be complete upon receipt.

(d) "Consumer" defined

For the purpose of this section, the term "consumer" includes the consumer's spouse, parent (if the consumer is a minor), guardian, executor, or administrator.

§ 1692d. Harassment or abuse

A debt collector may not engage in any conduct the natural consequence of which is to harass, oppress, or abuse any person in connection with the collection of a debt. Without limiting the general application of the foregoing, the following conduct is a violation of this section:

    (1) The use or threat of use of violence or other criminal means to harm the physical person, reputation, or property of any person.
    (2) The use of obscene or profane language or language the natural consequence of which is to abuse the hearer or reader.

(3) The publication of a list of consumers who allegedly refuse to pay debts, except to a consumer reporting agency or to persons meeting the requirements of section 1681a(f) or 1681b(3) of this title.

(4) The advertisement for sale of any debt to coerce payment of the debt.

(5) Causing a telephone to ring or engaging any person in telephone conversation repeatedly or continuously with intent to annoy, abuse, or harass any person at the called number.

(6) Except as provided in section 1692b of this title, the placement of telephone calls without meaningful disclosure of the caller's identity.

§ 1692e. False or misleading representations

A debt collector may not use any false, deceptive, or misleading representation or means in connection with the collection of any debt. Without limiting the general application of the foregoing, the following conduct is a violation of this section:

(1) The false representation or implication that the debt collector is vouched for, bonded by, or affiliated with the United States or any State, including the use of any badge, uniform, or facsimile thereof.

(2) The false representation of -
(A) the character, amount, or legal status of any debt; or
(B) any services rendered or compensation which may be lawfully received by any debt collector for the collection of a debt.

(3) The false representation or implication that any individual is an attorney or that any communication is from an attorney.

(4) The representation or implication that nonpayment of any debt will result in the arrest or imprisonment of any person or the seizure, garnishment, attachment, or sale of any property or wages of any person unless such action is lawful and the debt collector or creditor intends to take such action.

(5) The threat to take any action that cannot legally be taken or that is not intended to be taken.

(6) The false representation or implication that a sale, referral, or other transfer of any interest in a debt shall cause the consumer to -
(A) lose any claim or defense to payment of the debt; or
(B) become subject to any practice prohibited by this subchapter.

(7) The false representation or implication that the consumer committed any crime or other conduct in order to disgrace the consumer.

(8) Communicating or threatening to communicate to any person credit information which is known or which should be known to be false, including the failure to communicate that a disputed debt is disputed.

(9) The use or distribution of any written communication which simulates or is falsely represented to be a document authorized, issued, or approved by

any court, official, or agency of the United States or any State, or which creates a false impression as to its source, authorization, or approval.

(10) The use of any false representation or deceptive means to collect or attempt to collect any debt or to obtain information concerning a consumer.

(11) Except as otherwise provided for communications to acquire location information under section 1692b of this title, the failure to disclose clearly in all communications made to collect a debt or to obtain information about a consumer, that the debt collector is attempting to collect a debt and that any information obtained will be used for that purpose.

(12) The false representation or implication that accounts have been turned over to innocent purchasers for value.

(13) The false representation or implication that documents are legal process.

(14) The use of any business, company, or organization name other than the true name of the debt collector's business, company, or organization.

(15) The false representation or implication that documents are not legal process forms or do not require action by the consumer.

(16) The false representation or implication that a debt collector operates or is employed by a consumer reporting agency as defined by section 1681a(f) of this title.

§ 1692f. Unfair practices

A debt collector may not use unfair or unconscionable means to collect or attempt to collect any debt. Without limiting the general application of the foregoing, the following conduct is a violation of this section:

(1) The collection of any amount (including any interest, fee, charge, or expense incidental to the principal obligation) unless such amount is expressly authorized by the agreement creating the debt or permitted by law.

(2) The acceptance by a debt collector from any person of a check or other payment instrument postdated by more than five days unless such person is notified in writing of the debt collector's intent to deposit such check or instrument not more than ten nor less than three business days prior to such deposit.

(3) The solicitation by a debt collector of any postdated check or other postdated payment instrument for the purpose of threatening or instituting criminal prosecution.

(4) Depositing or threatening to deposit any postdated check or other postdated payment instrument prior to the date on such check or instrument.

(5) Causing charges to be made to any person for communications by concealment of the true purpose of the communication. Such charges include, but are not limited to, collect telephone calls and telegram fees.

(6) Taking or threatening to take any nonjudicial action to effect dispossession or disablement of property if -

(A) there is no present right to possession of the property claimed as collateral through an enforceable security interest;

(B) there is no present intention to take possession of the property; or

(C) the property is exempt by law from such dispossession or disablement.

(7) Communicating with a consumer regarding a debt by post card.

(8) Using any language or symbol, other than the debt collector's address, on any envelope when communicating with a consumer by use of the mails or by telegram, except that a debt collector may use his business name if such name does not indicate that he is in the debt collection business.

§ 1692g. Validation of debts

(a) Notice of debt; contents

Within five days after the initial communication with a consumer in connection with the collection of any debt, a debt collector shall, unless the following information is contained in the initial communication or the consumer has paid the debt, send the consumer a written notice containing -

(1) the amount of the debt;

(2) the name of the creditor to whom the debt is owed;

(3) a statement that unless the consumer, within thirty days after receipt of the notice, disputes the validity of the debt, or any portion thereof, the debt will be assumed to be valid by the debt collector;

(4) a statement that if the consumer notifies the debt collector in writing within the thirty-day period that the debt, or any portion thereof, is disputed, the debt collector will obtain verification of the debt or a copy of a judgment against the consumer and a copy of such verification or judgment will be mailed to the consumer by the debt collector; and

(5) a statement that, upon the consumer's written request within the thirty-day period, the debt collector will provide the consumer with the name and address of the original creditor, if different from the current creditor.

(b) Disputed debts

If the consumer notifies the debt collector in writing within the thirty-day period described in subsection (a) of this section that the debt, or any portion thereof, is disputed, or that the consumer requests the name and address of the original creditor, the debt collector shall cease collection of the debt, or any disputed portion thereof, until the debt collector obtains verification of the debt or a copy of a judgment, or the name and address of the original creditor, and a copy of such verification or judgment, or name and address of the original creditor, is mailed to the consumer by the debt collector.

(c) Admission of liability

The failure of a consumer to dispute the validity of a debt under this section may not be construed by any court as an admission of liability by the consumer.

§ 1692h. Multiple debts

If any consumer owes multiple debts and makes any single payment to any debt collector with respect to such debts, such debt collector may not apply such payment to any debt which is disputed by the consumer and, where applicable, shall apply such payment in accordance with the consumer's directions.

§ 1692i. Legal actions by debt collectors

(a) Venue

Any debt collector who brings any legal action on a debt against any consumer shall -
   (1) in the case of an action to enforce an interest in real property securing the consumer's obligation, bring such action only in a judicial district or similar legal entity in which such real property is located; or
   (2) in the case of an action not described in paragraph (1), bring such action only in the judicial district or similar legal entity -
      (A) in which such consumer signed the contract sued upon; or
      (B) in which such consumer resides at the commencement of the
action.

(b) Authorization of actions

Nothing in this subchapter shall be construed to authorize the bringing of legal actions by debt collectors.

§ 1692j. Furnishing certain deceptive forms

(a) It is unlawful to design, compile, and furnish any form knowing that such form would be used to create the false belief in a consumer that a person other than the creditor of such consumer is participating in the collection of or in an attempt to collect a debt such consumer allegedly owes such creditor, when in fact such person is not so participating.

(b) Any person who violates this section shall be liable to the same extent and in the same manner as a debt collector is liable under section 1692k of this title for failure to comply with a provision of this subchapter.

§ 1692k. Civil liability

(a) Amount of damages

Except as otherwise provided by this section, any debt collector who fails to comply with any provision of this subchapter with respect to any person is liable to such person in an amount equal to the sum of -

(1) any actual damage sustained by such person as a result of such failure;

(2) (A) in the case of any action by an individual, such additional damages as the court may allow, but not exceeding $1,000; or
(B) in the case of a class action,
(i) such amount for each named plaintiff as could be recovered under subparagraph (A), and
(ii) such amount as the court may allow for all other class members, without regard to a minimum individual recovery, not to exceed the lesser of $500,000 or 1 per centum of the net worth of the debt collector; and

(3) in the case of any successful action to enforce the foregoing liability, the costs of the action, together with a reasonable attorney's fee as determined by the court. On a finding by the court that an action under this section was brought in bad faith and for the purpose of harassment, the court may award to the defendant attorney's fees reasonable in relation to the work expended and costs.

(b) Factors considered by court

In determining the amount of liability in any action under subsection (a) of this section, the court shall consider, among other relevant factors -

(1) in any individual action under subsection (a)(2)(A) of this section, the frequency and persistence of noncompliance by the debt collector, the nature of such noncompliance, and the extent to which such noncompliance was intentional; or

(2) in any class action under subsection (a)(2)(B) of this section,   the frequency and persistence of noncompliance by the debt collector, the nature of such noncompliance, the resources of the debt collector, the number of persons adversely affected, and the extent to which the debt collector's noncompliance was intentional.

(c) Intent

A debt collector may not be held liable in any action brought under this subchapter if the debt collector shows by a preponderance of evidence that the violation was not intentional and resulted from a bona fide error notwithstanding the maintenance of procedures reasonably adapted to avoid any such error.

(d) Jurisdiction

An action to enforce any liability created by this subchapter may be brought in any appropriate United States district court without regard to the amount in controversy, or in any other court of competent jurisdiction, within one year from the date on which the violation occurs.

(e) Advisory opinions of Commission

No provision of this section imposing any liability shall apply to any act done or omitted in good faith in conformity with any advisory opinion of the Commission, notwithstanding that after such act or omission has occurred, such opinion is amended, rescinded, or determined by judicial or other authority to be invalid for any reason.

§ 1692l. Administrative enforcement

(a) Federal Trade Commission

Compliance with this subchapter shall be enforced by the Commission, except to the extent that enforcement of the requirements imposed under this subchapter is specifically committed to another agency under subsection (b) of this section. For purpose of the exercise by the Commission of its functions and powers under the Federal Trade Commission Act (15 U.S.C. 41 et seq.), a violation of this subchapter shall be deemed an unfair or deceptive act or practice in violation of that Act. All of the functions and powers of the Commission under the Federal Trade Commission Act are available to the Commission to enforce compliance by any person with this subchapter, irrespective of whether that person is engaged in commerce or meets any other jurisdictional tests in the Federal Trade Commission Act, including the power to enforce the provisions of this subchapter in the same manner as if the violation had been a violation of a Federal Trade Commission trade regulation rule.

(b) Applicable provisions of law

Compliance with any requirements imposed under this subchapter shall be enforced under -

(1) section 8 of the Federal Deposit Insurance Act (12 U.S.C. 1818), in the case of -
    (A) national banks, and Federal branches and Federal agencies of foreign banks, by the Office of the Comptroller of the Currency;
    (B) member banks of the Federal Reserve System (other than national banks), branches and agencies of foreign banks (other than Federal branches, Federal agencies, and insured State branches of foreign banks), commercial lending companies owned or controlled by foreign banks, and organizations operating under section 25 or 25(a) (FOOTNOTE 1) of the Federal Reserve Act (12 U.S.C. 601 et seq., 611 et seq.), by the Board of Governors of the Federal Reserve System; and (FOOTNOTE 1) See References in Text note below.
    (C) banks insured by the Federal Deposit Insurance Corporation (other than members of the Federal Reserve System) and insured State branches of foreign banks, by the Board of Directors of the Federal Deposit Insurance Corporation;

(2) section 8 of the Federal Deposit Insurance Act (12 U.S.C. 1818), by the Director of the Office of Thrift Supervision, in the case of a savings association the deposits of which are insured by the Federal Deposit Insurance Corporation;

(3) the Federal Credit Union Act (12 U.S.C. 1751 et seq.), by the National Credit Union Administration Board with respect to any Federal credit union;

(4) subtitle IV of title 49, by the Interstate Commerce Commission with respect to any common carrier subject to such subtitle;

(5) the Federal Aviation Act of 1958 (49 App. U.S.C. 1301 et seq.), by the Secretary of Transportation with respect to any air carrier or any foreign air carrier subject to that Act; and

(6) the Packers and Stockyards Act, 1921 (7 U.S.C. 181 et seq.) (except as provided in section 406 of that Act (7 U.S.C. 226, 227)), by the Secretary of Agriculture with respect to any activities subject to that Act. The terms used in paragraph (1) that are not defined in this subchapter or otherwise defined in section 3(s) of the Federal Deposit Insurance Act (12 U.S.C. 1813(s)) shall have the meaning given to them in section 1(b) of the International Banking Act of 1978 (12 U.S.C. 3101).

(c) Agency powers

For the purpose of the exercise by any agency referred to in subsection (b) of this section of its powers under any Act referred to in that subsection, a violation of any requirement imposed under this subchapter shall be deemed to be a violation of a requirement imposed under that Act. In addition to its powers under any provision of law specifically referred to in subsection (b) of this section, each of the agencies referred to in that subsection may exercise, for the purpose of enforcing compliance with any requirement imposed under this subchapter any other authority conferred on it by law, except as provided in subsection (d) of this section.

(d) Rules and regulations

Neither the Commission nor any other agency referred to in subsection (b) of this section may promulgate trade regulation rules or other regulations with respect to the collection of debts by debt collectors as defined in this subchapter.

§ 1692m. Reports to Congress by the Commission; views of other Federal agencies

(a) Not later than one year after the effective date of this subchapter and at one-year intervals thereafter, the Commission shall make reports to the Congress concerning the administration of its functions under this subchapter, including such recommendations as the Commission deems necessary or appropriate. In addition, each report of the Commission shall include its assessment of the extent to which compliance with this subchapter is being achieved and a summary of the enforcement actions taken by the Commission under section 1692l of this title.

(b) In the exercise of its functions under this subchapter, the Commission may obtain upon request the views of any other Federal agency which exercises enforcement functions under section 1692l of this title.

§ 1692n. Relation to State laws

This subchapter does not annul, alter, or affect, or exempt any person subject to the provisions of this subchapter from complying with the laws of any State with respect to debt collection practices, except to the extent that those laws are inconsistent with any provision of this subchapter, and then only to the extent of the inconsistency. For purposes of this section, a State law is not inconsistent with this subchapter if the protection such law affords any consumer is greater than the protection provided by this subchapter.

§ 1692o. Exemption for State regulation

The Commission shall by regulation exempt from the requirements of this subchapter any class of debt collection practices within any State if the Commission determines that under the law of that State that class of debt collection practices is subject to requirements substantially similar to those imposed by this subchapter, and that there is adequate provision for enforcement.

CALIFORNIA DEBT COLLECTION ACT

TITLE 1.60C
FAIR DEBT COLLECTION PRACTICES
————————
ARTICLE 1
GENERAL PROVISIONS
Section
1788. Title of Act.
1788.1. Legislative Findings.
1788.2. Definitions.
1788.3. Credit Union Provisions.

§ 1788. Title of Act.
This title may be cited as the Robbins-Rosenthal Fair Debt Collection Practices Act.

§ 1788.1. Legislative Findings.
(a) The Legislature makes the following findings:
(1) The banking and credit system and grantors of credit to consumers are dependent upon the collection of just and owing debts. Unfair or deceptive collection practices undermine the public confidence which is essential to the continued functioning of the banking and credit system and sound extensions of credit to consumers.
(2) There is need to ensure that debt collectors and debtors exercise their responsibilities to one another with fairness, honesty and due regard for the rights of the other.
(b) It is the purpose of this title to prohibit debt collectors from engaging in unfair or deceptive acts or practices in the collection of consumer debts and to require debtors to act fairly in entering into and honoring such debts, as specified in this title.

§ 1788.2. Definitions.
(a) Definitions and rules of construction set forth in this section are applicable for the purpose of this title.
(b) The term "debt collection" means any act or practice in connection with the collection of consumer debts.
(c) The term "debt collector" means any person who, in the ordinary course of business, regularly, on behalf of himself or herself or others,

engages in debt collection. The term includes any person who composes and sells, or offers to compose and sell, forms, letters, and other collection media used or intended to be used for debt collection, but does not include an attorney or counselor at law.

(d) The term "debt" means money, property or their equivalent which is due or owing or alleged to be due or owing from a natural person to another person.

(e) The term "consumer credit transaction" means a transaction between a natural person and another person in which property, services or money is acquired on credit by that natural person from such other person primarily for personal, family, or household purposes.

(f) The terms "consumer debt" and "consumer credit" mean money, property or their equivalent, due or owing or alleged to be due or owing from a natural person by reason of a consumer credit transaction.

(g) The term "person" means a natural person, partnership, corporation, limited liability company, trust, estate, cooperative, association or other similar entity.

(h) The term "debtor" means a natural person from whom a debt collector seeks to collect a consumer debt which is due and owing or alleged to be due and owing from such person.

(i) The term "creditor" means a person who extends consumer credit to a debtor.

(j) The term "consumer credit report" means any written, oral or other communication of any information by a consumer reporting agency bearing on a consumer's creditworthiness, credit standing, credit capacity, character, general reputation, personal characteristics or mode of living which is used or expected to be used or collected in whole or in part for the purpose of serving as a factor in establishing the consumer's eligibility for

(1) credit or insurance to be used primarily for person, family, or household purposes, or

(2) employment purposes, or

(3) other purposes authorized under any applicable federal or state law or regulation.

The term does not include (a) any report containing information solely as to transactions or experiences between the consumer and the person making the report; (b) any authorization or approval of a specific extension of credit directly or indirectly by the issuer of a credit card or similar device; or (c) any report in which a person who has been requested by a third party to make a specific extension of credit directly or indirectly to a consumer conveys his or her decision with respect to that request, if the third party advises the consumer of the name and address of the person to whom the request was made and such person makes the disclosures to the consumer required under any applicable federal or state law or regulation.

(k) The term "consumer reporting agency" means any person which, for monetary fees, dues, or on a cooperative nonprofit basis, regularly engages, in whole or in part, in the practice of assembling or evaluating consumer credit information or other information on consumers for the purpose of furnishing consumer credit reports to third parties, and which uses any means or facility for the purpose of preparing or furnishing consumer credit reports.

§ 1788.3. Credit Union Provisions.
Nothing contained in this title shall be construed to prohibit a credit union chartered under Division 5 (commencing with Section 14000) of the Financial Code or under the Federal Credit Union Act (Chapter 14 (commencing with Section 1751) of Title 12 of the United States Code) from providing information to an employer when the employer is ordinarily and necessarily entitled to receive such information because he is an employee, officer, committee member, or agent of such credit union.

————————

ARTICLE 2
DEBT COLLECTOR RESPONSIBILITIES
Section
1788.10. Threats by Debt Collectors.
1788.11. Phone Calls.
1788.12. Communications with Employer, Family.
1788.13. Misrepresentation.
1788.14. Collection Costs.
1788.15. Judicial Action.
1788.16. Communication Simulating False Authority.

§ 1788.10. Threats by Debt Collectors.
No debt collector shall collect or attempt to collect a consumer debt by means of the following conduct:
(a) The use, or threat of use, of physical force or violence or any criminal means to cause harm to the person, or the reputation, or the property of any person;
(b) The threat that the failure to pay a consumer debt will result in an accusation that the debtor has committed a crime where such accusation, if made, would be false;
(c) The communication of, or threat to communicate to any person the fact that a debtor has engaged in conduct, other than the failure to pay a consumer debt, which the debt collector knows or has reason to believe will defame the debtor;
(d) The threat to the debtor to sell or assign to another person the obligation of the debtor to pay a consumer debt, with an accompanying false

representation that the result of such sale or assignment would be that the debtor would lose any defense to the consumer debt;

(e) The threat to any person that nonpayment of the consumer debt may result in the arrest of the debtor or the seizure, garnishment, attachment or sale of any property or the garnishment or attachment of wages of the debtor, unless such action is in fact contemplated by the debt collector and permitted by the law; or

(f) The threat to take any action against the debtor which is prohibited by this title.

§ 1788.11. Phone Calls.

No debt collector shall collect or attempt to collect a consumer debt by means of the following practices:

(a) Using obscene or profane language;

(b) Placing telephone calls without disclosure of the caller's identity, provided that an employee of a licensed collection agency may identify himself by using his registered alias name as long as he correctly identifies the agency he represents;

(c) Causing expense to any person for long distance telephone calls, telegram fees or charges for other similar communications, by misrepresenting to such person the purpose of such telephone call, telegram or similar communication;

(d) Causing a telephone to ring repeatedly or continuously to annoy the person called; or

(e) Communicating, by telephone or in person, with the debtor with such frequency as to be unreasonable and to constitute an harassment to the debtor under the circumstances.

§ 1788.12. Communications with Employer, Family.

No debt collector shall collect or attempt to collect a consumer debt by means of the following practices:

(a) Communicating with the debtor's employer regarding the debtor's consumer debt unless such a communication is necessary to the collection of the debt, or unless the debtor or his attorney has consented in writing to such communication. A communication is necessary to the collection of the debt only if it is made for the purposes of verifying the debtor's employment, locating the debtor, or effecting garnishment, after judgment, of the debtor's wages, or in the case of a medical debt for the purpose of discovering the existence of medical insurance. Any such communication, other than a communication in the case of a medical debt by a health care provider or its agent for the purpose of discovering the existence of medical insurance, shall be in writing unless such written communication receives no response within 15 days and shall be made only as many times as is necessary to the collection of the debt. Communications to a debtor's employer regarding a debt shall not contain language that would be improper if the communication were made to the debtor. One communication solely for the purpose of verifying the debtor's employment may be oral without prior written contact;

(b) Communicating information regarding a consumer debt to any member of the debtor's family, other than the debtor's spouse or the parents or guardians of the debtor who is either a minor or who resides in the same household with such parent or guardian, prior to obtaining a judgment against the debtor, except where the purpose of the communication is to locate the debtor, or where the debtor or his attorney has consented in writing to such communication;

(c) Communicating to any person any list of debtors which discloses the nature or existence of a consumer debt, commonly known as "deadbeat lists," or advertising any consumer debt for sale, by naming the debtor; or

(d) Communicating with the debtor by means of a written communication that displays or conveys any information about the consumer debt or the debtor other than the name, address and telephone number of the debtor and the debt collector and which is intended both to be seen by any other person and also to embarrass the debtor.

Notwithstanding the foregoing provisions of this section, the disclosure, publication or communication by a debt collector of information relating to a consumer debt or the debtor to a consumer reporting agency or to any other person reasonably believed to have a legitimate business need for such information shall not be deemed to violate this title.

§ 1788.13. Misrepresentation.
No debt collector shall collect or attempt to collect a consumer debt by means of the following practices:

(a) Any communication with the debtor other than in the name either of the debt collector or the person on whose behalf the debt collector is acting;

(b) Any false representation that any person is an attorney or counselor at law;

(c) Any communication with a debtor in the name of an attorney or counselor at law or upon stationery or like written instruments bearing the name of the attorney or counselor at law, unless such communication is by an attorney or counselor at law or shall have been approved or authorized by such attorney or counselor at law;

(d) The representation that any debt collector is vouched for, bonded by, affiliated with, or is an instrumentality, agent or official of any federal, state or local government or any agency of federal, state or local government, unless the collector is actually employed by the particular governmental agency in question and is acting on behalf of such agency in the debt collection matter;

(e) The false representation that the consumer debt may be increased by the addition of attorney's fees, investigation fees, service fees, finance charges, or other charges if, in fact, such fees or charges may not legally be added to the existing obligation;

(f) The false representation that information concerning a debtor's failure or alleged failure to pay a consumer debt has been or is about to be referred to a consumer reporting agency;

(g) The false representation that a debt collector is a consumer reporting agency;

(h) The false representation that collection letters, notices or other printed forms are being sent by or on behalf of a claim, credit, audit or legal department;

(i) The false representation of the true nature of the business or services being rendered by the debt collector;

(j) The false representation that a legal proceeding has been, is about to be, or will be instituted unless payment of a consumer debt is made;

(k) The false representation that a consumer debt has been, is about to be, or will be sold, assigned, or referred to a debt collector for collection; or

(l) Any communication by a licensed collection agency to a debtor demanding money unless the claim is actually assigned to the collection agency.

§ 1788.14. Collection Costs.
No debt collector shall collect or attempt to collect a consumer debt by means of the following practices:

(a) Obtaining an affirmation from a debtor who has been adjudicated a bankrupt, of a consumer debt which has been discharged in such bankruptcy, without clearly and conspicuously disclosing to the debtor, in writing, at the time such affirmation is sought, the fact that the debtor is not legally obligated to make such affirmation;

(b) Collecting or attempting to collect from the debtor the whole or any part of the debt collector's fee or charge for services rendered, or other expense incurred by the debt collector in the collection of the consumer debt, except as permitted by law; or

(c) Initiating communications, other than statements of account, with the debtor with regard to the consumer debt, when the debt collector has been previously notified in writing by the debtor's attorney that the debtor is represented by such attorney with respect to the consumer debt and such notice includes the attorney's name and address and a request by such attorney that all communications regarding the consumer debt be addressed to such attorney, unless the attorney fails to answer correspondence, return telephone calls, or discuss the obligation in question. This subdivision shall not apply where prior approval has been obtained from the debtor's attorney, or where the communication is a response in the ordinary course of business to a debtor's inquiry.

§ 1788.15. Judicial Action.

(a) No debt collector shall collect or attempt to collect a consumer debt by means of judicial proceedings when the debt collector knows that service of process, where essential to jurisdiction over the debtor or his property, has not been legally effected.

(b) No debt collector shall collect or attempt to collect a consumer debt, other than one reduced to judgment, by means of judicial proceedings in a county other than the county in which the debtor has incurred the consumer debt or the county in which the debtor resides at the time such proceedings are instituted, or resided at the time the debt was incurred.

§ 1788.16. Communication Simulating False Authority.

It is unlawful, with respect to attempted collection of a consumer debt, for a debt collector, creditor, or an attorney, to send a communication which simulates legal or judicial process or which gives the appearance of being authorized, issued, or approved by a governmental agency or attorney when it is not. Any violation of the provisions of this section is a misdemeanor punishable by imprisonment in the county jail not exceeding six months, or by a fine not exceeding two thousand five hundred dollars ($2,500) or by both.

————————

ARTICLE 3
DEBTOR RESPONSIBILITIES
Section
1788.20. Credit Application - False Information.
1788.21. Debtor Address Change.
1788.22. Use After Credit Card Termination.

§ 1788.20. Credit Application - False Information.

In connection with any request or application for consumer credit, no person shall:

(a) Request or apply for such credit at a time when such person knows there is no reasonable probability of such person's being able, or such person then lacks the intention, to pay the obligation created thereby in accordance with the terms and conditions of the credit extension; or

(b) Knowingly submit false or inaccurate information or willfully conceal adverse information bearing upon such person's credit worthiness, credit standing, or credit capacity.

§ 1788.21. Debtor Address Change.

(a) In connection with any consumer credit existing or requested to be extended to a person, such person shall within a reasonable time notify the creditor or prospective creditor of any change in such person's name, address, or employment.

(b) Each responsibility set forth in subdivision (a) shall apply only if and after the creditor clearly and conspicuously in writing discloses such responsibility to such person.

§ 1788.22. Use After Credit Card Termination.

(a) In connection with any consumer credit extended to a person under an account:

(1) No such person shall attempt to consummate any consumer credit transaction thereunder knowing that credit privileges under the account have been terminated or suspended.

(2) Each such person shall notify the creditor by telephone, telegraph, letter, or any other reasonable means that an unauthorized use of the account has occurred or may occur as the result of loss or theft of a credit card, or other instrument identifying the account, within a reasonable time after such person's discovery thereof, and shall reasonably assist the creditor in determining the facts and circumstances relating to any unauthorized use of the account.

(b) Each responsibility set forth in subdivision (a) shall apply only if and after the creditor clearly and conspicuously in writing discloses such responsibility to such person.

———————

ARTICLE 4

ENFORCEMENT
Section
1788.30. Limits of Damages.
1788.31. Separability.
1788.32. Remedies - Cumulative.

§ 1788.30. Limits of Damages.

(a) Any debt collector who violates this title with respect to any debtor shall be liable to that debtor only in an individual action, and his liability therein to that debtor shall be in an amount equal to the sum of any actual damages sustained by the debtor as a result of the violation.

(b) Any debt collector who willfully and knowingly violates this title with respect to any debtor shall, in addition to actual damages sustained by the debtor as a result of the violation, also be liable to the debtor only in an individual action, and his additional liability therein to that debtor shall be for a penalty in such amount as the court may allow, which shall not be less than one hundred dollars ($100) nor greater than one thousand dollars ($1,000).

(c) In the case of any action to enforce any liability under this title, the prevailing party shall be entitled to costs of the action. Reasonable attorney's fees, which shall be based on time necessarily expended to enforce the liability, shall be awarded to a prevailing debtor; reasonable attorney's fees may be awarded to a prevailing creditor upon a finding by the court that the debtor's prosecution or defense of the action was not in good faith.

(d) A debt collector shall have no civil liability under this title if, within 15 days either after discovering a violation which is able to be cured, or after the receipt of a written notice of such violation, the debt collector notifies the debtor of the violation, and makes whatever adjustments or corrections are necessary to cure the violation with respect to the debtor.

(e) A debt collector shall have no civil liability to which such debt collector might otherwise be subject for a violation of this title, if the debt collector shows by a preponderance of evidence that the violation was not intentional and resulted notwithstanding the maintenance of procedures reasonably adapted to avoid any such violation.

(f) Any action under this section may be brought in any appropriate court of competent jurisdiction in an individual capacity only, within one year from the date of the occurrence of the violation.

(g) Any intentional violation of the provisions of this title by the debtor may be raised as a defense by the debt collector, if such violation is pertinent or relevant to any claim or action brought against the debt collector by or on behalf of the debtor.

§ 1788.31. Separability.
If any provision of this title, or the application thereof to any person or circumstances, is held invalid, the remaining provisions of this title, or the application of such provisions to other persons or circumstances, shall not be affected thereby.

§ 1788.32. Remedies - Cumulative.
The remedies provided herein are intended to be cumulative and are in addition to any other procedures, rights, or remedies under any other provision of law. The enactment of this title shall not supersede existing administrative regulations of the Director of Consumer Affairs except to the extent that those regulations are inconsistent with the provisions of this title.

TEXAS DEBT COLLECTION ACT

Art. 5069-11.01. Definitions.

As used in this subchapter:

(a) "Debt" means any obligation or alleged obligation arising out of a consumer transaction.

(b) "Debt collection" means any action, conduct, or practice in soliciting debts for collection or in collecting debts owed or due, or alleged to be owed or due a creditor by a consumer.

(c) "Debt collector" means any person engaging directly or indirectly in debt collection, as defined herein, and includes any person who sells, or offers to sell, forms represented to be a collection system, device, or scheme, intended or calculated to be used to collect debts.

(d) "Consumer" means an individual who owes or allegedly owes a debt created primarily for personal, family, or household purposes.

(e) "Consumer transaction" means a transaction in which one or more of the parties is a consumer.

(f) "Creditor" means a party to a consumer transaction other than a consumer.

(g) "Person" means individual, corporation, trust, partnership, incorporated or unincorporated association, or any other legal entity.

(h) "Credit bureau" means any person who, for compensation, gathers, records, and disseminates information relative to the creditworthiness, financial responsibility, paying habits, and other similar information regarding any person, for the purpose of furnishing consumer reports to third parties.

Subsec. (h) added by Acts 1993, 73rd Leg., ch. 813, Sec. 1, eff. Sept. 1, 1993.

Acts 1973, 63rd Leg., p. 1513, ch. 547, Sec. 1, eff. Aug. 27, 1973.

Art. 5069-11.02. Threats or coercion.

No debt collector may collect or attempt to collect any debt alleged to be due and owing by any threats, coercion, or attempts to coerce which employ any of the following practices:

(a) using or threatening to use violence or other criminal means to cause harm to the person or property of any person;

(b) accusing falsely or threatening to accuse falsely any person of fraud or any other crime;

(c) representing or threatening to represent to a third party or any other person, that a consumer is willfully refusing to pay a non-disputed debt when the debt is in dispute for any reason and the consumer has notified such debt collector in writing of the dispute;

(d) threatening to sell or assign to another the obligation of the consumer with an attending false representation that the result of such sale or assignment would be that the consumer would lose any defense to the alleged debt or would be subject to illegal collection attempts;

(e) threatening that the debtor will be arrested for nonpayment of an alleged debt without proper court proceedings; however, nothing herein shall prevent a debt collector from informing the debtor that the debtor may be arrested after proper court proceedings in cases where the debtor has violated the criminal laws of this state;

(f) threatening to file charges, complaints, or criminal action against a debtor when in fact the debtor has not violated any criminal laws; provided, however, nothing herein shall prevent a debt collector from threatening to institute civil lawsuits or other judicial proceedings to collect a debt;

(g) threatening that nonpayment of an alleged debt will result in the seizure, repossession, or sale of any property of that person without proper court proceedings; however, nothing herein shall prevent a debt collector from exercising or threatening to exercise a statutory or contractual right of seizure, repossession, or sale which does not require court proceedings; or

(h) threatening to take any action prohibited by law.

Acts 1973, 63rd Leg., p. 1513, ch. 547, Sec. 2, eff. Aug. 27, 1973.

Art. 5069-11.03. Harassment; abuse.

In connection with the collection of or attempt to collect any debt alleged to be due and owing by a consumer, no debt collector may oppress, harass, or abuse any person by methods which employ the following practices:

(a) using profane or obscene language or language that is intended to unreasonably abuse the hearer or reader;

(b) placing telephone calls without disclosure of the name of the individual making the call, and with the willful intent to annoy or harass or threaten any person at the called number;

(c) causing expense to any person in the form of long distance telephone tolls, telegram fees, or other charges incurred by a medium of communication, without first disclosing the name of the person making the telephone call or transmitting the communication; or

(d) causing a telephone to ring repeatedly or continuously or making repeated and continuous telephone calls, with the willful intent to harass any person at the called number.

Acts 1973, 63rd Leg., p. 1513, ch. 547, Sec. 3, eff. Aug. 27, 1973.

Art. 5069-11.04. Unfair or unconscionable means.

No debt collector may collect or attempt to collect any debt by unfair or unconscionable means employing the following practices:

(a) seeking or obtaining any written statement or acknowledgment in any form that specifies that a consumer's obligation is one incurred for necessaries of life where the obligation was not in fact incurred for such necessaries; or

(b) collecting or attempting to collect any interest or other charge, fee, or expense incidental to the obligation unless such interest or incidental fee, charge, or expenses is expressly authorized by the agreement creating the obligation or legally chargeable to the consumer. However, creditors may charge reasonable reinstatement fees as consideration for renewal of a real estate loan or contract of sale, after default, if the additional fees are included in a written contract executed at the time of renewal.

Acts 1973, 63rd Leg., p. 1513, ch. 547, Sec. 4, eff. Aug. 27, 1973.

Art. 5069-11.05. Fraudulent, deceptive, or misleading representations.

No debt collector may collect or attempt to collect debts or obtain information concerning a consumer by any fraudulent, deceptive, or misleading representations which employ the following practices:

(a) using any name while engaged in the collection of debts other than the true business or professional name or the true personal or legal name of the debt collector or, if engaged in the collection of a credit card debt, the name appearing on the face of the credit card; or failing to maintain a list of all business or professional names known to be used or formerly used by individual persons collecting debts or attempting to collect debts for the debt collector;

(b) falsely representing that the debt collector has information in his possession or something of value for the consumer in order to solicit or discover information about the consumer;

(c) failing to clearly disclose, in any communication with the debtor, the name of the person to whom the debt has been assigned or is owed at the time of making any demand for money (provided, however, this subsection shall not apply to persons servicing or collecting real estate first lien mortgage loans or credit card debts);

(d) failing to clearly disclose, in any communication with the debtor, that the debt collector is attempting to collect a debt, unless such communication is for the purpose of discovering the whereabouts of the debtor;

(e) using any written communication which fails to clearly indicate the name of the debt collector and the debt collector's street address or post office box and telephone number, when the written notice refers to an alleged delinquent debt; (the foregoing shall not require disclosure of names and addresses of employees of debt collectors);

(f) using any written communication which demands a response to a place other than the debt collector's or creditor's street address or post office box; (the foregoing shall not require response to the address of an employee of a debt collector);

(g) misrepresenting the character, extent, or amount of a debt against a consumer, or misrepresenting its status in any judicial or governmental proceedings;

(h) falsely representing that any debt collector is vouched for, bonded by, affiliated with, or an instrumentality, agent, or official of this state or any agency of federal, state, or local government;

(i) using, distributing, or selling any written communication which simulates or falsely represents to be a document authorized, issued, or approved by a court, an official, a governmental agency, or any other legally constituted or authorized governmental authority, or which creates a false impression about its source, authorization, or approval; or using any seal or insignia or design which simulates that of any governmental agency;

(j) representing that a debt may be increased by the addition of attorney's fees, investigation fees, service fees, or other charges when there is no written contract or statute authorizing such additional fees or charges;

(k) representing that a debt will definitely be increased by the addition of attorney's fees, investigation fees, service fees, or other charges when the award of such fee or charge is discretionary by a court of law;

(l) falsely representing the status or true nature of the services rendered by the debt collector or his business;

(m) using any written communication which violates or fails to conform to the United States postal laws and regulations;

(n) using any communication which purports to be from any attorney or law firm, when in fact it is not;

(o) representing that a debt is being collected by an attorney when it is not; or

(p) representing that a debt is being collected by an independent, bona fide organization engaged in the business of collecting past due accounts when the debt is being collected by a subterfuge organization under the control and direction of the person to whom the debt is owed; however, nothing herein shall prohibit a creditor from owning or operating its own bona fide debt collection agency.

Acts 1973, 63rd Leg., p. 1513, ch. 547, Sec. 5, eff. Aug. 27, 1973.

Amended by Acts 1995, 74th Leg., ch. 414, Sec. 18, eff. Sept. 1, 1995.

Art. 5069-11.06. Deceptive use of credit bureau name.

No person shall use the term "credit bureau," "retail merchants," or "retail merchants association" in his business or trade name unless such person is in fact engaged in gathering, recording, and disseminating favorable as well as unfavorable information relative to the credit worthiness, financial responsibility, paying habits and other similar information regarding individuals, firms, corporations and any other legal entity being considered for credit extension so that a prospective creditor may be able to make a sound decision in the extension of credit. This paragraph shall not apply to any nonprofit retail trade association consisting of individual members and qualifying as a bona fide business league as defined by the United States Internal Revenue Service, and which nonprofit retail trade association does not engage in the business of debt collection or credit reporting.

Acts 1973, 63rd Leg., p. 1513, ch. 547, Sec. 6, eff. Aug. 27, 1973.

Art. 5069-11.07. Use of independent debt collectors.

No creditor may use any independent debt collector who repeatedly and continuously engages in acts or practices which are prohibited by this Act after the creditor has actual knowledge that an independent debt collector is in fact repeatedly and continuously engaging in such acts or practices.

Acts 1973, 63rd Leg., p. 1513, ch. 547, Sec. 7, eff. Aug. 27, 1973.

Art. 5069-11.07A. Correction of third-party debt collector's files; bond requirement.

(a) If an individual disputes the accuracy of an item in a third-party debt collector's file on the individual, the individual may give notice of the inaccuracy in writing to the third-party debt collector. The third-party debt collector shall provide forms for the notice and shall assist an individual in preparing the notice when requested.

(b) Within 30 days after the date on which a notice of inaccuracy is received, the third-party debt collector shall send a written statement to the individual in which the third-party debt collector shall deny the inaccuracy, admit the inaccuracy, or state that it has not had sufficient time to complete its investigation.

(c) If the third-party debt collector admits that the item is inaccurate, it shall within five business days correct the item in its file and shall immediately send to each person who has previously received a report from the third-party debt collector containing the inaccurate information notice of the inaccuracy and a copy of the accurate report.

(d) If the third-party debt collector states that it has not had sufficient time to complete its investigation, it shall immediately change the item in its file as requested by the individual, shall immediately send to each person who previously received the report containing the information a notice that is equivalent to a notice under Subsection (c) of this section and a copy of the changed report, and shall immediately cease collection efforts if the item involves a debt. When the third-party debt collector completes its investigation and determines whether the item is accurate or inaccurate, it shall inform the individual of its determination. If the third-party debt collector determines that the information was accurate, it may again report that information and may resume its collection efforts.

(e) A third-party debt collector may not engage in debt collection unless the third-party debt collector entity whether a sole proprietorship, firm, partnership, or corporation has obtained a surety bond issued by a surety company authorized to do business in this state as required by this section. A copy of the bond must be filed with the secretary of state.

(f) The surety bond must be in favor of:

(1) any person who is damaged by a violation of this Act; and

(2) the state, for the benefit of any person who is damaged by a violation of this Act.

(g) A person claiming against the bond for a violation of this Act may maintain an action against the third-party debt collector and against the surety. The aggregate liability of the surety to all persons damaged by a violation of this Act may not exceed the amount of the surety bond.

(h) The bond must be in the amount of $10,000.

(i) For purposes of this section, "third-party debt collector" means a debt collector, as defined by 15 U.S.C. Section 1692a(6), other than an attorney at law collecting a debt as an attorney on behalf of and in the name of a client, unless the attorney has nonattorney employees who are regularly engaged to solicit debts for collection or who regularly make contact with debtors for the purpose of collection or adjustment of the debt.

(j) The provisions of this section apply to any person who for compensation gathers, records, or disseminates information relative to the creditworthiness, financial responsibility, and paying habits and other similar information, regarding any person, for the purpose of furnishing such information to any other person.

Added by Acts 1993, 73rd Leg., ch. 788, Sec. 1, eff. Sept. 1, 1993.

Art. 5069-11.08. Bona fide error.

No person shall be guilty of a violation of this Act if the action complained of resulted from a bona fide error notwithstanding the use of reasonable procedures adopted to avoid such error.

Acts 1973, 63rd Leg., p. 1513, ch. 547, Sec. 8, eff. Aug. 27, 1973.

Art. 5069-11.09. Penalties.

Any person who violates a provision of this Act is guilty of a misdemeanor, and upon conviction is punishable by a fine of not less than $100 nor more than $500 for each violation. Such misdemeanor charge must be filed within one year of the date of the alleged violation.

Acts 1973, 63rd Leg., p. 1513, ch. 547, Sec. 9, eff. Aug. 27, 1973.

Art. 5069-11.10. Civil remedies.

(a) Any person may seek injunctive relief to prevent or restrain a violation of this Act and any person may maintain an action for actual damages sustained as a result of a violation of this Act. A person who successfully maintains such action shall be awarded attorneys' fees reasonable in relation to the amount of work expended and costs. On a finding by the court that an action under this section was brought in bad faith or for purposes of harassment, the court shall award to the defendant attorneys' fees reasonable in relation to the work expended and costs.

(b) When the attorney general has reason to believe that a person is violating or is about to violate a provision of this Act, the attorney general may bring an action in the name of the state against the person to restrain or enjoin the person from violating this Act.

(c) A person who successfully maintains an action under this article for violation of Article 11.02(c) or 11.07A of this Act shall be awarded at least $100 for each violation of this Act.

Subsec. (c) added by Acts 1993, 73rd Leg., ch. 813, Sec. 2, eff. Sept. 1, 1993; amended by Acts 1995, 74th Leg., ch. 414, Sec. 19, eff. Sept. 1, 1995.

Acts 1973, 63rd Leg., p. 1513, ch. 547, Sec. 9, eff. Aug. 27, 1973. Amended by Acts 1983, 68th Leg., p. 2884, ch. 490, Sec. 2, eff. Aug. 29, 1983.

Art. 5069-11.11. Other remedies.

(a) A violation of any provision of this Act by any person is a deceptive trade practice in addition to those practices delineated in Chapter 17, Subchapter E, Business & Commerce Code, and is actionable pursuant to said subchapter. As such, the venue provision and all remedies available in said subchapter apply to and are cumulative of the remedies in this Act.

(b) None of the provisions of this Act shall affect or alter any remedies at law or in equity otherwise available to debtors, creditors, governmental entities, or any other legal entity.

Acts 1973, 63rd Leg., p. 1513, ch. 547, Sec. 11, eff. Aug. 27, 1973. Amended by Acts 1983, 68th Leg., p. 3259, ch. 564, Sec. 1, eff. Aug. 29, 1983.

Art. 5069-11.12. Report to consumer.

A credit bureau shall, upon request, provide to any person in its registry a copy of all information contained in its files concerning such person. This copy must be provided to the consumer within 45 days of the request.

Added by Acts 1993, 73rd Leg., ch. 813, Sec. 3, eff. Sept. 1, 1993.

FLORIDA DEBT COLLECTION ACT

PART V COMMERCIAL COLLECTION PRACTICES

559.541 Short title. ---

Sections 559.541-559.548 may be cited as the "Florida Commercial Collection Practices Act."

559.542 Legislative intent. ---

The Legislature finds that commercial collection practices in this state are not governed by the federal and state laws relating to the collection of consumer claims and that current criminal laws are inadequate to deal with certain unlawful and fraudulent activities specifically involving the collection of commercial claims in this state. Under such circumstances, there have been in the past, and will be in the future unless the Legislature acts, persons who succeed in flaunting the criminal laws of this state while engaging in the business of collecting commercial claims. Therefore, the Legislature intends by this part to specifically regulate commercial collection activities, separate and apart from consumer collection activities, to prevent unlawful and fraudulent commercial collection activities that otherwise may go unpenalized. The Legislature seeks to do so by requiring the registration of persons and businesses engaged in soliciting the collection of commercial claims or in collecting commercial claims, by prohibiting collection activities in this state by unregistered persons, and by providing effective mechanisms for enforcement of
this part.

559.543 Definitions. ---

As used in this part:

(1) "Claim" or "commercial claim" means any obligation for the payment of money or its equivalent arising out of a transaction wherein credit has been offered or extended to any person, and the money, property, or service which was the subject of the transaction was primarily for commercial purposes and not primarily for personal, family, or household purposes, whether or not such obligation has been reduced to judgment. The term "claim" or "commercial claim" includes an obligation of a person who is comaker, endorser,

guarantor, or surety as well as the person to whom such credit was originally extended.

(2) "Commercial collection agency" means any person engaged, as a primary or secondary business activity, in the business of soliciting commercial claims for collection or in the business of collecting commercial claims, asserted to be owed or due to another person, regardless of whether the collection efforts are directed at the primary debtor or some other source of payment.

(3) "Credit grantor" means any person or entity to whom a commercial claim is owed, due, or alleged to be owed or due, whether or not such person or entity is domiciled or doing business within this state and whether or not such commercial claim arose within this state. However, such term does not apply to any registrant under this part who has received an assignment or transfer of a commercial claim in default solely for the purpose of facilitating collection of such commercial claim for another.

(4) "Out-of-state collector" means any person or business entity engaged in the business of soliciting commercial claims for collection or of collecting commercial claims whose business activities in this state are limited to collecting commercial claims by means of interstate communications, including telephone, mail, or facsimile transmission, originating from outside this state.

(5) "Department" means the Department of Banking and Finance.

559.544 Registration required; exemptions. ---

(1) No person shall engage in business in this state as a commercial collection agency, as defined in this part, or continue to do business in this state as a commercial collection agency, without first registering in accordance with this part and thereafter maintaining such registration.

(2) Each commercial collection agency doing business in this state shall register with the department and annually renew such registration, providing the registration fee, information, and surety bond required by this part.

(3) No registration shall be valid for any commercial collection agency transacting business at any place other than that designated in the registration unless the department is first notified in advance of any change of location. A registration under this part is not transferable or assignable. Any commercial collection agency desiring to change its registered name, location, or agent for

service of process at any time other than renewal of registration shall notify the department of such change prior to the change.

(4) The department shall not accept any registration for any commercial collection agency as validly made and filed with the department under this section unless the registration information furnished to the department by the registrant is complete pursuant to s. 559.545 and facially demonstrates that such registrant is qualified to engage in business as a commercial collection agency, including specifically that neither the registrant nor any principal of the registrant has engaged in any unlawful collection practices, dishonest dealings, acts of moral turpitude, or other criminal acts that reflect an inability to engage in the commercial collection agency business. The department shall inform any person whose registration is rejected by the department of the fact of and basis for such rejection. A prospective registrant shall be entitled to be registered when his or its registration information is complete on its face, the applicable registration fee has been paid, and the required evidence of current bond is furnished to the department.

(5) This section shall not apply to:

(a) A member of The Florida Bar, unless such person is primarily engaged in the collection of commercial claims. "Primarily engaged in the collection of commercial claims" means that more than one-half of the income of such person arises from the business of soliciting commercial claims for collection or collecting commercial claims.

(b) A financial institution authorized to do business in this state and any wholly owned subsidiary and affiliate thereof.

(c) A licensed real estate broker.

(d) A title insurance company authorized to do business in this state.

(e) A collection agency which is not primarily engaged in the collection of commercial claims. "Not primarily engaged in the collection of commercial claims" means that less than one-half of the collection revenue of such agency arises from the collection of commercial claims.

(f) A consumer finance company and any wholly owned subsidiary and affiliate thereof.

(g) A person licensed pursuant to chapter 520.

(h) A credit grantor.

(i) An out-of-state collector as defined in this part.

(j) An FDIC-insured institution or subsidiary or affiliate thereof.

559.545 Registration of commercial collection agencies; procedure. ---

Any person who wishes to register as a commercial collection agency in compliance with this part shall do so on forms furnished by the department. Any renewal of registration shall be made between October 1 and December 31 of each year. In registering or renewing a registration as required by this part, each commercial collection agency shall furnish to the department a registration fee, information, and surety bond, as follows:

(1) The registrant shall pay to the department a registration fee of $500. All amounts collected shall be deposited to the credit of the Regulatory Trust Fund of the department.

(2) The registrant shall provide the following information:

(a) The business name or trade name of the commercial collection agency, the current mailing address of the agency, and the current business location of each place from which the agency operates either a main or branch office, with a designation of which location constitutes its principal place of business.

(b) The full names, current addresses, current telephone numbers, and social security numbers, or federal identification numbers of any corporate owner, of the registrant's owners or corporate officers and directors, and of the Florida resident agent of the registering agency.

(c) A statement as to whether the registrant is a domestic or foreign corporation, together with the state and date of incorporation, charter number of the corporation, and, if a foreign corporation, the date the corporation first registered to do business in this state.

(d) A statement listing each county in this state in which the registrant is currently doing business or plans to do business within the next calendar year, indicating each county in which the registrant holds an occupational license.

(e) A statement listing each county in this state in which the registrant is operating under a fictitious name or trade name other than that of the registrant, indicating the date and place of registration of any such fictitious name or trade name.

(f) A statement listing the names of any other corporations, entities, or trade names through which any owner or director of the registrant was known or did business as a commercial or consumer collection agency within the 5 calendar years immediately preceding the year in which the agency is registering.

(g) A statement clearly identifying and explaining any occasion on which any professional license or occupational license held by the registrant, any principal of the registrant, or any business entity in which any principal of the registrant was the owner of 10 percent or more of such business was the subject of any suspension, revocation, or other disciplinary action.

(h) A statement clearly identifying and explaining any occasion of a finding of guilt of any crime involving moral turpitude or dishonest conduct on the part of any principal of the registrant.

(3) The registrant shall furnish to the department evidence, as provided in s. 559.546, of the registrant having a current surety bond in the amount of $50,000, valid for the year of registration, paid for and issued for the use and benefit of any credit grantor who suffers or sustains any loss or damage by reason of any violation of the provisions of this part by the registrant, or by any agent or employee of the registrant acting within the scope of his employment, and issued to ensure conformance with the provisions of this part.

559.546 Bond; evidence of current and valid bond. ---

Pursuant to s. 559.545, the registrant shall provide to the department evidence that the registrant has been issued a current and valid surety bond as required by this part.

(1) In addition to each registration filed pursuant to s. 559.545 and any renewal of such registration, each registrant shall furnish to the department the following:

(a) A copy of the surety bond, which bond shall be one issued by a surety known by the registrant to be acceptable to the department.

(b) A statement from the surety that the annual premium for the bond has been paid in full by the registrant.

(c) A statement from the surety that the bond issued by the surety meets the requirements of this part.

(2) The liability of the surety under any bond issued pursuant to the requirements of this part shall not exceed in the aggregate the amount of the bond, regardless of the number or amount of any claims filed or which might be asserted against the surety on such bond. If multiple claims are filed against the surety on any such bond in excess of the amount of the bond, the surety may pay the full amount of the bond to the department and shall not be further liable under the bond. The department shall hold such funds for distribution to claimants and administratively determine and pay to each claimant the pro rata share of each valid claim made against the funds within 6 months after the date of the filing of the first claim against the surety.

559.547 Void registration. ---

(1) Any registration made under this part by any person or commercial collection agency based upon the presentation by such person or collection agency of false identification or information, or identification not current with respect to name, address, and business location, or any other fact material to such registration shall be void.

(2) Any registration made under this part, but which is void under subsection (1), shall not be construed as creating any defense to any prosecution for violation of any provision of this part.

559.548 Penalties. ---

(1) Each of the following acts constitutes a felony of the third degree, punishable as provided in s. 775.082, s. 775.083, or s. 775.084:

(a) Operating or soliciting business as a commercial collection agency in this state without first registering with the department, unless specifically exempted by this part.

(b) Registering or attempting to register by means of fraud, misrepresentation, or concealment.

(2) Each of the following acts constitutes a misdemeanor of the second degree, punishable as provided in s. 775.082 or s. 775.083:

(a) Relocating a business as a commercial collection agency, or operating under any name other than that designated in the registration, unless written notification is given to the department and to the surety or sureties on the original bond.

(b) Assigning or attempting to assign a registration under this part.

(3) The court may, in addition to other punishment provided for, invalidate the registration of any registrant under this part who has been found guilty of conduct prohibited in subsection (1) or subsection (2).

PART VI CONSUMER COLLECTION PRACTICES

559.55 Definitions. ---

The following terms shall, unless the context otherwise indicates, have the following meanings for the purpose of this part:

(1) "Debt" or "consumer debt" means any obligation or alleged obligation of a consumer to pay money arising out of a transaction in which the money, property, insurance, or services which are the subject of the transaction are primarily for personal, family, or household purposes, whether or not such obligation has been reduced to judgment.

(2) "Debtor" or "consumer" means any natural person obligated or allegedly obligated to pay any debt.

(3) "Creditor" means any person who offers or extends credit creating a debt or to whom a debt is owed, but does not include any person to the extent that they receive an assignment or transfer of a debt in default solely for the purpose of facilitating collection of such debt for another.

(4) "Department" means the Department of Banking and Finance.

(5) "Communication" means the conveying of information regarding a debt directly or indirectly to any person through any medium.

(6) "Debt collector" means any person who uses any instrumentality of commerce within this state, whether initiated from within or outside this state, in any business the principal purpose of which is the collection of debts, or who regularly collects or attempts to collect, directly or indirectly, debts owed or due or asserted to be owed or due another. The term "debt collector"

includes any creditor who, in the process of collecting his own debts, uses any name other than his own which would indicate that a third person is collecting or attempting to collect such debts. The term does not include:

(a) Any officer or employee of a creditor while, in the name of the creditor, collecting debts for such creditor;

(b) Any person while acting as a debt collector for another person, both of whom are related by common ownership or affiliated by corporate control, if the person acting as a debt collector for persons to whom it is so related or affiliated and if the principal business of such persons is not the collection of debts;

(c) Any officer or employee of any federal, state, or local governmental body to the extent that collecting or attempting to collect any debt is in the performance of his official duties;

(d) Any person while serving or attempting to serve legal process on any other person in connection with the judicial enforcement of any debt;

(e) Any not-for-profit organization which, at the request of consumers, performs bona fide consumer credit counseling and assists consumers in the liquidation of their debts by receiving payments from such consumers and distributing such amounts to creditors; or

(f) Any person collecting or attempting to collect any debt owed or due or asserted to be owed or due another to the extent that such activity is incidental to a bona fide fiduciary obligation or a bona fide escrow arrangement; concerns a debt which was originated by such person; concerns a debt which was not in default at the time it was obtained by such person; or concerns a debt obtained by such person as a secured party in a commercial credit transaction involving the creditor.

(7) "Consumer collection agency" means any debt collector or business entity engaged in the business of soliciting consumer debts for collection or of collecting consumer debts, which debt collector or business is not expressly exempted as set forth in s. 559.553(4).

(8) "Out-of-state consumer debt collector" means any person whose business activities in this state involve both collecting or attempting to collect consumer debt from debtors located in this state by means of interstate communication originating from outside this state and soliciting consumer debt accounts for collection from creditors who have a business presence in this

state. For purposes of this subsection, a creditor has a business presence in this state if either the creditor or an affiliate or subsidiary of the creditor has an office in this state.

(9) "Federal Fair Debt Collection Practices Act" or "Federal Act" means the federal legislation regulating fair debt collection practices, as set forth in Pub. L. No. 95-109, as amended and published in 15 U.S.C. ss. 1692 et seq.

559.551 Short title. ---

Sections 559.55-559.785 may be cited as the "Florida Consumer Collection Practices Act."

559.552 Relationship of state and federal law. ---

Nothing in this part shall be construed to limit or restrict the continued applicability of the Federal Fair Debt Collection Practices Act to consumer collection practices in this state. This part is in addition to the requirements and regulations of the Federal Act. In the event of any inconsistency between any provision of this part and any provision of the Federal Act, the provision which is more protective of the consumer or debtor shall prevail.

559.553 Registration of consumer collection agencies required; exemptions. ---

(1) After January 1, 1994, no person shall engage in business in this state as a consumer collection agency or continue to do business in this state as a consumer collection agency without first registering in accordance with this part, and thereafter maintaining a valid registration.

(2) Each consumer collection agency doing business in this state shall register with the department and renew such registration annually as set forth in s. 559.555.

(3) A prospective registrant shall be entitled to be registered when registration information is complete on its face and the applicable registration fee has been paid; however, the department may reject a registration submitted by a prospective registrant if the registrant or any principal of the registrant previously has held any professional license or state registration which was the subject of any suspension or revocation which has not been explained by the prospective registrant to the satisfaction of the department either in the registration information submitted initially or upon the subsequent written request of the department. In the event that an attempted registration is rejected

by the department the prospective registrant shall be informed of the basis for rejection.

(4) This section shall not apply to:

(a) Any original creditor.

(b) Any member of The Florida Bar.

(c) Any financial institution authorized to do business in this state and any wholly owned subsidiary and affiliate thereof.

(d) Any licensed real estate broker.

(e) Any insurance company authorized to do business in this state.

(f) Any consumer finance company and any wholly owned subsidiary and affiliate thereof.

(g) Any person licensed pursuant to chapter 520.

(h) Any out-of-state consumer debt collector who does not solicit consumer debt accounts for collection from credit grantors
who have a business presence in this state.

(i) Any FDIC-insured institution or subsidiary or affiliate thereof.

(5) Any out-of-state consumer debt collector as defined in s. 559.55(8) who is not exempt from registration by application of subsection (4) and who fails to register in accordance with this part shall be subject to an enforcement action by the state as specified in s. 559.565.

559.555 Registration of consumer collection agencies; procedure. ---

Any person required to register as a consumer collection agency shall furnish to the department the registration fee and information as follows:

(1) The registrant shall pay to the department a registration fee in the amount of $200. All amounts collected shall be deposited by the department to the credit of the Regulatory Trust Fund of the department.

(2) Each registrant shall provide to the department the business name or trade name, the current mailing address, the current business location which

constitutes its principal place of business, and the full name of each individual who is a principal of the registrant. "Principal of a registrant" means the registrant's owners if a partnership or sole proprietorship, corporate officers, corporate directors other than directors of a not-for-profit corporation organized pursuant to chapter 617 and Florida resident agent if a corporate registrant. The registration information shall include a statement clearly identifying and explaining any occasion on which any professional license or state registration held by the registrant, by any principal of the registrant, or by any business entity in which any principal of the registrant was the owner of 10 percent or more of such business, was the subject of any suspension or revocation.

(3) Renewal of registration shall be made between October 1 and December 31 of each year. There shall be no proration of the fee for any registration.

559.563 Void registration. ---

Any registration made under this part based upon false identification or false information, or identification not current with respect to name, address, and business location, or other fact which is material to such registration, shall be void. Any registration made and subsequently void under this section shall not be construed as creating any defense in any action by the department to impose any sanction for any violation of this part.

559.565 Enforcement action against out-of-state consumer debt collector. ---

The remedies of this section are cumulative to other sanctions and enforcement provisions of this part for any violation by an out-of-state consumer debt collector, as defined in s. 559.55(8).

(1) Any out-of-state consumer debt collector who collects or attempts to collect consumer debts in this state without first registering in accordance with this part shall be subject to an administrative fine not to exceed $1,000 together with reasonable attorney fees and court costs in any successful action by the state to collect such fines.

(2) Any person, whether or not exempt from registration under this part, who violates the provisions of s. 559.72 shall be subject to sanctions for such violations the same as any other consumer debt collector, including imposition of an administrative fine. The registration of a duly registered out-of-state consumer debt collector shall be subject to revocation or suspension in the same manner as the registration of any other registrant under this part.

(3) In order to effectuate the provisions of this section and enforce the requirements of this part as it relates to out-of-state consumer debt collectors, the Attorney General is expressly authorized to initiate such action on behalf of the state as he deems appropriate in any federal district court of competent jurisdiction.

559.715 Assignment of consumer debts. ---

This part does not prohibit the assignment, by a creditor, of the right to bill and collect a consumer debt. However, the assignee must give the debtor written notice of such assignment within 30 days after the assignment. The assignee is a real party in interest and may bring an action in a court of competent jurisdiction to collect a debt that has been assigned to such assignee and is in default.

559.72 Prohibited practices generally. ---

In collecting consumer debts, no person shall:

(1) Simulate in any manner a law enforcement officer or a representative of any governmental agency;

(2) Use or threaten force or violence;

(3) Tell a debtor who disputes a consumer debt that he or any person employing him will disclose to another, orally or in writing, directly or indirectly, information affecting the debtor's reputation for credit worthiness without also informing the debtor that the existence of the dispute will also be disclosed as required by subsection (6);

(4) Communicate or threaten to communicate with a debtor's employer prior to obtaining final judgment against the debtor, unless the debtor gives his permission in writing to contact his employer or acknowledges in writing the existence of the debt after the debt has been placed for collection, but this shall not prohibit a person from telling the debtor that his employer will be contacted if a final judgment is obtained;

(5) Disclose to a person other than the debtor or his family information affecting the debtor's reputation, whether or not for credit worthiness, with knowledge or reason to know that the other person does not have a legitimate business need for the information or that the information is false;

(6) Disclose information concerning the existence of a debt known to be reasonably disputed by the debtor without disclosing that fact. If a disclosure is made prior to such reasonable dispute having been asserted and written notice is received from the debtor that any part of the debt is disputed and if such dispute is reasonable, the person who made the original disclosure shall reveal upon the request of the debtor within 30 days the details of the dispute to each person to whom disclosure of the debt without notice of the dispute was made within the preceding 90 days;

(7) Willfully communicate with the debtor or any member of his family with such frequency as can reasonably be expected to harass the debtor or his family, or willfully engage in other conduct which can reasonably be expected to abuse or harass the debtor or any member of his family;

(8) Use profane, obscene, vulgar, or willfully abusive language in communicating with the debtor or any member of his family;

(9) Claim, attempt, or threaten to enforce a debt when such person knows that the debt is not legitimate or assert the existence of some other legal right when such person knows that the right does not exist;

(10) Use a communication which simulates in any manner legal or judicial process or which gives the appearance of being authorized, issued or approved by a government, governmental agency, or attorney at law, when it is not;

(11) Communicate with a debtor under the guise of an attorney by using the stationery of an attorney or forms or instruments which only attorneys are authorized to prepare;

(12) Orally communicate with a debtor in such a manner as to give the false impression or appearance that such person is or is associated with an attorney;

(13) Advertise or threaten to advertise for sale any debt as a means to enforce payment except under court order or when acting as an assignee for the benefit of a creditor;

(14) Publish or post, threaten to publish or post, or cause to be published or posted before the general public individual names or any list of names of debtors, commonly known as a deadbeat list, for the purpose of enforcing or attempting to enforce collection of consumer debts;

(15) Refuse to provide adequate identification of himself or his employer or other entity whom he represents when requested to do so by a debtor from whom he is collecting or attempting to collect a consumer debt;

(16) Mail any communication to a debtor in an envelope or postcard with words typed, written, or printed on the outside of the envelope or postcard calculated to embarrass the debtor. An example of this would be an envelope addressed to "Deadbeat, John Doe"; or

(17) Communicate with the debtor between the hours of 9 p.m. and 8 a.m. in the debtor's time zone without the prior consent of the debtor.

559.725 Consumer complaints; administrative duties. ---

(1) The Division of Consumer Services shall serve as the registry for receiving and maintaining records of inquiries, correspondence, and complaints from consumers concerning any and all persons who collect debts, including consumer collection agencies.

(2) The division shall classify complaints by type and identify the number of written complaints against persons collecting or attempting to collect debts in this state, including credit grantors collecting their own debts, debt collectors generally, and, specifically, consumer collection agencies as distinguished from other persons who collect debts such as commercial debt collection agencies regulated under part V of this chapter. The division shall identify the nature and number of various kinds of written complaints, including specifically those alleging violations of s. 559.72.

(3) The division shall inform and furnish relevant information to the appropriate regulatory body of the state, or The Florida Bar in the case of attorneys, when any consumer debt collector exempt from registration under this part has been named in five or more written consumer complaints alleging violations of s. 559.72 within a 12-month period.

(4) The division shall furnish a form to each complainant whose complaint concerns an alleged violation of s. 559.72 by a consumer collection agency. Such form may be filed with the Department of Banking and Finance. The form shall identify the accused consumer collection agency and provide for the complainant's summary of the nature of the alleged violation and facts which allegedly support the complaint. The form shall include a provision for the complainant to state under oath before a notary public that the allegations therein made are true.

(5) Upon receipt of such sworn complaint, the department shall promptly furnish a copy of the sworn complaint to the accused consumer collection agency.

(6) The department shall investigate sworn complaints by direct written communication with the complainant and the affected consumer collection agency. In addition, the department shall attempt to resolve each sworn complaint and shall record the resolution of such complaints.

(7) Periodically, the department shall identify consumer collection agencies that have unresolved sworn consumer complaints from five or more different consumers within a 12-month period under the provisions of this part.

(8) The department shall issue a written warning notice to the accused consumer collection agency if the department is unable to resolve all such sworn complaints and fewer than five unresolved complaints remain. Such notice shall include a statement that the warning may constitute evidence in any future investigation of similar complaints against that agency and in any future administrative determination of the imposition of other administrative remedies available to the department under this part.

(9) The department may issue a written reprimand when five or more such unresolved sworn complaints against a consumer collection agency collectively fall short of constituting apparent repeated violations that warrant more serious administrative sanctions. Such reprimand shall include a statement that the reprimand may constitute evidence in any future investigation of similar complaints against that agency and in any future administrative determination of the imposition of other administrative remedies available to the department.

(10) The department shall issue a notice of intent either to revoke or suspend the registration or to impose an administrative fine when the department preliminarily determines that repeated violations of s. 559.72 by an accused registrant have occurred which would warrant more serious administrative sanctions being imposed under this part. The department shall advise each registrant of the right to require an administrative hearing under chapter 120, prior to the agency's final action on the matter as authorized by s. 559.730.

(11) The department shall advise the appropriate state attorney, or the Attorney General in the case of an out-of-state consumer debt collector, of any determination by the department of a violation of the requirements of this part by any consumer collection agency which is not registered as required by this part. The department shall furnish the state attorney or Attorney General with

the department's information concerning the alleged violations of such requirements.

559.730 Administrative remedies. ---

(1) The department may revoke or suspend the registration of any registrant under this part who has engaged in repeated violations which establish a clear pattern of abuse of prohibited collection practices under s. 559.72. Final department action to revoke or suspend the registration of any registrant shall be subject to review in accordance with chapter 120 in the same manner as revocation of a license. The repeated violations of the law by one employee shall not be grounds for revocation or suspension of the registration of the employing consumer collection agency, unless the employee is also the owner of a majority interest in the collection agency.

(2) The registration of a registrant shall not be revoked or suspended if the registrant shows by a preponderance of the evidence that the violations were not intentional and resulted from bona fide error notwithstanding the maintenance of procedures reasonably adapted to avoid any such error.

(3) The department shall consider the number of complaints against the registrant in relation to the accused registrant's volume of business when determining whether suspension or revocation is the more appropriate sanction when circumstances warrant that one or the other should be imposed upon a registrant.

(4) The department shall impose suspension rather than revocation when circumstances warrant that one or the other should be imposed upon a registrant and the accused registrant demonstrates that the registrant has taken affirmative steps which can be expected to effectively eliminate the repeated violations and that the registrant's registration has never previously been suspended.

(5) The department may impose an administrative fine up to $1,000 against the offending registrant as a sanction for repeated violations of the provisions of s. 559.72 when violations do not rise to the level of misconduct governed by subsection (1). Final department action to impose an administrative fine shall be subject to review in accordance with s. 120.57.

(6) Any administrative fine imposed under this part shall be payable to the department. The department shall maintain an appropriate record and shall deposit such fine into the Regulatory Trust Fund of the department.

(7) An administrative action by the department to impose revocation, suspension, or fine shall be brought within 2 years after the date of the last violation upon which the action is founded.

(8) Nothing in this part shall be construed to preclude any person from pursuing remedies available under the Federal Fair Debt Collection Practices Act for any violation of such act, including specifically against any person who is exempt from the registration provisions of this part.

559.77 Civil remedies. ---

A debtor may bring a civil action against a person violating the provisions of s. 559.72 in a court of competent jurisdiction of the county in which the alleged violator resides or has his principal place of business or in the county wherein the alleged violation occurred. Upon adverse adjudication, the defendant shall be liable for actual damages or $500, whichever is greater, together with court costs and reasonable attorney's fees incurred by the plaintiff. The court may, in its discretion, award punitive damages and may provide such equitable relief as it deems necessary or proper, including enjoining the defendant from further violations of this part. If the court finds that the suit fails to raise a justiciable issue of law or fact, the plaintiff shall be liable for court costs and reasonable attorney's fees incurred by the defendant.

559.78 Judicial enforcement. ---

In addition to other penalties provided in this part, state attorneys and their assistants are authorized to apply to the court of competent jurisdiction within their respective jurisdictions, upon the sworn affidavit of any person alleging a violation of any of the provisions of this part. Such court shall have jurisdiction, upon hearing and for cause shown, to grant a temporary or permanent injunction restraining any person from violating any provision of this part, whether or not there exists an adequate remedy at law; and such injunction, suspension, or revocation shall issue without bond.

559.785 Criminal penalty. ---

It shall be a misdemeanor of the first degree, punishable as provided in s. 775.082 or s. 775.083, for any person not exempt from registering as provided in this part to engage in collecting consumer debts in this state without first registering with the department, or to register or attempt to register by means of fraud, misrepresentation, or concealment.

NEW YORK STATE CONSOLIDATED LAWS, CIVIL PRACTICE LAW & RULES ARTICLE 52, ENFORCEMENT OF MONEY JUDGMENTS

Sec. 5201. Debt or property subject to enforcement; proper garnishee.

(a) Debt against which a money judgment may be enforced. A money judgment may be enforced against any debt, which is past due or which is yet to become due, certainly or upon demand of the judgment debtor, whether it was incurred within or without the state, to or from a resident or non-resident, unless it is exempt from application to the satisfaction of the judgment. A debt may consist of a cause of action which could be assigned or transferred accruing within or without the state.

(b) Property against which a money judgment may be enforced. A money judgment may be enforced against any property which could be assigned or transferred, whether it consists of a present or future right or interest and whether or not it is vested, unless it is exempt from application to the satisfaction of the judgment. A money judgment entered upon a joint liability of two or more persons may be enforced against individual property of those persons summoned and joint property of such persons with any other persons against whom the judgment is entered.

(c) Proper garnishee for particular property or debt.

1. Where property consists of a right or share in the stock of an association or corporation, or interests or profits therein, for which a certificate of stock or other negotiable instrument is not outstanding, the corporation, or the president or treasurer of the association on behalf of the association, shall be the garnishee.

2. Where property consists of a right or interest to or in a decedent's estate or any other property or fund held or controlled by a fiduciary, the executor or trustee under the will, administrator or other fiduciary shall be the garnishee.

3. Where property consists of an interest in a partnership, any partner other than the judgment debtor, on behalf of the partnership, shall be the garnishee.

4. Where property or a debt is evidenced by a negotiable instrument for the payment of money, a negotiable document of title or a certificate of

stock of an association or corporation, the instrument, document or certificate shall be treated as property capable of delivery and the person holding it shall be the garnishee; except that in the case of a security which is transferable in the manner set forth in section 8-320 of the uniform commercial code, the firm or corporation which carries on its books an account in the name of the judgment debtor in which is reflected such security, shall be the garnishee; provided, however, that if such security has been pledged, the pledgee shall be the garnishee.

Sec. 5202. Judgment creditor's rights in personal property.

(a) Execution creditor's rights. Where a judgment creditor has delivered an execution to a sheriff, the judgment creditor's rights in a debt owed to the judgment debtor or in an interest of the judgment debtor in personal property, against which debt or property the judgment may be enforced, are superior to the extent of the amount of the execution to the rights of any transferee of the debt or property, except: 1. a transferee who acquired the debt or property for fair consideration before it was levied upon; or 2. a transferee who acquired a debt or personal property not capable of delivery for fair consideration after it was levied upon without knowledge of the levy.

(b) Other judgment creditor's rights. Where a judgment creditor has secured an order for delivery of, payment of, or appointment of a receiver of, a debt owed to the judgment debtor or an interest of the judgment debtor in personal property, the judgment creditor's rights in the debt or property are superior to the rights of any transferee of the debt or property, except a transferee who acquired the debt or property for fair consideration and without notice of such order.

Sec. 5203. Priorities and liens upon real property.

(a) Priority and lien on docketing judgment. No transfer of an interest of the judgment debtor in real property, against which property a money judgment may be enforced, is effective against the judgment creditor either from the time of the docketing of the judgment with the clerk of the county in which the property is located until ten years after filing of the judgment-roll, or from the time of the filing with such clerk of a notice of levy pursuant to an execution until the execution is returned, except:

> 1. a transfer or the payment of the proceeds of a judicial sale, which shall include an execution sale, in satisfaction either of a judgment previously so docketed or of a judgment where a notice of levy pursuant to an execution thereon was previously so filed; or

2. a transfer in satisfaction of a mortgage given to secure the payment of the purchase price of the judgment debtor's interest in the property; or

3. a transfer to a purchaser for value at a judicial sale, which shall include an execution sale; or

4. when the judgment was entered after the death of the judgment debtor; or

5. when the judgment debtor is the state, an officer, department, board or commission of the state, or a municipal corporation; or

6. when the judgment debtor is the personal representative of a decedent and the judgment was awarded in an action against him in his representative capacity.

(b) Extension of lien. Upon motion of the judgment creditor, upon notice to the judgment debtor, served personally or by registered or certified mail, return receipt requested, to the last known address of the judgment debtor, the court may order that the lien of a money judgment upon real property be effective after the expiration of ten years from the filing of the judgment-roll, for a period no longer than the time during which the judgment creditor was stayed from enforcing the judgment, or the time necessary to complete advertisement and sale of real property in accordance with section 5236, pursuant to an execution delivered to a sheriff prior to the expiration of ten years from the filing of the judgment-roll. The order shall be effective from the time it is filed with the clerk of the county in which the property is located and an appropriate entry is made upon the docket of the judgment.

Sec. 5204. Release of lien or levy upon appeal.

Upon motion of the judgment debtor, upon notice to the judgment creditor, the sheriff and the sureties upon the undertaking, the court may order, upon such terms as justice requires, that the lien of a money judgment, or that a levy made pursuant to an execution issued upon a money judgment, be released as to all or specified real or personal property upon the ground that the judgment debtor has given an undertaking upon appeal sufficient to secure the judgment creditor.

Sec. 5205. Personal property exempt from application to the satisfaction of money judgments.

(a) Exemption for personal property. The following personal property when owned by any person is exempt from application to the satisfaction of a money judgment except where the judgment is for the purchase price of the exempt property or was recovered by a domestic, laboring person or mechanic for work performed by that person in such capacity:

1. all stoves kept for use in the judgment debtor's dwelling house and necessary fuel therefor for sixty days; one sewing machine with its appurtenances;

2. the family bible, family pictures, and school books used by the judgment debtor or in the family; and other books, not exceeding fifty dollars in value, kept and used as part of the family or judgment debtor's library;

3. a seat or pew occupied by the judgment debtor or the family in a place of public worship;

4. domestic animals with the necessary food for those animals for sixty days, provided that the total value of such animals and food does not exceed four hundred fifty dollars; all necessary food actually provided for the use of the judgment debtor or his family for sixty days;

5. all wearing apparel, household furniture, one mechanical, gas or electric refrigerator, one radio receiver, one television set, crockery, tableware and cooking utensils necessary for the judgment debtor and the family;

6. a wedding ring; a watch not exceeding thirty-five dollars in value; and

7. necessary working tools and implements, including those of a mechanic, farm machinery, team, professional instruments, furniture and library, not exceeding six hundred dollars in value, together with the necessary food for the team for sixty days, provided, however, that the articles specified in this paragraph are necessary to the carrying on of the judgment debtor's profession or calling.

(b) Exemption of cause of action and damages for taking or injuring exempt personal property. A cause of action, to recover damages for taking or injuring personal property exempt from application to the satisfaction of a money judgment, is exempt from application to the satisfaction of a money judgment. A money judgment and its proceeds arising out of such a cause of action is exempt, for one year after the collection thereof, from application to the satisfaction of a money judgment.

(c) Trust exemption. 1. Except as provided in paragraphs four and five of this subdivision, all property while held in trust for a judgment debtor, where the trust has been created by, or the fund so held in trust has proceeded from, a person other than the judgment debtor, is exempt from application to the satisfaction of a money judgment.

2. For purposes of this subdivision, all trusts, custodial accounts, annuities, insurance contracts, monies, assets or interests established as part of, and all payments from, either any trust or plan, which is qualified as an individual retirement account under section four hundred eight of the United States Internal Revenue Code of 1986, as amended, or a Keogh (HR-10), retirement or other plan established by a corporation, which is qualified under section 401 of the United States Internal Revenue Code of 1986, as amended, or created as a result of rollovers from such plans pursuant to sections 402 (a) (5), 403 (a) (4) or 408 (d)(3) of the Internal Revenue Code of 1986, as amended, shall be considered a trust which has been created by or which has proceeded from a person other than the judgment debtor, even though such judgment debtor is (i) in the case of an individual retirement account plan, an individual who is the settlor of and depositor to such account plan, or (ii) a self-employed individual, or (iii) a partner of the entity sponsoring the Keogh (HR-10) plan, or (iv) a shareholder of the corporation sponsoring the retirement or other plan.

3. All trusts, custodial accounts, annuities, insurance contracts, monies, assets, or interests described in paragraph two of this subdivision shall be conclusively presumed to be spendthrift trusts under this section and the common law of the state of New York for all purposes, including, but not limited to, all cases arising under or related to a case arising under sections one hundred one to thirteen hundred thirty of title eleven of the United States Bankruptcy Code, as amended.

4. This subdivision shall not impair any rights an individual has under a qualified domestic relations order as that term is defined in section 414(p) of the United States Internal Revenue Code of 1986, as amended.

5. Additions to an asset described in paragraph two of this subdivision shall not be exempt from application to the satisfaction of a money judgment if (i) made after the date that is ninety days before the interposition of the claim on which such judgment was entered, or (ii) deemed to be fraudulent conveyances under article ten of the debtor and creditor law.

(d) Income exemptions. The following personal property is exempt from application to the satisfaction of a money judgment, except such part as a court determines to be unnecessary for the reasonable requirements of the judgment debtor and his dependents:

1. ninety per cent of the income or other payments from a trust the principal of which is exempt under subdivision (c); provided, however, that with respect to any income or payments made from trusts, custodial accounts, annuities, insurance contracts, monies, assets or interest established as part of an individual retirement account plan or as part of a Keogh (HR-10), retirement or other plan described in paragraph two of subdivision (c) of this

section, the exception in this subdivision for such part as a court determines to be unnecessary for the reasonable requirements of the judgment debtor and his dependents shall not apply, and the ninety percent exclusion of this paragraph shall become a one hundred percent exclusion;

2. ninety per cent of the earnings of the judgment debtor for his personal services rendered within sixty days before, and at any time after, an income execution is delivered to the sheriff or a motion is made to secure the application of the judgment debtor's earnings to the satisfaction of the judgment; and

3. payments pursuant to an award in a matrimonial action, for the support of a wife, where the wife is the judgment debtor, or for the support of a child, where the child is the judgment debtor; where the award was made by a court of the state, determination of the extent to which it is unnecessary shall be made by that court.

(e) Exemptions to members of armed forces. The pay and bounty of a non-commissioned officer, musician or private in the armed forces of the United States or the state of New York; a land warrant, pension or other reward granted by the United States, or by a state, for services in the armed forces; a sword, horse, medal, emblem or device of any kind presented as a testimonial for services rendered in the armed forces of the United States or a state; and the uniform, arms and equipments which were used by a person in the service, are exempt from application to the satisfaction of a money judgment; provided, however, that the provisions of this subdivision shall not apply to the satisfaction of any order or money judgment for the support of a person's child, spouse, or former spouse.

(f) Exemption for unpaid milk proceeds. Ninety per cent of any money or debt due or to become due to the judgment debtor for the sale of milk produced on a farm operated by him and delivered for his account to a milk dealer licensed pursuant to article twenty-one of the agriculture and markets law is exempt from application to the satisfaction of a money judgment.

(g) Security deposit exemption. Money deposited as security for the rental of real property to be used as the residence of the judgment debtor or the judgment debtor's family; and money deposited as security with a gas, electric, water, steam, telegraph or telephone corporation, or a municipality rendering equivalent utility services, for services to judgment debtor's residence or the residence of judgment debtor's family, are exempt from application to the satisfaction of a money judgment.

(h) The following personal property is exempt from application to the satisfaction of money judgment, except such part as a court determines to be unnecessary for the reasonable requirements of the judgment debtor and his dependents:

1. any and all medical and dental accessions to the human body and all personal property or equipment that is necessary or proper to maintain or assist in sustaining or maintaining one or more major life activities or is utilized to provide mobility for a person with a permanent disability; and

2. any guide dog, service dog or hearing dog, as those terms are defined in section one hundred eight of the agriculture and markets law, or any animal trained to aid or assist a person with a permanent disability and actually being so used by such person, together with any and all food or feed for any such dog or other animal.

(i) Exemption for life insurance policies. The right of a judgment debtor to accelerate payment of part or all of the death benefit or special surrender value under a life insurance policy, as authorized by paragraph one of subsection (a) of section one thousand one hundred thirteen of the insurance law, or to enter into a viatical settlement pursuant to the provisions of article seventy-eight of the insurance law, is exempt from application to the satisfaction of a money judgment.

Sec. 5206. Real property exempt from application to the satisfaction of money judgments.

(a) Exemption of homestead. Property of one of the following types, not exceeding ten thousand dollars in value above liens and encumbrances, owned and as a principal residence, is exempt from application to the satisfaction of a money judgment, unless the judgment was recovered wholly for the purchase price thereof:

1.   a lot of land with a dwelling thereon,

2.   shares of stock in a cooperative apartment corporation,

3.   units of a condominium apartment, or

4.   a mobile home.

But no exempt homestead shall be exempt from taxation or from sale for non-payment of taxes or assessments.

(b) Homestead exemption after owner's death.

The homestead exemption continues after the death of the person in whose favor the property was exempted for the benefit of the surviving spouse and surviving children until the majority of the youngest surviving child and until the death of the surviving spouse.

(c) Suspension of occupation as affecting homestead.

The homestead exemption ceases if the property ceases to be occupied as a residence by a person for whose benefit it may so continue, except where the suspension of occupation is for a period not exceeding one year, and occurs in consequence of injury to, or destruction of, the dwelling house upon the premises.

(d) Exemption of homestead exceeding ten thousand dollars in value.

The exemption of a homestead is not void because the value of the property exceeds ten thousand dollars but the lien of a judgment attaches to the surplus.

(e) Sale of homestead exceeding ten thousand dollars in value.

A judgment creditor may commence a special proceeding in the county in which the homestead is located against the judgment for the sale, by a sheriff or receiver, of a homestead exceeding ten thousand dollars in value. The court may direct that the notice of petition be served upon any other person. The court, if it directs such a sale, shall so marshal the proceeds of the sale that the right and interest of each person in the proceeds shall correspond as nearly as may be to his right and interest in the property sold. Money, not exceeding ten thousand dollars, paid to a judgment debtor, as representing his interest in the proceeds, is exempt for one year after the payment, unless, before the expiration of the year, he acquires an exempt homestead, in which case, the exemption ceases with respect to so much of the money as was not expended for the purchase of that property; and the exemption of the property so acquired extends to every debt against which the property sold was exempt. Where the exemption of property sold as prescribed in this subdivision has been continued after the judgment debtor's death, or where he dies after the sale and before payment to him of his portion of the proceeds of the sale, the court may direct that portion of the proceeds which represents his interest be invested for the benefit of the person or persons entitled to the benefit of the exemption, or be otherwise disposed of as justice requires.

(f) Exemption of burying ground.

Land, set apart as a family or private burying ground, is exempt from application to the satisfaction of a money judgment, upon the following conditions only:

      1. a portion of it must have been actually used for that purpose;

      2. it must not exceed in extent one-fourth of an acre; and

      3. it must not contain any building or structure, except one or more vaults or other places of deposit for the dead, or mortuary monuments.

Sec. 5207. Enforcement involving the state.

None of the procedures for the enforcement of money judgments are applicable to a judgment against the state. All procedures for the enforcement of money judgments against other judgment debtors are applicable to the state, its officers, agencies and subdivisions, as a garnishee, except where otherwise prescribed by law, and except that an order in such a procedure shall only provide for the payment of moneys not claimed by the state, and no judgment shall be entered against the state, or any officer, department, board or commission thereof, in such a procedure. This section shall not be deemed to grant any court jurisdiction to hear and determine claims or actions against the state not otherwise given by law to such court.

Sec. 5208. Enforcement after death of judgment debtor; leave of court; extension of lien.

Except where otherwise prescribed by law, after the death of a judgment debtor, an execution upon a money judgment shall not be levied upon any debt owed to him or any property in which be has an interest, nor shall any other enforcement procedure be undertaken with respect to such debt or property, except upon leave of the surrogate's court which granted letters testamentary or letters of administration upon the estate. If such letters have not been granted within eighteen months after the death, leave to issue such an execution or undertake such enforcement procedure may thereafter be granted, upon motion of the judgment creditor upon such notice as the court may require, by any court from which the execution could issue or in which the enforcement procedure could be commenced. A judgment lien existing against real property at the time of a judgment debtor's death shall expire two years thereafter or ten years after filing of the judgment-roll, whichever is later.

TEXAS PROPERTY CODE, TITLE 5
EXEMPT PROPERTY AND LIENS

Sec. 41.001. Interests in Land Exempt from Seizure.

(a) A homestead and one or more lots used for a place of burial of the dead are exempt from seizure for the claims of creditors except for encumbrances properly fixed on homestead property.

(b) Encumbrances may be properly fixed on homestead property for:

(1) purchase money,

(2) taxes on the property;

(3) work and material used in constructing improvements on the property if contracted for in writing as provided by Sections 53.059(a), (b), and (c);

(4) an owelty of partition imposed against the entirety of the property by a court order or by a written agreement of the parties to the partition, including a debt of one spouse in favor of the other spouse resulting from a division or an award of a family homestead in a divorce proceeding; or

(5) the refinance of a lien against a homestead, including a federal tax lien resulting from the tax debt of both spouses, if the homestead is a family homestead, or from the tax debt of the owner.

(c) The homestead claimant's proceeds of a sale of a homestead are not subject to seizure for a creditor's claim for six months after the date of sale.

Sec. 41.002. Definition of Homestead.

(a) If used for the purposes of an urban home or as a place to exercise a calling or business in the same urban area, the homestead of a family or a single, adult person, not otherwise entitled to a homestead, shall consist of not more than one acre of land which may be in one or more lots, together with any improvements thereon.

(b) If used for the purposes of a rural home, the homestead shall consist of:

(1) for a family, not more than 200 acres, which may be in one or more parcels, with the improvements thereon; or

(2) for a single, adult person, not otherwise entitled to a homestead, not more than 100 acres, which may be in one or more parcels, with the improvements thereon.

(c) A homestead is considered to be rural if, at the time the designation is made, the property is not served by municipal utilities and fire and police protection.

(d) The definition of a homestead as provided in this section applies to all homesteads in this state whenever created.

Sec. 41.003. Temporary Renting of a Homestead.

Temporary renting of a homestead does not change its homestead character if the homestead claimant has not acquired another homestead.

Sec. 41.004. Abandonment of a Homestead.

If a homestead claimant is married, a homestead cannot be abandoned without the consent of the claimant's spouse.

Sec. 41.005. Voluntary Designation of Homestead.

(a) If a rural homestead of a family is part of one or more parcels containing a total of more than 200 acres, the head of the family and, if married, that person's spouse may voluntarily designate not more than 200 acres of the property as the homestead. If a rural homestead of a single adult person, not otherwise entitled to a homestead, is part of one or more parcels containing a total of more than 100 acres, the person may voluntarily designate not more than 100 acres of the property as the homestead.

(b) If an urban homestead of a family, or an urban homestead of a single adult person not otherwise entitled to a homestead, is part of one or more lots containing a total of more than one acre, the head of the family and, if married, that person's spouse or the single adult person, as applicable, may voluntarily designate not more than one acre of the property as the homestead.

(c) To designate property as a homestead, a person or persons, as applicable, must make the designation in an instrument that is signed and acknowledged or proved in the manner required for the recording of other instruments. The person or persons must file the designation with the county clerk of the county in which all or part of the property is located. The clerk shall record the designation in the county deed records. The designation must contain:

(1) a description sufficient to identify the property designated;

(2) a statement by the person or persons who executed the instrument that the property is designated as the homestead of the person's family or as the homestead of a single adult person not otherwise entitled to a homestead; and

(3) the name of the current record title holder of the property; and

(4) for a rural homestead, the number of acres designated and, if there is more than one survey, the number of acres in each.

(d) A person or persons, as applicable, may change the boundaries of a homestead designated under this section by executing and recording an instrument in the manner required for a voluntary designation. A change under this subsection does not impair rights acquired by a party before the change.

(e) If a person or persons, as applicable, have not made a voluntary designation of a homestead under this section as of the time a writ of execution is issued against the person, any designation of the person's or persons' homestead must be made in accordance with Subchapter B.

(f) An instrument that made a voluntary designation of a homestead in accordance with prior law and that is on file with the county clerk on September 1, 1987, is considered a voluntary designation of a homestead under this section.

Sec. 41.006. Certain Sales of Homestead.

(a) Except as provided by Subsection (c), any sale or purported sale in whole or in part of a homestead at a fixed purchase price that is less than the appraised fair market value of the property at the time of the sale or purported sale, and in connection with which the buyer of the property executes a lease of the property to the seller at lease payments that exceed the fair rental value of the property, is considered to be a loan with all payments made from the seller to the buyer in excess of the sales price considered to be interest subject to Title 79, Revised Statutes (Article 5069-1.01 et seq., Vernon's Texas Civil Statutes).

(b) The taking of any deed in connection with a transaction described by this section is a deceptive trade practice under Subchapter E, Chapter 17, Business & Commerce Code, and the deed is void and no lien attaches to the homestead property as a result of the purported sale.

(c) This section does not apply to the sale of a family homestead to a parent, stepparent, grandparent, child, stepchild, brother, half brother, sister, half sister, or grandchild of an adult member of the family.

Sec. 41.007. Home Improvement Contract.

(a) A contract described by Section 41.001(b)(3) must contain the following warning, conspicuously printed, stamped, or typed in a size equal to at least 10-point bold type or computer equivalent, next to the owner's signature line on the contract:

"IMPORTANT NOTICE: You and your contractor are responsible for meeting the terms and conditions of this contract. If you sign this contract and you fail to meet the terms and conditions of this contract, you may lose your legal ownership rights in your home. KNOW YOUR RIGHTS AND DUTIES UNDER THE LAW."

(b) A violation of Subsection (a) of this section is a false, misleading, or deceptive act or practice within the meaning of Section 17.46, Business & Commerce Code, and is actionable in a public or private suit brought under the provisions of the Deceptive Trade Practices-Consumer Protection Act (Subchapter E, Chapter 17, Business & Commerce Code).

Sec. 41.021. Notice to Designate.

If an execution is issued against a holder of an interest in land of which a homestead may be a part and the judgment debtor has not made a voluntary designation of a homestead under Section 41.005, the judgment creditor may give the judgment debtor notice to designate the homestead as defined in Section 41.002. The notice shall state that if the judgment debtor fails to designate the homestead within the time allowed by Section 41.022, the court will appoint a commissioner to make the designation at the expense of the judgment debtor.

Sec. 41.022. Designation by Homestead Claimant.

At any time before 10 a.m. on the Monday next after the expiration of 20 days after the date of service of the notice to designate, the judgment debtor may designate the homestead as defined in Section 41.002 by filing a written designation, signed by the judgment debtor, with the justice or clerk of the court from which the writ of execution was issued, together with a plat of the area designated.

Sec. 41.023. Designation by Commissioner.

(a) If a judgment debtor who has not made a voluntary designation of a homestead under Section 41.005 does not designate a homestead as provided in Section 41.022, on motion of the judgment creditor, filed within 90 days after the issuance of the writ of execution, the court from which the writ of execution issued shall appoint a commissioner to designate the judgment debtor's homestead. The court may appoint a surveyor and others as may be necessary to assist the commissioner. The commissioner shall file his designation of the judgment debtor's homestead in a written report, together with a plat of the area designated, with the justice or clerk of the court not more than 60 days after the order of appointment is signed or within such time as the court may allow.

(b) Within 10 days after the commissioner's report is filed, the judgment debtor or the judgment creditor may request a hearing on the issue of whether the report should be confirmed, rejected, or modified as may be deemed appropriate in the particular circumstances of the case. The commissioner's report may be contradicted by evidence from either party, when exceptions to it or any item thereof have been filed before the hearing, but not otherwise. After the hearing, or if there is no hearing requested, the court shall designate the homestead as deemed appropriate and order sale of the excess.

(c) The commissioner, a surveyor, and others appointed to assist the commissioner are entitled to such fees and expenses as are deemed reasonable by the court. The court shall tax these fees and expenses against the judgment debtor as part of the costs of execution.

Sec. 41.024. Sale of Excess.

An officer holding an execution sale of property of a judgment debtor whose homestead has been designated under this chapter may sell the excess of the judgment debtor's interest in land not included in the homestead.

Sec. 42.001. Personal Property Exemption.

(a) Personal property, as described in Section 42.002, is exempt from garnishment, attachment, execution, or other seizure if:

    (1) the property is provided for a family and has an aggregate fair market value of not more than $60,000, exclusive of the amount of any liens, security interests, or other charges encumbering the property; or

(2) the property is owned by a single adult, who is not a member of a family, and has an aggregate fair market value of not more than $30,000, exclusive of the amount of any liens, security interests, or other charges encumbering the property.

(b) The following personal property is exempt from seizure and is not included in the aggregate limitations prescribed by Subsection (a):

(1) current wages for personal services, except for the enforcement of court-ordered child support payments;

(2) professionally prescribed health aids of a debtor or a dependent of a debtor.

(c) This section does not prevent seizure by a secured creditor with a contractual landlord's lien or other security in the property to be seized.

(d) Unpaid commissions for personal services not to exceed 25 percent of the aggregate limitations prescribed by Subsection (a) are exempt from seizure and are included in the aggregate.

Sec. 42.002. Personal Property.

(a) The following personal property is exempt under Section 42.001(a):

(1) home furnishings, including family heirlooms;

(2) provisions for consumption;

(3) farming or ranching vehicles and implements;

(4) tools, equipment, books, and apparatus, including boats and motor vehicles used in a trade or profession;

(5) wearing apparel;

(6) jewelry not to exceed 25 percent of the aggregate limitations prescribed by Section 42.001(a);

(7) two firearms;

(8) athletic and sporting equipment, including bicycles;

(9) a two-wheeled, three-wheeled, or four-wheeled motor vehicle for each member of a family or single adult who holds a driver's license or who does not hold a driver's license but who relies on another person to operate the vehicle for the benefit of the nonlicensed person;

(10) the following animals and forage on hand for their consumption:

(A) two horses, mules, or donkeys and a saddle, blanket, and bridle for each;

(B) 12 head of cattle;

(C) 60 head of other types of livestock; and

(D) 120 fowl;

(11) household pets; and

(12) the present value of any life insurance policy to the extent that a member of the family of the insured or a dependent of a single insured adult claiming the exemption is a beneficiary of the policy.

(b) Personal property, unless precluded from being encumbered by other law, may be encumbered by a security interest under Section 9.203, Business & Commerce Code, or Sections 41 and 42, Certificate of Title Act (Article 6687-1, Vernon's Texas Civil Statutes), or by a lien fixed by other law, and the security interest or lien may not be avoided on the ground that the property is exempt under this chapter.

Sec. 42.0021. Additional Exemption for Retirement Plan.

(a) In addition to the exemption prescribed by Section 42.001, a person's right to the assets held in or to receive payments, whether vested or not, under any stock bonus, pension, profit-sharing, or similar plan, including a retirement plan for self-employed individuals, and under any annuity or similar contract purchased with assets distributed from that type of plan, and under any retirement annuity or account described by Section 403(b) of the Internal Revenue Code of 1986, and under any individual retirement account or any individual retirement annuity, including a simplified employee pension plan, is exempt from attachment, execution, and seizure for the satisfaction of debts unless the plan, contract, or account does not qualify under the applicable provisions of the Internal Revenue Code of 1986. A person's right to the assets held in or to receive payments, whether vested or not, under a government or church plan or contract is also exempt unless the plan or contract does not qualify under the definition of a government or church plan under the applicable provisions of the federal Employee Retirement Income Security Act of 1974. If this subsection is held invalid or preempted by federal law in whole or in part or in certain circumstances, the subsection remains in effect in all other respects to the maximum extent permitted by law.

(b) Contributions to an individual retirement account or annuity that exceed the amounts deductible under the applicable provisions of the Internal Revenue

Code of 1986 and any accrued earnings on such contributions are not exempt under this section unless otherwise exempt by law. Amounts qualifying as nontaxable rollover contributions under Section 402(a)(5), 403(a)(4), 403(b)(8), or 408(d)(3) of the Internal Revenue Code of 1986 before January 1, 1993, are treated as exempt amounts under Subsection (a). In addition, amounts qualifying as nontaxable rollover contributions under Section 402(c), 402(e)(6), 402(f), 403(a)(4), 403(a)(5), 403(b)(8), 403(b)(10), or 408(d)(3) of the Internal Revenue Code of 1986 on or after January 1, 1993, are treated as exempt amounts under Subsection (a).

(c) Amounts distributed from a plan or contract entitled to the exemption under Subsection (a) are not subject to seizure for a creditor's claim for 60 days after the date of distribution if the amounts qualify as a nontaxable rollover contribution under Subsection (b).

(d) A participant or beneficiary of a stock bonus, pension, profit-sharing, retirement plan, or government plan is not prohibited from granting a valid and enforceable security interest in the participant's or beneficiary's right to the assets held in or to receive payments under the plan to secure a loan to the participant or beneficiary from the plan, and the right to the assets held in or to receive payments from the plan is subject to attachment, execution, and seizure for the satisfaction of the security interest or lien granted by the participant or beneficiary to secure the loan.

(e) If Subsection (a) is declared invalid or preempted by federal law, in whole or in part or in certain circumstances, as applied to a person who has not brought a proceeding under Title 11, United States Code, the subsection remains in effect, to the maximum extent permitted by law, as to any person who has filed that type of proceeding.

(f) A reference in this section to a specific provision of the Internal Revenue Code of 1986 includes a subsequent amendment of the substance of that provision.

Sec. 42.003. Designation of Exempt Property.

(a) If the number or amount of a type of personal property owned by a debtor exceeds the exemption allowed by Section 42.002 and the debtor can be found in the county where the property is located, the officer making a levy on the property shall ask the debtor to designate the personal property to be levied on. If the debtor cannot be found in the county or the debtor fails to make a designation within a reasonable time after the officer's request, the officer shall make the designation.

(b) If the aggregate value of a debtor's personal property exceeds the amount exempt from seizure under Section 42.001(a), the debtor may designate the portion of the property to be levied on. If, after a court's request, the debtor fails to make a designation within a reasonable time or if for any reason a creditor contests that the property is exempt, the court shall make the designation.

Sec. 42.004. Transfer of Nonexempt Property.

(a) If a person uses the property not exempt under this chapter to acquire, obtain an interest in, make improvement to, or pay an indebtedness on personal property which would be exempt under this chapter with the intent to defraud, delay, or hinder an interested person from obtaining that to which the interested person is or may be entitled, the property, interest, or improvement acquired is not exempt from seizure for the satisfaction of liabilities. If the property, interest, or improvement is acquired by discharging an encumbrance held by a third person, a person defrauded, delayed, or hindered is subrogated to the rights of the third person.

(b) A creditor may not assert a claim under this section more than two years after the transaction from which the claim arises. A person with a claim that is unliquidated or contingent at the time of the transaction may not assert a claim under this section more than one year after the claim is reduced to judgment.

(c) It is a defense to a claim under this section that the transfer was made in the ordinary course of business by the person making the transfer.

Sec. 42.005. Child Support Liens.

Sections 42.001, 42.002, and 42.0021 of this code do not apply to a child support lien established under Subchapter F, Chapter 14, Family Code.

CALIFORNIA CODES
CODE OF CIVIL PROCEDURE
SECTION 704.010-704.210

704.010. (a) Any combination of the following is exempt in the amount of one thousand nine hundred dollars ($1,900):

(1) The aggregate equity in motor vehicles.

(2) The proceeds of an execution sale of a motor vehicle.

(3) The proceeds of insurance or other indemnification for the loss, damage, or destruction of a motor vehicle.

(b) Proceeds exempt under subdivision (a) are exempt for a period of 90 days after the time the proceeds are actually received by the judgment debtor.

(c) For the purpose of determining the equity, the fair market value of a motor vehicle shall be determined by reference to used car price guides customarily used by California automobile dealers unless the motor vehicle is not listed in such price guides.

(d) If the judgment debtor has only one motor vehicle and it is sold at an execution sale, the proceeds of the execution sale are exempt in the amount of one thousand nine hundred dollars ($1,900) without making a claim. The levying officer shall consult and may rely upon the records of the Department of Motor Vehicles in determining whether the judgment debtor has only one motor vehicle. In the case covered by this subdivision, the exemption provided by subdivision (a) is not available.

704.020. (a) Household furnishings, appliances, provisions, wearing apparel, and other personal effects are exempt in the following cases:

(1) If ordinarily and reasonably necessary to, and personally used or procured for use by, the judgment debtor and members of the judgment debtor's family at the judgment debtor's principal place of residence.

(2) Where the judgment debtor and the judgment debtor's spouse live separate and apart, if ordinarily and reasonably necessary to, and personally used or procured for use by, the spouse and members of the spouse's family at the spouse's principal place of residence.

(b) In determining whether an item of property is "ordinarily and reasonably necessary" under subdivision (a), the court shall take into account both of the following:

(1) The extent to which the particular type of item is ordinarily found in a household.

(2) Whether the particular item has extraordinary value as compared to the value of items of the same type found in other households.

(c) If an item of property for which an exemption is claimed pursuant to this section is an item of the type ordinarily found in a household but is determined not to be exempt because the item has extraordinary value as compared to the value of items of the same type found in other households, the proceeds obtained at an execution sale of the item are exempt in the amount determined by the court to be a reasonable amount sufficient to purchase a replacement of ordinary value if the court determines that a replacement is reasonably necessary. Proceeds exempt under this subdivision are exempt for a period of 90 days after the proceeds are actually received by the judgment debtor.

704.030. Material that in good faith is about to be applied to the repair or improvement of a residence is exempt if the equity in the material does not exceed two thousand dollars ($2,000) in the following cases:

(a) If purchased in good faith for use in the repair or improvement of the judgment debtor's principal place of residence.

(b) Where the judgment debtor and the judgment debtor's spouse live separate and apart, if purchased in good faith for use in the repair or improvement of the spouse's principal place of residence.

704.040. Jewelry, heirlooms, and works of art are exempt to the extent that the aggregate equity therein does not exceed five thousand dollars ($5,000).

704.050. Health aids reasonably necessary to enable the judgment debtor or the spouse or a dependent of the judgment debtor to work or sustain health, and prosthetic and orthopedic appliances, are exempt.

704.060. (a) Tools, implements, instruments, materials, uniforms, furnishings, books, equipment, one commercial motor vehicle, one vessel, and other personal property are exempt to the extent that the aggregate equity therein does not exceed:

(1) Five thousand dollars ($5,000), if reasonably necessary to and actually used by the judgment debtor in the exercise of the trade, business, or profession by which the judgment debtor earns a livelihood.

(2) Five thousand dollars ($5,000), if reasonably necessary to and actually used by the spouse of the judgment debtor in the exercise of the trade, business, or profession by which the spouse earns a livelihood.

(3) Ten thousand dollars ($10,000), if reasonably necessary to and actually used by the judgment debtor and by the spouse of the judgment debtor in the exercise of the same trade, business, or profession by which both earn a livelihood. In the case covered by this paragraph, the exemptions provided in paragraphs (1) and (2) are not available.

(b) If property described in subdivision (a) is sold at an execution sale, or if it has been lost, damaged, or destroyed, the proceeds of the execution sale or of insurance or other indemnification are exempt for a period of 90 days after the proceeds are actually received by the judgment debtor or the judgment debtor's spouse. The amount exempt under this subdivision is the amount specified in subdivision (a) that applies to the particular case less the aggregate equity of any other property to which the exemption provided by subdivision (a) for the particular case has been applied.

(c) Notwithstanding subdivision (a), a motor vehicle is not exempt under subdivision (a) if there is a motor vehicle exempt under Section 704.010 which is reasonably adequate for use in the trade, business, or profession for which the exemption is claimed under this section.

(d) Notwithstanding subdivisions (a) and (b):

(1) The amount of the exemption for a commercial motor vehicle under paragraph (1) or (2) of subdivision (a) is limited to four thousand dollars ($4,000).

(2) The amount of the exemption for a commercial motor vehicle under paragraph (3) of subdivision (a) is limited to eight thousand dollars ($8,000).

704.070. (a) As used in this section:

(1) "Earnings withholding order" means an earnings withholding order under Chapter 5 (commencing with Section 706.010) (Wage Garnishment Law).

(2) "Paid earnings" means earnings as defined in Section 706.011 that were paid to the employee during the 30-day period ending on the date of the levy. For the purposes of this paragraph, where earnings that have been paid to the employee are sought to be subjected to the enforcement of a money judgment other than by a levy, the date of levy is deemed to be the date the earnings were otherwise subjected to the enforcement of the judgment.

(3) "Earnings assignment order for support" means an earnings assignment order for support as defined in Section 706.011.

(b) Paid earnings that can be traced into deposit accounts or in the form of cash or its equivalent as provided in Section 703.080 are exempt in the following amounts:

(1) All of the paid earnings are exempt if prior to payment to the employee they were subject to an earnings withholding order or an earnings assignment order for support.

(2) Seventy-five percent of the paid earnings that are levied upon or otherwise sought to be subjected to the enforcement of a money judgment are exempt if prior to payment to the employee they were not subject to an earnings withholding order or an earnings assignment order for support.

704.080. (a) For the purposes of this section:

(1) "Deposit account" means a deposit account in which payments authorized by the Social Security Administration are directly deposited by the United States government.

(2) "Payments authorized by the Social Security Administration" means regular retirement and survivors' benefits, supplemental security income benefits, coal miners' health benefits, and disability insurance benefits.

(b) A deposit account is exempt without making a claim in the following amount:

(1) Two thousand dollars ($2,000) where one depositor is the designated payee of the directly deposited payments.

(2) Three thousand dollars ($3,000) where two or more depositors are the designated payees of the directly deposited payments, unless those depositors are joint payees of directly deposited payments which represent a benefit to only one of the depositors, in which case the exempt amount is two thousand dollars ($2,000).

(c) The amount of a deposit account that exceeds the exemption provided in subdivision (b) is exempt to the extent that it consists of payments authorized by the Social Security Administration.

(d) Notwithstanding Article 5 (commencing with Section 701.010) of Chapter 3, when a deposit account is levied upon or otherwise sought to be subjected to the enforcement of a money judgment, the financial institution that holds the deposit account shall either place the amount that exceeds the exemption provided in subdivision (b) in a suspense account or otherwise prohibit withdrawal of that amount pending notification of the failure of the judgment creditor to file the affidavit required by this section or the judicial determination of the exempt status of the amount. Within 10 business days after the levy, the financial institution shall provide the levying officer with a written notice stating (1) that the deposit account is one in which payments authorized by the Social Security Administration are directly deposited by the United States government and (2) the balance of the deposit account that exceeds the exemption provided by subdivision (b). Promptly upon receipt of the notice, the levying officer shall serve the notice on the judgment creditor. service shall be made personally or by mail.

(e) Notwithstanding the procedure prescribed in Article 2 (commencing with Section 703.510), whether there is an amount exempt under subdivision (c) shall be determined as follows:

(1) Within five days after the levying officer serves the notice on the judgment creditor under subdivision (d), a judgment creditor who desires to claim that the amount is not exempt shall file with the court an affidavit alleging that the amount is not exempt and file a copy with the levying officer. The affidavit shall be in the form of the notice of opposition provided by Section 703.560, and a hearing shall be set and held, and notice given, as

provided by Sections 703.570 and 703.580. For the purpose of this subdivision, the "notice of opposition to the claim of exemption" in Sections 703.570 and 703.580 means the affidavit under this subdivision.

(2) If the judgment creditor does not file the affidavit with the levying officer and give notice of hearing pursuant to Section 703.570 within the time provided in paragraph (1), the levying officer shall release the deposit account and shall notify the financial institution.

(3) The affidavit constitutes the pleading of the judgment creditor, subject to the power of the court to permit amendments in the interest of justice. The affidavit is deemed controverted and no counteraffidavit is required.

(4) At a hearing under this subdivision, the judgment debtor has the burden of proving that the excess amount is exempt.

(5) At the conclusion of the hearing, the court by order shall determine whether or not the amount of the deposit account is exempt pursuant to subdivision (c) in whole or in part and shall make an appropriate order for its prompt disposition. No findings are required in a proceeding under this subdivision.

(6) Upon determining the exemption claim for the deposit account under subdivision (c), the court shall immediately transmit a certified copy of the order of the court to the financial institution and to the levying officer. If the order determines that all or part of the excess is exempt under subdivision (c), with respect to the amount of the excess which is exempt, the financial institution shall transfer the exempt excess from the suspense account or otherwise release any restrictions on its withdrawal by the judgment debtor. The transfer or release shall be effected within three business days of the receipt of the certified copy of the court order by the financial institution.

(f) If the judgment debtor claims that a portion of the amount is exempt other than pursuant to subdivision (c), the claim of exemption shall be made pursuant to Article 2 (commencing with Section 703.510). If the judgment debtor also opposes the judgment creditor's affidavit regarding an amount exempt pursuant to subdivision (c), both exemptions shall be determined at the same hearing, provided the judgment debtor has complied with Article 2 (commencing with Section 703.510).

704.090. (a) The funds of a judgment debtor confined in a prison or facility under the jurisdiction of the Department of Corrections or the Department of the Youth Authority or confined in any county or city jail, road camp, industrial farm, or other local correctional facility, held in trust for or to the credit of the judgment debtor, in an inmate's trust account or similar account by the state, county, or city, or any agency thereof, are exempt without making a claim in the amount of one thousand dollars ($1,000). If the judgment debtor is married, each spouse is entitled to a separate exemption under this section or the spouses may combine their exemptions.

(b) Notwithstanding subdivision (a), if the judgment is for a restitution fine or order imposed pursuant to subdivision (a) of Section 13967 of the Government Code, as operative on or before September 28, 1994, or Section 1203.04 of the Penal Code, as operative on or before August 2, 1995, or Section 1202.4 of the Penal Code, the funds held in trust for, or to the credit of, a judgment debtor described in subdivision (a) are exempt in the amount of three hundred dollars ($300) without making a claim.

704.100. (a) Unmatured life insurance policies (including endowment and annuity policies), but not the loan value of such policies, are exempt without making a claim.

(b) The aggregate loan value of unmatured life insurance policies (including endowment and annuity policies) is subject to the enforcement of a money judgment but is exempt in the amount of eight thousand dollars ($8,000). If the judgment debtor is married, each spouse is entitled to a separate exemption under this subdivision, and the exemptions of the spouses may be combined, regardless of whether the policies belong to either or both spouses and regardless of whether the spouse of the judgment debtor is also a judgment debtor under the judgment. The exemption provided by this subdivision shall be first applied to policies other than the policy before the court and then, if the exemption is not exhausted, to the policy before the court.

(c) Benefits from matured life insurance policies (including endowment and annuity policies) are exempt to the extent reasonably necessary for the support of the judgment debtor and the spouse and dependents of the judgment debtor.

704.110. (a) As used in this section:

(1) "Public entity" means the state, or a city, city and county, county, or other political subdivision of the state, or a public trust, public corporation, or public board, or the governing body of any of them, but does not include the United States except where expressly so provided.

(2) "Public retirement benefit" means a pension or an annuity, or a retirement, disability, death, or other benefit, paid or payable by a public retirement system.

(3) "Public retirement system" means a system established pursuant to statute by a public entity for retirement, annuity, or pension purposes or payment of disability or death benefits.

(b) All amounts held, controlled, or in process of distribution by a public entity derived from contributions by the public entity or by an officer or employee of the public entity for public retirement benefit purposes, and all rights and benefits accrued or accruing to any person under a public retirement system, are exempt without making a claim.

(c) Notwithstanding subdivision (b), where an amount described in subdivision (b) becomes payable to a person and is sought to be applied to the satisfaction of a judgment for child, family, or spousal support against that person:

(1) Except as provided in paragraphs (2) and (3), the amount is exempt only to the extent that the court determines under subdivision (c) of Section 703.070.

(2) If the amount sought to be applied to the satisfaction of the judgment is payable periodically, the amount payable is subject to an earnings assignment order for support as defined in Section 706.011, or any other applicable enforcement procedure, but the amount to be withheld pursuant to the assignment order or other procedure shall not exceed the amount permitted to be withheld on an earnings withholding order for support under Section 706.052. The paying entity may deduct from the payment being made to the judgment debtor, for each payment made pursuant to an earnings assignment order under this paragraph, an amount reflecting the actual cost of administration caused by the assignment order of up to two dollars ($2) for each payment.

(3) If the intercept procedure provided for in Section 11357 of the Welfare and Institutions Code is used for benefits that are payable periodically, the amount to be withheld shall not exceed the amount permitted to be withheld on an earnings withholding order for support under Section 706.052.

(4) If the amount sought to be applied to the satisfaction of the judgment is payable as a lump-sum distribution, the amount payable is subject to the intercept procedure provided in Section 11357 of the Welfare and Institutions Code or any other applicable enforcement procedure.

(d) All amounts received by any person, a resident of the state, as a public retirement benefit or as a return of contributions and interest thereon from the United States or a public entity or from a public retirement system are exempt.

704.113. (a) As used in this section, "vacation credits" means vacation credits accumulated by a state employee pursuant to Section 18050 of the Government Code or by any other public employee pursuant to any law for the accumulation of vacation credits applicable to the employee.

(b) All vacation credits are exempt without making a claim.

(c) Amounts paid periodically or as a lump sum representing vacation credits are subject to any earnings withholding order served under Chapter 5 (commencing with Section 706.010) or any earnings assignment order for support as defined in Section 706.011 and are exempt to the same extent as earnings of a judgment debtor.

704.114. (a) Notwithstanding any other provision of law, service of an earnings assignment order for support on any public entity described in Section 704.110, other than the United States government, creates a lien on all employee contributions in the amount necessary to satisfy a support judgment as determined under Section 695.210 to the extent that the judgment remains enforceable.

(b) The public entity shall comply with any request for a return of employee contributions by an employee named in the order by delivering the contributions to the clerk of the court from which the order issued, unless the entity has received a certified copy of an order terminating the earnings assignment order for support.

(c) Upon receipt of moneys pursuant to this section, the clerk of the court, within 10 days, shall send written notice of the fact to the parties and to the district attorney enforcing any order pursuant to Section 11475.1 of the Welfare and Institutions Code.

(d) Moneys received pursuant to this section are subject to any procedure available to enforce an order for support, but if no enforcement procedure is commenced after 30 days have elapsed from the date the notice of receipt is sent, the clerk shall, upon request, return the moneys to the public entity that delivered the moneys to the court unless the public entity has informed the court in writing that the moneys shall be released to the employee.

(e) A court shall not directly or indirectly condition the issuance, modification, or termination of, or condition the terms or conditions of, any order for support upon the making of a request for the return of employee contributions by an employee.

704.115. (a) As used in this section, "private retirement plan" means:

(1) Private retirement plans, including, but not limited to, union retirement plans.

(2) Profit-sharing plans designed and used for retirement purposes.

(3) Self-employed retirement plans and individual retirement annuities or accounts provided for in the Internal Revenue Code of 1954 as amended, to the extent the amounts held in the plans, annuities, or accounts do not exceed the maximum amounts exempt from federal income taxation under that code.

(b) All amounts held, controlled, or in process of distribution by a private retirement plan, for the payment of benefits as an annuity, pension, retirement allowance, disability payment, or death benefit from a private retirement plan are exempt.

(c) Notwithstanding subdivision (b), where an amount described in subdivision (b) becomes payable to a person and is sought to be applied to the satisfaction of a judgment for child, family, or spousal support against that person:

(1) Except as provided in paragraph (2), the amount is exempt only to the extent that the court determines under subdivision (c) of Section 703.070.

(2) If the amount sought to be applied to the satisfaction of the judgment is payable periodically, the amount payable is subject to an earnings assignment order for support as defined in Section 706.011 or any other applicable enforcement procedure, but the amount to be withheld pursuant to the assignment order or other procedure shall not exceed the amount permitted to be withheld on an earnings withholding order for support under Section 706.052.

(d) After payment, the amounts described in subdivision (b) and all contributions and interest thereon returned to any member of a private retirement plan are exempt.

(e) Notwithstanding subdivisions (b) and (d), except as provided in subdivision (f), the amounts described in paragraph (3) of subdivision (a) are exempt only to the extent necessary to provide for the support of the judgment debtor when the judgment debtor retires and for the support of the spouse and dependents of the judgment debtor, taking into account all resources that are likely to be available for the support of the judgment debtor when the judgment debtor retires. In determining the amount to be exempt under this subdivision, the court shall allow the judgment debtor such additional amount as is necessary to pay any federal and state income taxes payable as a result of the applying of an amount described in paragraph (3) of subdivision (a) to the satisfaction of the money judgment.

(f) Where the amounts described in paragraph (3) of subdivision (a) are payable periodically, the amount of such periodic payment that may be applied to the satisfaction of a money judgment is the amount that may be withheld from a like amount of earnings under Chapter 5 (commencing with Section 706.010) (Wage Garnishment Law).

704.120. (a) Contributions by workers payable to the Unemployment Compensation Disability Fund and by employers payable to the Unemployment Fund are exempt without making a claim.

(b) Before payment, amounts held for payment of the following benefits are exempt without making a claim:

(1) Benefits payable under Division 1 (commencing with Section 100) of the Unemployment Insurance Code.

(2) Incentives payable under Division 2 (commencing with Section 5000) of the Unemployment Insurance Code.

(3) Benefits payable under an employer's plan or system to supplement unemployment compensation benefits of the employees generally or for a class or group of employees.

(4) Unemployment benefits payable by a fraternal organization to its bona fide members.

(5) Benefits payable by a union due to a labor dispute.

(c) After payment, the benefits described in subdivision (b) are exempt.

(d) During the payment of benefits described in paragraph (1) of subdivision (b) to a judgment debtor under a support judgment, the judgment creditor may, through the appropriate district attorney, seek to apply the benefit payment to satisfy the judgment as provided by Section 11350.5 of the Welfare and Institutions Code.

(e) During the payment of benefits described in paragraphs (2) to (5), inclusive, of subdivision (b) to a judgment debtor under a support judgment, the judgment creditor may, directly or through the appropriate district attorney, seek to apply the benefit payments to satisfy the judgment by an earnings assignment order for support as defined in Section 706.011 or any other applicable enforcement procedure. If the benefit is payable periodically, the amount to be withheld pursuant to the assignment order or other procedure shall be 25 percent of the amount of each periodic payment or any lower amount specified in writing by the judgment creditor or court order, rounded down to the nearest whole dollar. Otherwise the amount to be withheld shall be the amount the court determines under subdivision (c) of Section 703.070. The paying entity may deduct from each payment made pursuant to an assignment order under this subdivision an amount reflecting the actual cost of administration caused by the assignment order up to two dollars ($2) for each payment.

704.130. (a) Before payment, benefits from a disability or health insurance policy or program are exempt without making a claim. After payment, the benefits are exempt.

(b) Subdivision (a) does not apply to benefits that are paid or payable to cover the cost of health care if the judgment creditor is a provider of health care whose claim is the basis on which the benefits are paid or payable.

704.140. (a) Except as provided in Article 5 (commencing with Section 708.410) of Chapter 6, a cause of action for personal injury is exempt without making a claim.

(b) Except as provided in subdivisions (c) and (d), an award of damages or a settlement arising out of personal injury is exempt to the extent necessary for the support of the judgment debtor and the spouse and dependents of the judgment debtor.

(c) Subdivision (b) does not apply if the judgment creditor is a provider of health care whose claim is based on the providing of health care for the personal injury for which the award or settlement was made.

(d) Where an award of damages or a settlement arising out of personal injury is payable periodically, the amount of such periodic payment that may be applied to the satisfaction of a money judgment is the amount that may be withheld from a like amount of earnings under Chapter 5 (commencing with Section 706.010) (Wage Garnishment Law).

704.150. (a) Except as provided in Article 5 (commencing with Section 708.410) of Chapter 6, a cause of action for wrongful death is exempt without making a claim.

(b) Except as provided in subdivision (c), an award of damages or a settlement arising out of the wrongful death of the judgment debtor's spouse or a person on whom the judgment debtor or the judgment debtor's spouse was dependent is exempt to the extent reasonably necessary for support of the judgment debtor and the spouse and dependents of the judgment debtor.

(c) Where an award of damages or a settlement arising out of the wrongful death of the judgment debtor's spouse or a person on whom the judgment debtor or the judgment debtor's spouse was dependent is payable periodically, the amount of such a periodic payment that may be applied to the satisfaction of a money judgment is the amount that may be withheld from a like amount of earnings under Chapter 5 (commencing with Section 706.010) (Wage Garnishment Law).

704.160. (a) Except as provided by Chapter 1 (commencing with Section 4900) of Part 3 of Division 4 of the Labor Code, before payment, a claim for workers' compensation or workers' compensation awarded or adjudged is exempt without making a claim. Except as specified in subdivision (b), after payment, the award is exempt.

(b) Notwithstanding any other provision of law, during the payment of workers' compensation temporary disability benefits described in subdivision (a) to a support judgment debtor, the support judgment creditor may, through the appropriate district attorney, seek to apply the workers' compensation temporary disability benefit payment to satisfy the support judgment as provided by Section 11350.1 of the Welfare and Institutions Code.

(c) Notwithstanding any other provision of law, during the payment of workers' compensation temporary disability benefits described in subdivision (a) to a support judgment debtor under a support judgment, including a judgment for reimbursement of public assistance, the judgment creditor may, directly or through the appropriate district attorney, seek to apply the temporary disability benefit payments to satisfy the support judgment by an earnings assignment order for support, as defined in Section 5208 of the Family Code, or any other applicable enforcement procedure. The amount to be withheld pursuant to the earnings assignment order for support or other enforcement procedure shall be 25 percent of the amount of each periodic payment or any lower amount specified in writing by the judgment creditor or court order, rounded down to the nearest dollar. Otherwise, the amount to be withheld shall be the amount the court determines under subdivision (c) of

Section 703.070.   The paying entity may deduct from each payment made pursuant to an order assigning earnings under this subdivision an amount reflecting the actual cost of administration of this assignment, up to two dollars ($2) for each payment.

(d) Unless the provision or context otherwise requires, the following definitions govern the construction of this section.

(1) "Judgment debtor" or "support judgment debtor" means a person who is owing a duty of support.

(2) "Judgment creditor" or "support judgment creditor" means the person to whom support has been ordered to be paid.

(3) "Support" refers to an obligation owing on behalf of a child, spouse, or family; or an amount owing pursuant to Section 11350 of the Welfare and Institutions Code. It also includes past due support or arrearage when it exists.

704.170. Before payment, aid provided pursuant to Division 9 (commencing with Section 10000) of the Welfare and Institutions Code or similar aid provided by a charitable organization or a fraternal benefit society as defined in Section 10990 of the Insurance Code, is exempt without making a claim. After payment, the aid is exempt.

704.180. Before payment, relocation benefits for displacement from a dwelling which are to be paid pursuant to Chapter 16 (commencing with Section 7260) of Division 7 of Title 1 of the Government Code or the federal "Uniform Relocation Assistance and Real Property Acquisition Policies Act of 1970" (42 U.S.C. Sec. 4601 et seq.), as amended, are exempt without making a claim. After payment, the benefits are exempt.

704.190. (a) As used in this section, "institution of higher education" means "institution of higher education" as defined in Section 1141(a) of Title 20 of the United States Code, as amended.

(b) Before payment, financial aid for expenses while attending school provided to a student by an institution of higher education is exempt without making a claim. After payment, the aid is exempt.

704.200. (a) As used in this section:

(1) "Cemetery" has the meaning provided by Section 7003 of the Health and Safety Code.

(2) "Family plot" is a plot that satisfies the requirements of Section 8650 of the Health and Safety Code.

(3) "Plot" has the meaning provided by Section 7022 of the Health and Safety Code.

(b) A family plot is exempt without making a claim.

(c) Except as provided in subdivision (d), a cemetery plot for the judgment debtor and the spouse of the judgment debtor is exempt.

(d) Land held for the purpose of sale or disposition as cemetery plots or otherwise is not exempt.

704.210. Property that is not subject to enforcement of a money judgment is exempt without making a claim.

FLORIDA STATUTES
(FULL VOLUME 1995)
CHAPTER 222: METHOD OF SETTING APART HOMESTEAD AND EXEMPTIONS

222.01 Designation of homestead by owner before levy. ---

Whenever any person residing in this state desires to avail himself or herself of the benefit of the provisions of the constitution and laws exempting property as a homestead from forced sale under any process of law, he or she may make a statement, in writing, containing a description of the real property, mobile home, or modular home claimed to be exempt and declaring that the real property, mobile home, or modular home is the homestead of the party in whose behalf such claim is being made. Such statement shall be signed by the person making it and shall be recorded in the circuit court.

222.02 Designation of homestead after levy. ---

Whenever a levy is made upon the lands, tenements, mobile home, or modular home of such person whose homestead has not been set apart and selected, such person, or the person's agent or attorney, may in writing notify the officer making such levy, by notice under oath made before any officer of this state duly authorized to administer oaths, at any time before the day appointed for the sale thereof, of what such person regards as his or her homestead, with a description thereof; and the remainder only shall be subject to sale under such levy.

222.03 Survey at instance of dissatisfied creditor. ---

If the creditor in any execution or process sought to be levied is dissatisfied with the quantity of land selected and set apart, and shall himself or herself, or by his or her agent or attorney, notify the officer levying, the officer shall at the creditor's request cause the same to be surveyed, and when the homestead is not within the corporate limits of any town or city, the person claiming said exemption shall have the right to set apart that portion of land belonging to him or her which includes the residence, or not, at the person's option, and if the first tract or parcel does not contain 160 acres, the said officer shall set apart the remainder from any other tract or tracts claimed by the debtor, but in every case taking all the land lying contiguous until the whole quantity of 160 acres is made up. The person claiming the exemption shall not be forced to take as his or her homestead any tract or portion of a tract, if any defect exists in the title, except at the person's option. The expense of such survey shall be chargeable on the execution as costs; but if it shall appear that the person claiming such exemption does not own more than 160 acres in the state, the expenses of said survey shall be paid by the person directing the same to be made.

222.04 Sale after survey. ---

After such survey has been made, the officer making the levy may sell the property levied upon not included in such property set off in such manner.

222.05 Setting apart leasehold. ---

Any person owning and occupying any dwelling house, including a mobile home used as a residence, or modular home, on land not his or her own which he or she may lawfully possess, by lease or otherwise, and claiming such house, mobile home, or modular home as his or her homestead, shall be entitled to the exemption of such house, mobile home, or modular home from levy and sale as aforesaid.

222.061 Method of exempting personal property; inventory. ---

(1) When a levy is made by writ of execution, writ of attachment, or writ of garnishment upon personal property which is allowed by law or by the State Constitution to be exempt from levy and sale, the debtor may claim such personal property to be exempt from sale by making, within 15 days after the date of the levy, an inventory of his or her personal property. The inventory shall show the fair market valuation of the property listed and shall have an affidavit attached certifying that the inventory contains a correct list of all personal property owned by the debtor in this state and that the value shown is the fair market value of the property. The debtor shall designate the property listed in the schedule which he or she claims to be exempt from levy and sale.

(2) The original inventory and affidavit shall be filed with the court which issued the writ. The debtor, by mail or hand delivery, shall promptly serve one copy on the judgment creditor and furnish one copy to the sheriff who executed the writ. If the creditor desires to object to the inventory, he or she shall file an objection with the court which issued the writ within 5 days after service of the inventory, or he or she shall be deemed to admit the inventory as true. If the creditor does not file an objection, the clerk of the court shall immediately send the case file to the court issuing the writ, and the court shall promptly issue an order exempting the items claimed. Such order shall be sent by the

court to the sheriff directing him or her to promptly redeliver to the debtor any exempt property under the levy and to sell any nonexempt property under the levy according to law.

(3) If the creditor files an objection, he or she shall promptly serve, by mail or hand delivery, one copy on the debtor and furnish one copy to the sheriff who executed the writ. Upon the filing of an objection, the clerk shall immediately send the case file to the court issuing the writ, and the court shall automatically schedule a prompt evidentiary hearing to determine the validity of the objection and shall enter its order therein describing the exempt and nonexempt property. Upon its issuance, the order shall be sent by the court to the sheriff directing him or her to promptly redeliver to the debtor any exempt property under the levy and to sell the nonexempt property under the levy according to law.

(4) The court shall appoint a disinterested appraiser to assist in its evidentiary hearing unless the debtor and creditor mutually waive the appointment of such appraiser. The appraiser shall take and file an oath that he or she will faithfully appraise the property at its fair market value and that he or she will file a signed and sworn appraisal with the court as required by law. Notice of the time and place of the inspection of the property for the purpose of its appraisal shall be given by the appraiser to the debtor, creditor, and sheriff, at least 24 hours before the inspection is made. The appraiser shall be entitled to a reasonable fee as determined by the court for his or her services. The appraiser's fee shall be taxed as costs, but no costs shall be assessed against the debtor for the proceedings under this section if the debtor prevails on his or her claim of exemption. The court may require the creditor to deposit a cash bond, a surety bond, or other security, conditioned on the creditor's obligation to pay reasonable appraisal expenses, not to exceed $100.

(5) During the pendency of proceedings under this section, the sheriff shall safeguard the property seized under the writ, and the creditor shall deposit sufficient moneys with the sheriff to pay the cost of such safeguarding until the property is sold or redelivered to the debtor. When the sheriff receives a copy of a court order identifying which property has been declared exempt and which property has been declared not exempt and ordering the sale of the property not exempt from levy, he or she shall sell the property.

(6) The party who successfully maintains his or her claim at the time of the evidentiary hearing may be entitled to reasonable attorney's fees and shall be entitled to costs. The costs shall include, but not be limited to, appraisal fees, storage fees, and such other costs incurred as a result of the levy.

(7) No inventory or schedule to exempt personal property from sale shall be accepted prior to a levy on the property.

222.07 Defendant's rights of selection. ---

Upon the completion of the inventory the person entitled to the exemption, or the person's agent or attorney, may select from such an inventory an amount of property not exceeding, according to such appraisal, the amount of value exempted; but if the person so entitled, or the person's agent or attorney, does not appear and make such selection, the officer shall make the selection for him or her, and the property not so selected as exempt may be sold.

222.08 Jurisdiction to set apart homestead and exemption. ---

The circuit courts have equity jurisdiction to order and decree the setting apart of homesteads and of exemptions of personal property from forced sales.

222.09 Injunction to prevent sale. ---

The circuit courts have equity jurisdiction to enjoin the sale of all property, real and personal, that is exempt from forced sale.

222.10 Jurisdiction to subject property claimed to be exempt. ---

The circuit courts have equity jurisdiction upon bill filed by a creditor or other person interested in enforcing any unsatisfied judgment or decree, to determine whether any property, real or personal, claimed to be exempt, is so exempt, and in case it be not exempt, the court shall, by its decree subject it, or so much thereof as may be necessary, to the satisfaction of said judgment or decree and may enjoin the sheriff or other officer from setting apart as exempt property, real or personal, which is not exempt, and may annul all exemptions made and set apart by the sheriff or other officer.

222.11 Exemption of wages from garnishment. ---

(1) As used in this section, the term:

(a) "Earnings" includes compensation paid or payable, in money of a sum certain, for personal services or labor whether denominated as wages, salary, commission, or bonus.

(b) "Disposable earnings" means that part of the earnings of any head of family remaining after the deduction from those earnings of any amounts required by law to be withheld.

(c) "Head of family" includes any natural person who is providing more than one-half of the support for a child or other dependent.

(2)

(a) All of the disposable earnings of a head of family whose disposable earnings are less than or equal to $500 a week are exempt from attachment or garnishment.

(b) Disposable earnings of a head of a family, which are greater than $500 a week, may not be attached or garnished unless such person has agreed otherwise in writing. In no event shall the amount attached or garnished exceed the amount allowed under the Consumer Credit Protection Act, 15 U.S.C. s. 1673.

(c) Disposable earnings of a person other than a head of family may not be attached or garnished in excess of the amount allowed under the Consumer Credit Protection Act, 15 U.S.C. s. 1673.

(3) Earnings that are exempt under subsection (2) and are credited or deposited in any financial institution are exempt from attachment or garnishment for 6 months after the earnings are received by the financial institution if the funds can be traced and properly identified as earnings. Commingling of earnings with other funds does not by itself defeat the ability of a head of family to trace earnings.

222.12 Proceedings for exemption. ---

Whenever any money or other thing due for labor or services as aforesaid is attached by such process, the person to whom the same is due and owing may make oath before the officer who issued the process that the money attached is due for the personal labor and services of such person, and she or he is the head of a family residing in said state. When such an affidavit is made, notice of same shall be forthwith given to the party, or her or his attorney, who sued out the process, and if the facts set forth in such affidavit are not denied under oath within 2 days after the service of said notice, the process shall be returned, and all proceedings under the same shall cease. If the facts stated in the affidavit are denied by the party who sued out the process within the time above set forth and under oath, then the matter shall be tried by the court from which the writ or process issued, in like manner as claims to property levied upon by writ of execution are tried, and the money or thing attached shall remain subject to the process until released by the judgment of the court which shall try the issue.

222.13 Life insurance policies; disposition of proceeds. ---

(1) Whenever any person residing in the state shall die leaving insurance on his or her life, the said insurance shall inure exclusively to the benefit of the person for whose use and benefit such insurance is designated in the policy, and the proceeds thereof shall be exempt from the claims of creditors of the insured unless the insurance policy or a valid assignment thereof provides otherwise. Notwithstanding the foregoing, whenever the insurance, by designation or otherwise, is payable to the insured or to the insured's estate or to his or her executors, administrators, or assigns, the insurance proceeds shall become a part of the insured's estate for all purposes and shall be administered by the personal representative of the estate of the insured in accordance with the probate laws of the state in like manner as other assets of the insured's estate.

(2) Payments as herein directed shall, in every such case, discharge the insurer from any further liability under the policy, and the insurer shall in no event be responsible for, or be required to see to, the application of such payments.

222.14 Exemption of cash surrender value of life insurance policies and annuity contracts from legal process. ---

The cash surrender values of life insurance policies issued upon the lives of citizens or residents of the state and the proceeds of annuity contracts issued to citizens or residents of the state, upon whatever form, shall not in any case be liable to attachment, garnishment or legal process in favor of any creditor of the person whose life is so insured or of any creditor of the person who is the beneficiary of such annuity contract, unless the insurance policy or annuity contract was effected for the benefit of such creditor.

222.15 Wages or unemployment compensation payments due deceased employee may be paid spouse or certain relatives. ---

(1) It is lawful for any employer, in case of the death of an employee, to pay to the wife or husband, and in case there is no wife or husband, then to the child or children, provided the child or children are over the age of 18 years, and in case there is no child or children, then to the father or mother, any

wages or travel expenses that may be due such employee at the time of his or her death.

(2) It is also lawful for the Division of Unemployment Compensation of the Department of Labor and Employment Security, in case of death of any unemployed individual, to pay to those persons referred to in subsection (1) any unemployment compensation payments that may be due such individual at the time of his or her death.

222.16 Wages or unemployment compensation payments so paid not subject to administration. ---

Any wages, travel expenses, or unemployment compensation payments so paid under the authority of s. 222.15 shall not be considered as assets of the estate and subject to administration; provided, however, that the travel expenses so exempted from administration shall not exceed the sum of $300.

222.17 Manifesting and evidencing domicile in Florida. ---

(1) Any person who shall have established a domicile in this state may manifest and evidence the same by filing in the office of the clerk of the circuit court for the county in which the said person shall reside, a sworn statement showing that he or she resides in and maintains a place of abode in that county which he or she recognizes and intends to maintain as his or her permanent home.

(2) Any person who shall have established a domicile in the State of Florida, but who shall maintain another place or places of abode in some other state or states, may manifest and evidence his or her domicile in this state by filing in the office of the clerk of the circuit court for the county in which he or she resides, a sworn statement that his or her place of abode in Florida constitutes his or her predominant and principal home, and that he or she intends to continue it permanently as such.

(3) Such sworn statement shall contain, in addition to the foregoing, a declaration that the person making the same is, at the time of making such statement, a bona fide resident of the state, and shall set forth therein his or her place of residence within the state, the city, county and state wherein he or she formerly resided, and the place or places, if any, where he or she maintains another or other place or places of abode.

(4) Any person who shall have been or who shall be domiciled in a state other than the State of Florida, and who has or who may have a place of abode within the State of Florida, or who has or may do or perform other acts within

the State of Florida, which independently of the actual intention of such person respecting his or her domicile might be taken to indicate that such person is or may intend to be or become domiciled in the State of Florida, and if such person desires to maintain or continue his or her domicile in such state other than the State of Florida, the person may manifest and evidence his or her permanent domicile and intention to permanently maintain and continue his or her domicile in such state other than the State of Florida, by filing in the office of the clerk of the circuit court in any county in the State of Florida in which the person may have a place of abode or in which the person may have done or performed such acts which independently may indicate that he or she is or may intend to be or become domiciled in the State of Florida, a sworn statement that the person's domicile is in such state other than the State of Florida, as the case may be, naming such state where he or she is domiciled and stating that he or she intends to permanently continue and maintain his or her domicile in such other state so named in said sworn statement. Such sworn statement shall also contain a declaration that the person making the same is at the time of the making of such statement a bona fide resident of such state other than the State of Florida, and shall set forth therein his or her place of abode within the State of Florida, if any. Such sworn statement may contain such other and further facts with reference to any acts done or performed by such person which such person desires or intends not to be construed as evidencing any intention to establish his or her domicile within the State of Florida.

(5) The sworn statement permitted by this section shall be signed under oath before an official authorized to take affidavits. Upon the filing of such declaration with the clerk of the circuit court, it shall be the duty of the clerk in whose office such declaration is filed to record the same in a book to be provided for that purpose. For the performance of the duties herein prescribed, the clerk of the circuit court shall collect a service charge for each declaration as provided in s. 28.24.

(6) It shall be the duty of the Department of Legal Affairs to prescribe a form for the declaration herein provided for, and to furnish the same to the several clerks of the circuit courts of the state.

(7) Nothing herein shall be construed to repeal or abrogate other existing methods of proving and evidencing domicile except as herein specifically provided.

222.18 Exempting disability income benefits from legal processes. --

Disability income benefits under any policy or contract of life, health, accident, or other insurance of whatever form, shall not in any case be liable to attachment, garnishment, or legal process in the state, in favor of any creditor or creditors of the recipient of such disability income benefits, unless such policy or contract of insurance was effected for the benefit of such creditor or creditors.

222.20 Nonavailability of federal bankruptcy exemptions. ---

In accordance with the provision of s. 522(b) of the Bankruptcy Code of 1978 (11 U.S.C. s. 522(b)), residents of this state shall not be entitled to the federal exemptions provided in s. 522(d) of the Bankruptcy Code of 1978 (11 U.S.C. s. 522(d)). Nothing herein shall affect the exemptions given to residents of this state by the State Constitution and the Florida Statutes.

222.201 Availability of federal bankruptcy exemptions. ---

(1) Notwithstanding s. 222.20, an individual debtor under the federal Bankruptcy Reform Act of 1978 may exempt, in addition to any other exemptions allowed under state law, any property listed in subsection (d)(10) of s. 522 of that act.

(2) The provisions of this section apply to any bankruptcy action that is filed on or after October 1, 1987.

222.21 Exemption of pension money and retirement or profit-sharing benefits from legal processes. ---

(1) Money received by any debtor as pensioner of the United States within 3 months next preceding the issuing of an execution, attachment, or garnishment process may not be applied to the payment of the debts of the pensioner when it is made to appear by the affidavit of the debtor or otherwise that the pension money is necessary for the maintenance of the debtor's support or a family supported wholly or in part by the pension money. The filing of the affidavit by the debtor, or the making of such proof by the debtor, is prima facie evidence; and it is the duty of the court in which the proceeding is pending to release all pension moneys held by such attachment or garnishment process, immediately, upon the filing of such affidavit or the making of such proof.

(2) (a) Except as provided in paragraph (b), any money or other assets payable to a participant or beneficiary from, or any interest of any participant or beneficiary in, a retirement or profit-sharing plan that is qualified under s. 401(a), s. 403(a), s. 403(b), s. 408, or s. 409 of the Internal Revenue Code of 1986, as amended, is exempt from all claims of creditors of the beneficiary or participant.

(b) Any plan or arrangement described in paragraph (a) is not exempt from the claims of an alternate payee under a qualified domestic relations order. However, the interest of any alternate payee under a qualified domestic relations order is exempt from all claims of any creditor, other than the Department of Health and Rehabilitative Services, of the alternate payee. As used in this paragraph, the terms "alternate payee" and "qualified domestic relations order" have the meanings ascribed to them in s. 414(p) of the Internal Revenue Code of 1986.

(c) The provisions of paragraphs (a) and (b) apply to any proceeding that is filed on or after October 1, 1987.

222.22 Exemption of moneys in the Prepaid Postsecondary Education Expense Trust Fund from legal process. ---

Moneys paid into or out of the Prepaid Postsecondary Education Expense Trust Fund by or on behalf of a purchaser or qualified beneficiary pursuant to an advance payment contract made under s. 240.551, which contract has not been terminated, are not liable to attachment, garnishment, or legal process in the state in favor of any creditor of the purchaser or beneficiary of such advance payment contract.

222.25 Other individual property exempt from legal process. ---

The following property is exempt from attachment, garnishment, or other legal process:

(1) A debtor's interest, not to exceed $1,000 in value, in a single motor vehicle as defined in s. 320.01; and

(2) A debtor's interest in any professionally prescribed health aids for the debtor or a dependent of the debtor.

222.29 No exemption for fraudulent transfers. ---

An exemption from attachment, garnishment, or legal process provided by this chapter is not effective if it results from a fraudulent transfer or conveyance as provided in chapter 726.

222.30 Fraudulent asset conversions. ---

(1) As used in this section, "conversion" means every mode, direct or indirect, absolute or conditional, of changing or disposing of an asset, such that the products or proceeds of the asset become immune or exempt by law from claims of creditors of the debtor and the products or proceeds of the asset remain property of the debtor. The definitions of chapter 726 apply to this section unless the application of a definition would be unreasonable.

(2) Any conversion by a debtor of an asset that results in the proceeds of the asset becoming exempt by law from the claims of a creditor of the debtor is a fraudulent asset conversion as to the creditor, whether the creditor's claim to the asset arose before or after the conversion of the asset, if the debtor made the conversion with the intent to hinder, delay, or defraud the creditor.

(3) In an action for relief against a fraudulent asset conversion, a creditor may obtain:

(a) Avoidance of the fraudulent asset conversion to the extent necessary to satisfy the creditor's claim.

(b) An attachment or other provisional remedy against the asset converted in accordance with applicable law.

(c) Subject to applicable principles of equity and in accordance with applicable rules of civil procedure: 1. An injunction against further conversion by the debtor of the asset or of other property. 2. Any other relief the circumstances may require.

(4) If a creditor has obtained a judgment on a claim against the debtor, the creditor, if the court so orders, may levy execution on the asset converted or its proceeds.

(5) A cause of action with respect to a fraudulent asset conversion is extinguished unless an action is brought within 4 years after the fraudulent asset conversion was made.

(6) If an asset is converted and the converted asset is subsequently transferred to a third party, the provisions of chapter 726 apply to the transfer to the third party.

FLORIDA STATUTES (FULL VOLUME 1993)
CHAPTER 726: FRAUDULENT TRANSFERS

726.101 Short title. ---

This act may be cited as the "Uniform Fraudulent Transfer Act."

History: s. 1, ch. 87-79.

726.102 Definitions. ---

As used in ss. 726.101-726.112:

(1) "Affiliate" means:

(a) A person who directly or indirectly owns, controls, or holds with power to vote, 20 percent or more of the outstanding voting securities of the debtor, other than a person who holds the securities:

    1. As a fiduciary or agent without sole discretionary power to vote the securities; or

    2. Solely to secure a debt, if the person has not exercised the power to vote.

(b) A corporation 20 percent or more of whose outstanding voting securities are directly or indirectly owned, controlled, or held with power to vote, by the debtor or a person who directly or indirectly owns, controls, or holds, with power to vote, 20 percent or more of the outstanding voting securities of the debtor, other than a person who holds the securities:

    1. As a fiduciary or agent without sole power to vote the securities; or

    2. Solely to secure a debt, if the person has not in fact exercised the power to vote.

(c) A person whose business is operated by the debtor under a lease or other agreement, or a person substantially all of whose assets are controlled by the debtor; or

(d) A person who operates the debtor's business under a lease or other agreement or controls substantially all of the debtor's assets.

(2) "Asset" means property of a debtor, but the term does not include:

(a) Property to the extent it is encumbered by a valid lien;

(b) Property to the extent it is generally exempt under nonbankruptcy law; or

(c) An interest in property held in tenancy by the entireties to the extent it is not subject to process by a creditor holding a claim against only one tenant.

(3) "Claim" means a right to payment, whether or not the right is reduced to judgment, liquidated, unliquidated, fixed, contingent, matured, unmatured, disputed, undisputed, legal, equitable, secured, or unsecured.

(4) "Creditor" means a person who has a claim.

(5) "Debt" means liability on a claim.

(6) "Debtor" means a person who is liable on a claim.

(7) "Insider" includes:

(a) If the debtor is an individual:

1. A relative of the debtor or of a general partner of the debtor;
2. A partnership in which the debtor is a general partner;
3. A general partner in a partnership described in subparagraph 2; or
4. A corporation of which the debtor is a director, officer, or person in control;

(b) If the debtor is a corporation:

1. A director of the debtor;
2. An officer of the debtor;
3. A person in control of the debtor;
4. A partnership in which the debtor is a general partner;
5. A general partner in a partnership described in subparagraph 4; or
6. A relative of a general partner, director, officer, or person in control of the debtor.

(c) If the debtor is a partnership:

1. A general partner in the debtor;

2. A relative of a general partner in, a general partner of, or a person in control of the debtor;

3. Another partnership in which the debtor is a general partner;

4. A general partner in a partnership described in subparagraph 3; or

5. A person in control of the debtor.

(d) An affiliate, or an insider of an affiliate as if the affiliate were the debtor.

(e) A managing agent of the debtor.

(8) "Lien" means a charge against or an interest in property to secure payment of a debt or performance of an obligation, and includes a security interest created by agreement, a judicial lien obtained by legal or equitable process or proceedings, a common-law lien, or a statutory lien.

(9) "Person" means an individual, partnership, corporation, association, organization, government or governmental subdivision or agency, business trust, estate, trust, or any other legal or commercial entity.

(10) "Property" means anything that may be the subject of ownership.

(11) "Relative" means an individual related by consanguinity within the third degree as determined by the common law, a spouse, or an individual related to a spouse within the third degree as so determined, and includes an individual in an adoptive relationship within the third degree.

(12) "Transfer" means every mode, direct or indirect, absolute or conditional, voluntary or involuntary, of disposing of or parting with an asset or an interest in an asset, and includes payment of money, release, lease, and creation of a lien or other encumbrance.

(13) "Valid lien" means a lien that is effective against the holder of a judicial lien subsequently obtained by legal or equitable process or proceedings.

History: s. 2, ch. 87-79.

726.103 Insolvency. ---

(1) A debtor is insolvent if the sum of the debtor's debts is greater than all of the debtor's assets at a fair valuation.

(2) A debtor who is generally not paying his debts as they become due is presumed to be insolvent.

(3) A partnership is insolvent under subsection (1) if the sum of the partnership's debts is greater than the aggregate, at a fair valuation, of all of the partnership's assets and the sum of the excess of the value of each general partner's nonpartnership assets over the partner's nonpartnership debts.

(4) Assets under this section do not include property that has been transferred, concealed, or removed with intent to hinder, delay, or defraud creditors or that has been transferred in a manner making the transfer voidable under ss. 726.101-726.112.

(5) Debts under this section do not include an obligation to the extent it is secured by a valid lien on property of the debtor not included as an asset.

History: s. 3, ch. 87-79.

726.104 Value. ---

(1) Value is given for a transfer or an obligation if, in exchange for the transfer or obligation, property is transferred or an antecedent debt is secured or satisfied, but value does not include an unperformed promise made otherwise than in the ordinary course of the promisor's business to furnish support to the debtor or another person.

(2) For the purposes of ss. 726.105(1)(b) and 726.106, a person gives a reasonably equivalent value if the person acquires an interest of the debtor in an asset pursuant to a regularly conducted, noncollusive foreclosure sale or execution of a power of sale for the acquisition or disposition of the interest of the debtor upon default under a mortgage, deed of trust, or security agreement.

(3) A transfer is made for present value if the exchange between the debtor and the transferee is intended by them to be contemporaneous and is in fact substantially contemporaneous.

History: s. 4, ch. 87-79.

726.105 Transfers fraudulent as to present and future creditors. ---

(1) A transfer made or obligation incurred by a debtor is fraudulent as to a creditor, whether the creditor's claim arose before or after the transfer was

made or the obligation was incurred, if the debtor made the transfer or incurred the obligation:

(a) With actual intent to hinder, delay, or defraud any creditor of the debtor; or

(b) Without receiving a reasonably equivalent value in exchange for the transfer or obligation, and the debtor:

1. Was engaged or was about to engage in a business or a transaction for which the remaining assets of the debtor were unreasonably small in relation to the business or transaction; or

2. Intended to incur, or believed or reasonably should have believed that he would incur, debts beyond his ability to pay as they became due.

(2) In determining actual intent under paragraph (1)(a), consideration may be given, among other factors, to whether:

(a) The transfer or obligation was to an insider.

(b) The debtor retained possession or control of the property transferred after the transfer.

(c) The transfer or obligation was disclosed or concealed.

(d) Before the transfer was made or obligation was incurred, the debtor had been sued or threatened with suit.

(e) The transfer was of substantially all the debtor's assets.

(f) The debtor absconded.

(g) The debtor removed or concealed assets.

(h) The value of the consideration received by the debtor was reasonably equivalent to the value of the asset transferred or the amount of the obligation incurred.

(i) The debtor was insolvent or became insolvent shortly after the transfer was made or the obligation was incurred.

(j) The transfer occurred shortly before or shortly after a substantial debt was incurred.

(k) The debtor transferred the essential assets of the business to a lienor who transferred the assets to an insider of the debtor.

History: s. 5, ch. 87-79.

726.106 Transfers fraudulent as to present creditors. ---

(1) A transfer made or obligation incurred by a debtor is fraudulent as to a creditor whose claim arose before the transfer was made or the obligation was incurred if the debtor made the transfer or incurred the obligation without receiving a reasonably equivalent value in exchange for the transfer or obligation and the debtor was insolvent at that time or the debtor became insolvent as a result of the transfer or obligation.

(2) A transfer made by a debtor is fraudulent as to a creditor whose claim arose before the transfer was made if the transfer was made to an insider for an antecedent debt, the debtor was insolvent at that time, and the insider had reasonable cause to believe that the debtor was insolvent.

History: s. 6, ch. 87-79.

726.107 When transfer made or obligation incurred. ---

For the purposes of ss. 726.101-726.112:

(1) A transfer is made:

(a) With respect to an asset that is real property other than a fixture, but including the interest of a seller or purchaser under a contract for the sale of the asset, when the transfer is so far perfected that a good faith purchaser of the asset from the debtor against whom applicable law permits the transfer to be perfected cannot acquire an interest in the asset that is superior to the interest of the transferee.

(b) With respect to an asset that is not real property or that is a fixture, when the transfer is so far perfected that a creditor on a simple contract cannot acquire a judicial lien otherwise than under ss. 726.101-726.112 that is superior to the interest of the transferee.

(2) If applicable law permits the transfer to be perfected as provided in subsection (1) and the transfer is not so perfected before the commencement of

an action for relief under ss. 726.101-726.112, the transfer is deemed made immediately before the commencement of the action.

(3) If applicable law does not permit the transfer to be perfected as provided in subsection (1), the transfer is made when it becomes effective between the debtor and the transferee.

(4) A transfer is not made until the debtor has acquired rights in the asset transferred.

(5) An obligation is incurred:

(a) If oral, when it becomes effective between the parties; or

(b) If evidenced by a writing, when the writing executed by the obligor is delivered to or for the benefit of the obligee.

History: s. 7, ch. 87-79; s. 28, ch. 91-110.

726.108 Remedies of creditors. ---

(1) In an action for relief against a transfer or obligation under ss. 726.101-726.112, a creditor, subject to the limitations in s.726.109 may obtain:

(a) Avoidance of the transfer or obligation to the extent necessary to satisfy the creditor's claim;

(b) An attachment or other provisional remedy against the asset transferred or other property of the transferee in accordance with applicable law;

(c) Subject to applicable principles of equity and in accordance with applicable rules of civil procedure:

1. An injunction against further disposition by the debtor or a transferee, or both, of the asset transferred or of other property;
2. Appointment of a receiver to take charge of the asset transferred or of other property of the transferee; or
3. Any other relief the circumstances may require.

(2) If a creditor has obtained a judgment on a claim against the debtor, the creditor, if the court so orders, may levy execution on the asset transferred or its proceeds.

History: s. 8, ch. 87-79.

726.109 Defenses, liability, and protection of transferee. ---

(1) A transfer or obligation is not voidable under s. 726.105(1)(a) against a person who took in good faith and for a reasonably equivalent value or against any subsequent transferee or obligee.

(2) Except as otherwise provided in this section, to the extent a transfer is voidable in an action by a creditor under s.726.108(1)(a), the creditor may recover judgment for the value of the asset transferred, as adjusted under subsection (3), or the amount necessary to satisfy the creditor's claim, whichever is less. The judgment may be entered against:

(a) The first transferee of the asset or the person for whose benefit the transfer was made; or

(b) Any subsequent transferee other than a good faith transferee who took for value or from any subsequent transferee.

(3) If the judgment under subsection (2) is based upon the value of the asset transferred, the judgment must be for an amount equal to the value of the asset at the time of the transfer, subject to adjustment as the equities may require.

(4) Notwithstanding voidability of a transfer or an obligation under ss. 726.101-726.112, a good-faith transferee or obligee is entitled, to the extent of the value given the debtor for the transfer or obligation, to:

(a) A lien on or a right to retain any interest in the asset transferred;

(b) Enforcement of any obligation incurred; or

(c) A reduction in the amount of the liability on the judgment.

(5) A transfer is not voidable under s. 726.105(1)(b) or s. 726.106 if the transfer results from:

(a) Termination of a lease upon default by the debtor when the termination is pursuant to the lease and applicable law; or

(b) Enforcement of a security interest in compliance with Article 9 of the Uniform Commercial Code.

(6) A transfer is not voidable under s. 726.106(2):

(a) To the extent the insider gave new value to or for the benefit of the debtor after the transfer was made unless the new value was secured by a valid lien;

(b) If made in the ordinary course of business or financial affairs of the debtor and the insider; or

(c) If made pursuant to a good faith effort to rehabilitate the debtor and the transfer secured present value given for that purpose as well as an antecedent debt of the debtor.

History: s. 9, ch. 87-79.

726.110 Extinguishment of cause of action. ---

A cause of action with respect to a fraudulent transfer or obligation under ss. 726.101-726.112 is extinguished unless action is brought:

(1) Under s. 726.105(1)(a), within 4 years after the transfer was made or the obligation was incurred or, if later, within 1 year after the transfer or obligation was or could reasonably have been discovered by the claimant;

(2) Under s. 726.105(1)(b) or s. 726.106(1), within 4 years after the transfer was made or the obligation was incurred; or

(3) Under s. 726.106(2), within 1 year after the transfer was made or the obligation was incurred.

History: s. 10, ch. 87-79.

726.111 Supplementary provisions. ---

Unless displaced by the provisions of ss. 726.101-726.112, the principles of law and equity, including the law merchant and the law relating to principal and agent, estoppel, laches, fraud, misrepresentation, duress, coercion, mistake, insolvency, or other validating or invalidating cause, supplement those provisions.

History: s. 11, ch. 87-79.

726.112 Uniformity of application and construction. ---

Chapter 87-79, Laws of Florida, shall be applied and construed to effectuate its general purpose to make uniform the law with respect to the subject of the law among states enacting it.

History: s. 12, ch. 87-79.

726.201 Fraudulent loans void. ---

When any loan of goods and chattels shall be pretended to have been made to any person with whom or those claiming under him, possession shall have remained for the space of 2 years without demand and pursued by due process of law on the part of the pretended lender, or where any reservation or limitation shall be pretended to have been made of a use or property by way of condition, reversion, remainder or otherwise in goods and chattels, and the possession thereof shall have remained in another as aforesaid, the same shall be taken, as to the creditors and purchasers of the persons aforesaid so remaining in possession, to be fraudulent within this chapter, and the absolute property shall be with the possession, unless such loan, reservation or limitation of use or property were declared by will or deed in writing proved and recorded.

History: s. 4, Jan. 28, 1823; s. 1, ch. 872, 1859; RS 1994; GS 2516; RGS 3871; CGL 5778.

Note. Former s. 726.09

STATEMENT OF FINANCIAL AFFAIRS

UNITED STATES BANKRUPTCY COURT
NORTHERN DISTRICT OF TEXAS
DALLAS DIVISION

In re: I. AM BROKE §
               §   Case No. 393-39999-SAF (Chapter 11)
Debtor   §
               §

STATEMENT OF FINANCIAL AFFAIRS

This Statement is to be completed by every debtor. Spouses filing a joint petition may file a single statement on which the information for both spouses is combined. If the case is filed under chapter 12 or chapter 13, a married debtor must furnish information for both spouses whether or not a joint petition is filed, unless the spouses are separated and a joint petition is not filed. An individual debtor engaged in business as a sole proprietor, partner, family farmer, or self-employed professional, should provide the information requested on this statement concerning all such activities as well as the individual's personal affairs.

Questions 1 - 15 are to be completed by all debtors. Debtors that are or have been in business, as defined below, also must complete Questions 16 - 21. Each question must be answered. If the answer to any question is "None," or the question is not applicable, mark the box labeled "None." If additional space is needed for the answer to any question, use and attach a separate sheet properly identified with the case name, case number (if known), and the number of the question.

DEFINITIONS

"In business." A debtor is "in business" for the purpose of this form if the debtor is a corporation or partnership. An individual debtor is "in business" for the purpose of this form if the debtor is or has been, within the two years immediately preceding the filing of this bankruptcy case, any of the following: an officer, director, managing executive, or person in control of a corporation;

a partner, other than a limited partner, of a partnership; a sole proprietor or self-employed.

"Insider." The term "insider" includes but is not limited to: relatives of the debtor; general partners of the debtor and their relatives; corporations of which the debtor is an officer, director, or person in control; officers, directors, and any person in control of a corporate debtor and their relatives; affiliates of the debtor and insiders of such affiliates; any managing agent of the debtor. 11 U.S.C. § 101(30).

1. Income from employment or operation of a business

None

☐

State the gross amount of income the debtor has received from employment, trade, or profession, or from operation of the debtor's business from the beginning of this calendar year to the date this case was commenced. State also the gross amounts received during the two years immediately preceding this calendar year. (A debtor that maintains, or has maintained, financial records on the basis of a fiscal rather than a calendar year may report fiscal year income. Identify the beginning and ending dates of the debtor's fiscal year.) If a joint petition is filed, state income for each spouse separately. (Married debtors filing under chapter 12 or chapter 13 must state income of both spouses whether or not a joint petition is filed, unless the spouses are separated and a joint petition is not filed.)

DATES/AMOUNT(S)	SOURCE
1991 Earnings - $340,000.00	AMC Attorneys
1992 Earnings - $ 99,000.00	ABC Attorneys
1/1/93 - 8/31/93: $0.00	

2. Income other than from employment or operation of business

None

☐

State the amount of income received by the debtor other than from employment, trade, profession, or operation of the debtor's business during the two years immediately preceding the commencement of this case. Give particulars. If a joint petition is filed, state income for each spouse separately. (Married debtors filing under chapter 12 or chapter 13 must state income for each spouse whether or not a joint petition is filed, unless the spouses are separated and a joint petition is not filed.)

	DATES/AMOUNT(S)		SOURCE
1991	1/1/91 - 12/31/91	$ 40,000	Leased Commercial Bldg.
1992	1/1/92 - 12/31/92	$ 30,000	Leased Commercial Bldg.
1993	1/1/93 - 12/31/93	$ 15,000	Leased Commercial Bldg.
1991	1/1/91 - 12/31/91		Rental from Condominium
1992	1/1/92 - 12/31/92	$800,000	Rental from Condominium
1993		$400	Rental from Condominium
1993:		$1,100	Interest in closed bank account at Last Bank & Trust
1993:		$1,400	Sale of stock in Loser Bancshares

3. Payments to Creditors

None
☐

a. List all payments on loans, installment purchases of goods or services, and other debts, aggregating more than $600 to any creditor, made within 90 days immediately preceding the commencement of this case. (Married debtors filing under chapter 12 or chapter 13 must include payments by either or both spouses whether or not a joint petition is filed, unless the spouses are separated and a joint petition is not filed.)

NAME AND ADDRESS OF CREDITOR	Internal Revenue Service, Austin, Texas	Dallas Savings & Loan	Banking On You
DATES OF PAYMENTS	1/1/93	Debt Service Payments @ $1,000/Mo.	April and May Debt Service Payments at $400.00/Mo
AMOUNT PAID	$3,000.00	$3,000.00	$ 800.00
AMOUNT STILL OWING	$ 39,000.00	$ 90,000.00	$ 80,000.00

None

☐

b. List all payments made within one year immediately preceding the commencement of this case to or for the benefit of creditors who are or were insiders. (Married debtors filing under chapter 12 or chapter 13 must include payments by either or both spouses whether or not a joint petition is filed, unless the spouses are separated and a joint petition is not filed.)

4. Suits, executions, garnishments and attachments

None

☐

a. List all suits to which the debtor is or was a party within one year immediately preceding the filing of this bankruptcy case. (Married debtors filing under chapter 12 or chapter 13 must include information concerning either or both spouses whether or not a joint petition is filed, unless the spouses are separated and a joint petition is not filed.)

None

☐

b. Describe all property that has been attached, garnished or seized under any legal or equitable process within one year immediately preceding the commencement of this case. (Married debtors filing under chapter 12 or chapter 13 must include information concerning property of either or both spouses whether or not a joint petition is filed, unless the spouses are separated and a joint petition is not filed.)

NAME AND ADDRESS OF PERSON FOR WHOSE BENEFIT PROPERTY WAS SEIZED	DATE OF SEIZURE	DESCRIPTION AND VALUE OF THE PROPERTY
We Are Bankers	Writ of Garnishment filed against Debtor 1/2/92 to collect on unpaid judgment. Judgment was satisfied by Debtor on 4/1/92 and filed with the County Clerk (Dallas County) on 4/2/92.	$100.00 garnished from bank account.

5. Repossessions, foreclosures and returns

None

☐

List all property that has been repossessed by a creditor, sold at a foreclosure sale, transferred through a deed in lieu of foreclosure or returned to the seller, within one year immediately preceding the commencement of this case. (Married debtors filing under chapter 12 or chapter 13 must include information concerning property either or both spouses whether or not a joint petition is filed, unless the spouses are separated and a joint petition is not filed.)

6. Assignments and receiverships

None

☐

a. Describe any assignment of property for the benefit of creditors made within 120 days immediately preceding the commencement of this case. (Married debtors filing under chapter 12 or chapter 13 must include any assignment by either or both spouses whether or not a joint petition is filed, unless the spouses are separated and a joint petition is not filed.)

None

☐

b. List all property which has been in the hands of a custodian, receiver, or court-appointed official within one year immediately preceding the commencement of this case. (Married debtors filing under chapter 12 or chapter 13 must include information concerning property either or both spouses whether or not a joint petition is filed, unless the spouses are separated and a joint petition is not filed.)

7. Gifts

None

☐

List all gifts or charitable contributions made within one year immediately preceding the commencement of this case except ordinary and usual gifts to family members aggregating less than $200 in value per individual family member and charitable contributions aggregating less than $100 per recipient. (Married debtors filing under chapter 12 or chapter 13 must include gifts or contributions by either or both spouses whether or not a joint petition is filed, unless the spouses are separated and a joint petition is not filed.)

8. Losses

None

☐

List all losses from fire, theft, other casualty or gambling within one year immediately preceding the commencement of this case or since the commencement of this case. (Married debtors filing under chapter 12 or chapter 13 must include losses by either or both spouses whether or not a joint petition is filed, unless the spouses are separated and a joint petition is not filed.)

9. Payments related to debt counseling or bankruptcy

None

☐

List all payments made or property transferred by or on behalf of the debtor to any persons, including attorneys, for consultation concerning debt consolidation, relief under the bankruptcy law or preparation of a petition in bankruptcy within one year immediately preceding the commencement of this case.

NAME AND ADDRESS OF PAYEE	DATE OF PAYMENT, NAME OF PAYOR IF OTHER THAN DEBTOR	AMOUNT OF MONEY OR DESCRIPTION AND VALUE OF PROPERTY
Two Guys Who Are Lawyers, P.C.	2/1/93	$1,000.00

10. Other transfers

None

☐

List all other property, other than property transferred in the ordinary course of the business or financial affairs of the debtor, transferred either absolutely or as security within one year immediately preceding the commencement of this case. (Married debtors filing under chapter 12 or chapter 13 must include transfers by either or both spouses whether or not a joint petition is filed, unless the spouses are separated and a joint petition is not filed.)

11. Closed financial accounts

None

☐

List all financial accounts and instruments held in the name of the debtor or for the benefit of the debtor which were closed, sold, or otherwise transferred within one year immediately preceding the commencement of this case. Include checking, savings, or other financial accounts, certificates of deposit, or other instruments; shares and share accounts held in banks, credit unions, pension funds, cooperatives, associations, brokerage houses and other financial institutions. (Married debtors filing under chapter 12 or chapter 13 must include information concerning accounts or instruments held by or for either or both spouses whether or not a joint petition is filed, unless the spouses are separated and a joint petition is not filed.)

NAME AND ADDRESS OF INSTITUTION	TYPE AND NUMBER OF ACCOUNT AND AMOUNT OF FINAL BALANCE	AMOUNT AND DATE OF SALE OR CLOSING
Best Bank, Dallas, Texas	Trust Account - Styled: "I. Am Broke & Assoc., P.C."	Liquidated 2/2/93.
	Cash: $1,000.00	$1,000.00
	Stock: 2,800 shares of Loser Bancshares sold @ 50C a share - $1,400.00	$1,400.00

12. Safe deposit boxes

None
☐

List each safe deposit or other box or depository in which the debtor has or had securities, cash or other valuables within one year immediately preceding the commencement of this case. (Married debtors filing under chapter 12 or chapter 13 must include boxes or depositories of either or both spouses whether or not a joint petition is filed, unless the spouses are separated and a joint petition is not filed.)

13. Setoffs

None
☐

List all setoffs made by any creditor, including a bank, against a debt or deposit of the debtor within 90 days preceding the commencement of this case. (Married debtors filing under chapter 12 or chapter 13 must include information concerning either or both spouses whether or not a joint petition is filed, unless the spouses are separated and a joint petition is not filed.)

14. Property held for another person

None

☐   List all property owned by another person that the debtor holds or controls.

15. Prior address of debtor

None

☐   If the debtor has moved within the two years immediately preceding the commencement of this case, list all premises which the debtor occupied during that period and vacated prior to the commencement of this case. If a joint petition is filed, report also any separate address of either spouse.

ADDRESS	NAME USED	DATES OF OCCUPANCY
1100 Commerce Dallas, TX 75242	I. Am Broke & Associates, P.C.	Conducts business from home.
"	Management Company U.S.A.	
"	WLW Joint Venture	

The following questions are to be completed by every debtor that is a corporation or partnership and by any individual debtor who is or has been, within the two years immediately preceding the commencement of this case, any of the following: an officer, director, managing executive, or owner of more than 5 percent of the voting securities of a corporation; a partner, other than a limited partner, of a partnership; a sole proprietor or otherwise self-employed.

(An individual or joint debtor should complete this portion of the statement only if the debtor is or has been in business, as defamed above, within the two years immediately preceding the commencement of this case.)

16. Nature, location and name of business

None

☐

a. If the debtor is an individual, list the names and addresses of all businesses in which the debtor was an officer, director, partner, or managing executive of a corporation, partnership, sole proprietorship, or was a self-employed professional within the two years immediately preceding the commencement of this case, or in which the debtor owned 5 percent or more of the voting or equity securities within the two years immediately preceding the commencement of this case.

None

☐ b. If the debtor is a partnership, list the names and addresses of all businesses in which the debtor was a partner or owned 5 percent or more of the voting securities, within the two years immediately preceding the commencement of this case.

None

☐ c. If the debtor is a corporation, list the names and addresses of all businesses in which the debtor was a partner or owned 5 percent or more of the voting securities within the two years immediately preceding the commencement of this case.

NAME	ADDRESS	NATURE OF BUSINESS	BEGINNING AND ENDING DATES OF OPERATION

17. Books, records and financial statements

None

☐ a. List all bookkeepers and accountants who within six years immediately preceding the filing of this bankruptcy case kept or supervised the keeping of books of account and records of the debtor.

NAME AND ADDRESS	DATES SERVICES RENDERED
Numbers Mann, CPA. 300 Bean Counter Ave. Dallas, TX 75200	Since 1985

None

☐ b. List all firms or individuals who within the two years immediately preceding the filing of this bankruptcy case have audited the books of account and records, or prepared a financial statement of the debtor.

NAME	ADDRESS	DATES SERVICES RENDERED
I. Am Broke	1100 Commerce Dallas, TX 75242	As required.

None

☐ c. List all firms or individuals who at the time of the commencement of this case were in possession of the books of account and records of the debtor. If any of the books of account and records are not available, explain.

NAME	ADDRESS
I. Am Broke	110 Commerce, Dallas, TX 75242

None

☐ d. List all financial institutions, creditors and other parties, including mercantile and trade agencies, to whom a financial statement was issued within the two years immediately preceding the commencement of this case by the debtor.

NAME AND ADDRESS	DATE ISSUED
Banking On You, 6666 Downtown Dr., Dallas, TX 75234	1989 to present, as required.
Dallas Savings & Loan, P.O. Box 77777, Dallas, Texas 75234	1989 to present.

18. Inventories

None

☐

a. List the dates of the last two inventories taken of your property, the name of the person who supervised the taking of each inventory, and the dollar amount and basis of each inventory.

None

☐

b. List the name and address of the person having possession of the records of each of the two inventories reported in a., above.

19. Current partners, officers, directors and shareholders

None

☐ a. If the debtor is a partnership, list the nature and percentage of partnership interest of each member of the partnership.

None

☐ b. If the debtor is a corporation, list all officers and directors of the corporation, and each stockholder who directly or indirectly owns, controls, or holds 5 percent or more of the voting securities of the corporation.

20. Former partners, officers, directors and shareholders

None

☐ a. If the debtor is a partnership, list each member who withdrew from the partnership within one year immediately preceding the commencement of this case.

None

☐ b. If the debtor is a corporation, list all officers, or directors whose relationship with the corporation terminated within one year immediately preceding the commencement of this case.

21. Withdrawals from a partnership or distributions by a corporation

None

☐ If the debtor is a partnership or corporation, list all withdrawals or distributions credited or given to an insider, including compensation in any form, bonuses, loans, stock redemptions, options exercised and any other perquisite during one year immediately preceding the commencement of this case.

[If completed by an individual or individual and spouse]

l declare under penalty of perjury that l have read the answers contained in the foregoing statement of financial affairs and any attachments thereto and that they are true and correct.

Date_____Signature_____

Date_____Signature_____
                                   of Joint Debtor (if any)

SCHEDULE OF REAL PROPERTY

UNITED STATES BANKRUPTCY COURT
FOR THE NORTHERN DISTRICT OF TEXAS
DALLAS DIVISION

IN RE: I. AM BROKE   §
     § CASE NO. 393-39999-SAF-1 1
Debtor.   §
     §

SCHEDULE A – REAL PROPERTY

Except as directed below, list all real property in which the debtor has any legal, equitable, or future interest, including all property owned as a co-tenant, community property, or in which the debtor has a life estate. Include any property in which the debtor holds rights and powers exercisable for the debtor's own benefit. If the debtor is married, state whether husband, wife, or both own the property by placing "H," "W," "J," or "C" in the column labeled "Husband," Wife, Joint, or Community." If the debtor holds no interest in real property, write "None" under "Description land location of Property."

Do not include interests in executory contracts and unexpired leases on this schedule. List them in Schedule G -- Executory Contracts and Unexpired Leases.

If an entity claims to have a lien or hold a secured interest in any property, state the amount of the secured claim. See Schedule D. If no entity claims to hold a secured interest in the property, write "None" in the column labeled "Amount of Secured Claim."

If the debtor is an individual or if a joint petition is filed, state the amount of any exemption claimed in the property only in Schedule C – Property Claimed as Exempt.

				TOTALS
Description and location of property	Homestead 1100 Commerce Dallas, TX 75242	Commercial Building 9999 Central Dallas, TX 75242	Condo III Tenancy Lane Dallas, TX 75000	
Nature of debtor's interest in property	Tenancy in Common undivided fee simple interest	Owner 100% fee simple interest	Owner 100% fee simple interest	
Husband, wife, joint or community	Community	Community	Community	
Current market value of debtor's interest in property without deducting any secured claim or exemption	$525,000	$100,000	$54,000	
Amount of secured claim	$500,000 (excluding accruals)	$90,000	$60,000	$650,000

SCHEDULE OF PERSONAL PROPERTY

UNITED STATES BANKRUPTCY COURT
FOR THE NORTHERN DISTRICT OF TEXAS
DALLAS DIVISION

IN RE: I. AM BROKE,   §   CASE NO. 393-39999-SAF-I 1
Debtor.   §

SCHEDULE B – PERSONAL PROPERTY

Except as directed below, list all personal property of the debtor of whatever kind. If the debtor has no property in one or more of the categories, place an "x" in the appropriate position in the column labeled "None." If additional space is needed in any category, attach a separate sheet properly identified with the case name, case number, and the number of the category. If the debtor is married, state whether husband, wife, or both own the property by placing an "H," "W," "J," or "C" in the column labeled "Husband, Wife, Joint, or Community." If the debtor is an individual or a joint petition is filed, state the amount of any exemption claimed only in Schedule C – Property Claimed as Exempt.

Do not list interest in executory contracts and unexpired leases on this schedule. List them in Schedule G – Executory Contracts and Unexpired Leases.

If the property is being held for the debtor by someone else, state that person's name and address under "Description and Location of Property."

Type of Property	None	Description and Location of Property	Husband, Wife, Joint, or Community	Current Market Value of Debtor's Interest in Property, without Deducting Any Secured Claim or Exemption
1. Cash on hand		100.00	Debtor	100.00

Type of Property	None	Description and Location of Property	Husband, Wife, Joint, or Community	Current Market Value of Debtor's Interest in Property, without Deducting Any Secured Claim or Exemption
2. Checking, savings or other financial accounts, certificates of deposit or shares in banks, savings and loan, thrift, building and loan and homestead associations, or credit unions, brokerage houses, or cooperatives		I. Am Broke D-I-P Acct. U.S. Trustee Approved Bank P.O. Box Dallas, TX 75252	DIP Account	600.00
3. Security deposits with public utilities, telephone companies, landlords, and others	X			0.00
4. Household goods and furnishings including audio, video, and computer equipment		1100 Commerce Dallas, TX 75242	1/2 of Community Property	10,00000
5. Books, pictures, and other art objects, antiques, stamp, coin, record, tape, compact disc, and other collections or collectibles		1100 Commerce Dallas, TX 75242	Debtor's 1/2 of Community Property	500.00
6. Wearing apparel		1100 Commerce Dallas, TX 75242	Debtor's 1/2 of Community Property	500.00

Type of Property	None	Description and Location of Property	Husband, Wife, Joint, or Community	Current Market Value of Debtor's Interest in Property, without Deducting Any Secured Claim or Exemption
7. Furs and jewelry		1100 Commerce Dallas, TX 75242	Debtor's 1/2 of Community Property	5,000.00
8. Firearms and sports, photographic, and other hobby equipment		1100 Commerce Dallas. TX 75242	Debtor's 1/2 of Community Property	3,100.00
9. Interests in insurance policies (name insurance company of each policy and itemize surrender or refund value of each)		Term Policies 1100 Commerce Dallas, TX 75242	Debtor's 1/2 of Community Property	0.00
10. Annuities (itemize and name each issuer)	X			0.00
11. Interests in IRA, ERISA, KEOGH, or other pension or profit sharing plan. (itemize)	X			0.00
12. Stock and interests in incorporated and unincorporated business. (itemize)		I) Money Managers Inc. 2) Company U.S.A	1) 900.00 2) 0.00	
13. Interest in partnerships or joint ventures (itemize)		75% JV Interest in Broke Joint Venture		0.00

Type of Property	None	Description and Location of Property	Husband, Wife, Joint, or Community	Current Market Value of Debtor's Interest in Property, without Deducting Any Secured Claim or Exemption
14. Government and corporate bonds and other negotiable and nonnegotiable instruments		44% interest in XX Joint Venture		0.00
15. Accounts receivable	x			0.00
16. Alimony maintenance support, and property settlement to which the debtor is or may be entitled. (give particulars)	X			0.00
17. Other liquidated debts owing debtor including tax refunds (give particulars)	X			0.00
18. Equitable or future interests, life estates, and rights or powers exercisable for the benefit of the debtor other than those listed in schedule of real property	X			0.00
19. Contingent and noncontingent interests in estate of a decedent, death benefit plan, life insurance policy, or trust	X			0.00

Type of Property	None	Description and Location of Property	Husband, Wife, Joint, or Community	Current Market Value of Debtor's Interest in Property, without Deducting Any Secured Claim or Exemption
20. Other contingent and unliquidated claims of every nature, including tax refunds, counterclaims of the debtor, and rights to setoff claims. (give estimated value of each)	X			0.00
21. Patents, copyrights, and other intellectual property. (give particulars)	X			0.00
22. Licenses, franchises and other general intangibles (give particulars)		Real Estate Broker license		0.00
23. Automobiles, trucks, trailers, and other vehicles and accessories		1) 1990 Chevrolet Cavalier 2) Horse Trailer	Debtor's 1/2 Community Property	1) 2,500.00 2) 75.00
24. Boats, motors, and accessories	X			0.00
25. Aircraft and accessories	X			0.00
26. Office equipment, furnishings, and supplies		1100 Commerce Dallas, TX 75242	Debtor's 1/2 Community Property	500.00
27. Machinery, fixtures, equipment, and supplies used in business	X			0.00

Type of Property	None	Description and Location of Property	Husband, Wife, Joint, or Community	Current Market Value of Debtor's Interest in Property, without Deducting Any Secured Claim or Exemption
28. Inventory	X			0.00
29. Animals	X			0.00
30. Crops - growing or harvested give particulars	X			0.00
31. Farming equipment and implements	X			0.00
32. Farm supplies, chemicals, and feed	X			0.00
33. Other personal property of any kind not already listed (itemize)				0.00
Total				$3,975.00

PROPERTY CLAIMED AS EXEMPT

UNITED STATES BANKRUPTCY COURT
FOR THE NORTHERN DISTRICT OF TEXAS
DALLAS DIVISION

IN RE:	§	
I. AM BROKE	§	CASE NO. 393-39999-SAF-11
DEBTOR	§	

SCHEDULE C – PROPERTY CLAIMED AS EXEMPT

Debtor elects the exemptions to which debtor is entitled under:
(Check one box)

[]   11 U.S.C. §522(b)(1): Exemptions provided in 11 U.S.C. §522(d). Note: These exemptions are available only in certain states.

[]   11 U.S.C. §522(b)(2): Exemptions available under applicable nonbankruptcy federal laws, state or local law where the debtor's domicile has been located for the 180 days immediately preceding the filing of the petition, or for a longer portion of the 180-day period than in any other place, and the debtor's interest as a tenant by the entirety or joint tenant to the extent the interest is exempt from process under applicable nonbankruptcy law.

Description of property	Specific law providing each exemption	Value of claimed exemption	Current market value of property without deducting exemption
Homestead 1100 Commerce Dallas, TX 75242	Texas Property Code § 41.001	500,000.00	500,000.00
Home furnishings	Texas Property Code § 42.002(a)(1)	10,500.00	10,500.00
Provisions for consumption	Texas Property Code § 42.002(a)(2)	100.00	100.00

Description of property	Specific law providing each exemption	Value of claimed exemption	Current market value of property without deducting exemption
Tools, equipment used in trade or profession	Texas Property Code § 42.002(a)(4)	500.00	500.00
Wearing apparel	Texas Property Code § 42.002(a)(5)	500.00	500.00
Jewelry	Texas Property Code § 42.002(a)(6)	5,000.00	5,000.00
Firearms (2)	Texas Property Code § 42.002(a)(7)	3,100.00	3,100.00
Vehicle and Trailer	Texas Property Code § 42.002(a)(9)	5,175.00	5,175.00
Life Ins. Policies present value	Texas Property Code § 42.002(a)(12)	0.00	0.00
Other Property	Texas Property Code § 41.001 (a)(1)	900.00	900.00
Total		$525,775.00	$525,775.00

CREDITORS HOLDING SECURED CLAIMS

UNITED STATES BANKRUPTCY COURT
FOR THE NORTHERN DISTRICT OF TEXAS
DALLAS DIVISION

IN RE: §

I. AM BROKE,   §   CASE NO. 393-39999-SAF-1 1

Debtor.   §

SCHEDULE D – CREDITORS HOLDING SECURED CLAIMS

State the name, mailing address, including zip code, and account number, if any, of all entities holding claims secured by property of the debtor as of the date of filing the petition. List creditors holding all types of secured interests such as judgment liens, garnishments, statutory liens, mortgages, deeds of trust, and other security interests. List creditors in alphabetical order to the extent practicable. If all secured creditors will not fit on this page, use the continuation sheet provided.

If any entity other than a spouse in a joint case may be jointly liable on a claim, place an "X" in the column labeled "Codebtor," include the entity on the appropriate schedule of creditors, and complete Schedule H – Codebtors. If a joint petition is filed, state whether husband, wife, both of them, or the marital community may be liable on each claim by placing an "H," "W," "J," or "C" in the column labeled "Husband, Wife, Joint, or Community."

If the claim is contingent, place an "X" in the column labeled "Contingent." If the claim is unliquidated, place an "X" in the column labeled "Unliquidated." If the claim is disputed, place an "X" in the column labeled "Disputed." (You may need to place an "X" in more than one of these three columns.)

Report the total of all claims listed on this schedule in the box labeled "Total" on the last sheet of the completed schedule. Report this total also on the Summary of Schedules.

[]   Check this box if debtor has no creditors holding secured claims to report on this Schedule D.

					TOTALS
Creditor's name and mailing address including zip code	Bank of Debtor 100 LBJ Frwy. Dallas, TX 77234	Dallas Savings & Loan P.O. Box 77777 Dallas, TX 75234	Texas Bank 2222 Dallas Park Road Dallas, Texas 75234	Banking On You P.O. Box 88888 Dallas, TX 75234	
Co-debtor	X	X	X	X	
Husband, wife, joint or community	Community	Community	Community	Community	
Date claim was incurred, nature of lien and description and market value of property subject to lien	2-30-89; Purchase Money Mortgage, 1st lien 1100 Commerce Dallas, TX 75242 market value undetermined	1-2-89, 1st lien, 9999 Central, Dallas, TX 75234 market value undetermined	2-2-94, 2nd lien 9999 Central Dallas, TX 75234	1-2-88 1st Lien Condominium Debt secured by property owned by WW Joint Venture	
Contingent					
Liquidated					
Disputed					
Amount of claim without deducting value of collateral	$500,000	$90,000.00	15,000.00	60,000	$665,000.00
Unsecured portion, if any	N/A	N/A	N/A	N/A	N/A

CREDITORS HOLDING
UNSECURED PRIORITY CLAIMS

UNITED STATES BANKRUPTCY COURT
FOR THE NORTHERN DISTRICT OF TEXAS
DALLAS DIVISION

IN RE: §
I. AM BROKE,   §   CASE NO. 393-39999-SAF-11
Debtor   §

SCHEDULE E – CREDITORS HOLDING
UNSECURED PRIORITY CLAIMS

A complete list of claims entitled to priority, listed separately by type of priority, is to be set forth on the sheets provided. Only holders of unsecured claims entitled to priority should be listed in this schedule. In the boxes provided on the attached sheets, state the name and mailing address, including zip code, and account number, if any, of all entities holding priority claims against the debtor or the property of the debtor, as of the date of filing of the petition.

If any entity other than a spouse in a joint case may be jointly liable on a claim, place an "X" in the column labeled "Codebtor," include the entity on the appropriate schedule of creditors, and complete Schedule H – Codebtors. If a joint petition is filed, state whether husband, wife, both of them, or the marital community may be liable on each claim by placing an "H," "W," "J," or "C" in the column labeled "Husband, Wife, Joint, or Community."

If the claim is contingent, place an "X" in the column labeled "contingent." If the claim is unliquidated, place an "X" in the column labeled "Unliquidated." If the claim is disputed, place an "X" in the column labeled "Disputed." (You may need to place an "X" in more than one of these three columns.)

Report the total of claims listed on each sheet in the box labeled "Subtotal" on each sheet. Report the total of all claims listed on this Schedule E in the box labeled "Total" on the last sheet of the completed schedule. Repeat this total also on the Summary Schedules.

[] Check this box if debtor has no creditors holding unsecured priority claims to report on this Schedule E.

TYPES OF PRIORITY CLAIMS (Check the appropriate box (es) below if claims in that category are listed on the attached sheets)

[] Extensions of credit in an involuntary case

Claims arising in the ordinary course of the debtor's business or financial affairs after the commencement of the case but before the earlier of the appointment of a trustee or the order for relief. 11 U.S.C. §507(a)(2).

[] Wages, salaries, and commissions

Wages, salaries, and commissions, including vacation, severance, and sick leave pay owing to employees, up to a maximum of $2,000.00 per employee, earned within 90 days immediately preceding the filing of the original petition, or the cessation of business, whichever occurred first, to the extent provided in 11 U.S.C. §507(a)(3).

[] Contributions to employee benefit plans

Money owed to employee benefit plans for services rendered within 180 days immediately preceding the filing of the original petition, or the cessation of business, whichever occurred first, to the extent provided in 11 U.S.C. §507(a)(4).

[] Certain farmers and fishermen

Claims of certain farmers and fishermen, up to a maximum of $2,000.00 per farmer or fishermen, against the debtor, as provided in 11 U.S.C. §507(a)(5).

[] Deposits by individuals

Claims of individuals up to a maximum of $900.00 for deposits for the purchase, lease, or rental of property or services for personal, family, or household use, that were not delivered or provided. 11 U.S.C. §507(a)(6).

[] Taxes and Certain Other Debts Owed to Governmental Units

Taxes, customs duties, and penalties owing to federal, state, and local governmental units as set forth in 11 U.S.C. §507(a)(7).

		TOTALS
Creditor's name and mailing address including zip code	IRS Austin, TX 77301 Acct 222-99A234	
Co-debtor	X	
Husband, wife, joint, or community	Community	
Date claim was incurred and consideration for claim	For tax period ending 12/31/90 Lien filed 11/14/92	
Contingent		
Unliquidated		
Disputed		
Amount of claim	39,000	39,000
Amount entitled to priority	39,000	39,000

CREDITORS HOLDING UNSECURED NONPRIORITY CLAIMS

UNITED STATES BANKRUPTCY COURT
FOR THE NORTHERN DISTRICT OF TEXAS
DALLAS DIVISION

IN RE: §
I. AM BROKE § CASE NO. 393-39999-SAF-11
Debtor. §

SCHEDULE F – CREDITORS HOLDING UNSECURED NONPRIORITY CLAIMS

State the name, mailing address, including zip code, and account number, if any, of all entities holding unsecured claims without priority against the debtor or the property of the debtor, as of the date of filing of the petition. Do not include claims listed in Schedule D and E. If all creditors will not fit on this page, use the continuation sheet provided.

If any entity other than a spouse in a joint case may be jointly liable on a claim, place an "X" in the column labeled "Codebtor" include the entity on the appropriate schedule of creditors, and complete Schedule H – Codebtors. If a joint petition is filed, state whether husband, wife, both of them, or the marital community may be liable on each claim by placing an "H," "W," "J," or "C" in the column labeled "Husband, Wife, Joint, or Community."

If the claim is contingent, place an "X" in the column labeled "contingent". If the claim is unliquidated, place an "X" in the column labeled "Unliquidated." If the claim is disputed, place an "X" in the column labeled "Disputed". (You may need to place an "X" in more than one of these three columns.)

Report the total of claims listed on each sheet in the box labeled "Subtotal" on each sheet. Report the total of all claims listed on this Schedule B in the box labeled "Total" on the last sheet of the completed schedule. Repeat this total also on the Summary Schedules.

[] Check this box if debtor has no creditors holding unsecured nonpriority claims to report on this Schedule F.

				TOTALS
Creditor's name and mailing address including zip code	Banking On You 6666 Downtown Dr. Dallas, Texas 75234 Attn: Mr. Niceguy, Vice Pres	Loans "R" Us 4554 Money Dr. Dallas, Texas 75234	Free Visa Assoc. P.O. Box 0279	
Co-debtor	X	X	X	
Husband, wife, joint, or community	Community	Community	Community	
Date claim was incurred and consideration for claim. If claim is subject to setoff, so state.	Loan dated 6/6/66	Loans during calendar years 1988, 1989, 1991	Charges through 1/1/93	
Contingent				
Unliquidated				
Disputed				
Amount of claim	$60,000	$150,000	$5,200	$219,200

EXECUTORY CONTRACTS AND UNEXPIRED LEASES

UNITED STATES BANKRUPTCY COURT
FOR THE NORTHERN DISTRICT OF TEXAS
DALLAS DIVISION

IN RE:	§	
I. AM BROKE	§	CASE NO. 393-39999-SAF-11
	§	
Debtor	§	

SCHEDULE G – EXECUTORY CONTRACTS AND UNEXPIRED LEASES

Describe all executory contracts of any nature and all unexpired leases of real or personal property. Include any timeshare interests.

State nature of debtor's interest in contract, i.e., "Purchaser," "Agent," etc. State whether debtor is the lessor or lessee of the lease.

Provide the names and complete mailing addresses of all other parties to each lease or contract described.

NOTE: A party listed on this schedule will not receive notice of the filing of this case unless the party is also scheduled in the appropriate schedule of creditors.

[] Check this box if debtor has no executory contracts or unexpired leases.

Name and mailing address, including zip code, of other parties to lease or contract	Description of contract or lease and nature of debtor's interest, state whether lease is for nonresidential real property. State contract number of any government contract.

1) Lessee:
  Widget Works, Inc.
  100 Maple Street
  Anytown, Texas 75200
	Debtor is Lessor. Property is nonresidential or commercial business property.

Name and mailing address, including zip code, of other parties to lease or contract	Description of contract or lease and nature of debtor's interest, state whether lease is for nonresidential real property. State contract number of any government contract.
(2) Consignment, Inc. 100 Elm St. Yourtown, Texas	Consignment contract for disposition of artwork

CODEBTORS

UNITED STATES BANKRUPTCY COURT
FOR THE NORTHERN DISTRICT OF TEXAS
DALLAS DIVISION

IN RE:	§	
I. AM BROKE,	§	CASE NO 393-39999-SAF-11
DEBTOR	§	

SCHEDULE H – CODEBTORS

Provide the information requested concerning any person or entity, other than a spouse in a joint case, that is also liable on any debts listed by debtor in the schedules of creditors. Include all guarantors and co-signers. In community property states, a married debtor not filing a joint case should report the name and address of the nondebtor spouse on this schedule. Include all names used by the nondebtor spouse during the six years immediately preceding the commencement of this case.

[]   Check this box if debtor has no codebtors.

Name and address of codebtor	Name and address of creditor
Nondebtor spouse: Hese Broke 1100 Commerce Dallas, TX 75242	(All creditors listed on schedules D, E, and F)
John R. Friend 444 Apple St. Dallas, Texas 75200	Banking On You 6666 Downtown Dr. Dallas, Texas 75000 Attn: Mr. Niceguy, Vice President
Guarantor of condominium loan: John R. Friend 444 Apple St. Dallas, Texas 75200	Loans "R" Us 21554 Money Drive Dallas, Texas 75234

CURRENT INCOME OF INDIVIDUAL DEBTORS

UNITED STATES BANKRUPTCY COURT
FOR THE NORTHERN DISTRICT OF TEXAS
DALLAS DIVISION

IN RE: §

I. AM BROKE,   §   CASE NO. 393-39999-SAF-11

Debtor.   §

SCHEDULE I – CURRENT INCOME OF
INDIVIDUAL DEBTOR(S)

The column labeled "Spouse" must be completed in all cases filed by joint debtors and by a married debtor in a chapter 12 or 13 case whether or not a joint petition is filed, unless the spouses are separated and a joint petition is not filed.

DEBTORS MARITAL STATUS: M		DEPENDENTS OF DEBTOR AND SPOUSE: 1	
	NAMES: JOHN	AGE(s): 2	RELATIONSHIP: Son
		DEBTOR	SPOUSE
EMPLOYMENT:			
OCCUPATION		Attorney	Housewife
NAME OF EMPLOYER		I. Am Broke & Associates, P.C.	N/A
HOW LONG EMPLOYED		10 yrs.	N/A
ADDRESS OF EMPLOYER		1100 Commerce Dallas, Texas 75242	N/A

	DEBTOR	SPOUSE
INCOME Estimate of average monthly income monthly gross wages salary, and commissions (pro rata if -0- monthly.)	5,700.00	N/A
Estimated monthly overtime		N/A
SUBTOTAL	5,700.00	N/A
LESS PAYROLL DEDUCTIONS		N/A
a. Payroll taxes and social security	1,500.00	N/A
b. Insurance		N/A
c. Union dues		N/A
d. Other (Specify)		N/A
		N/A
SUBTOTAL OF PAYROLL DEDUCTIONS	1,500.00	N/A
TOTAL NET MONTHLY TAKE HOME PAY	**$4,200.00	N/A
Regular income from operation of business or profession or farm (attach detailed statement)		N/A
Income from real property	$ 5,008.00	N/A
Alimony, maintenance or support payments to the debtor for the debtor's use or that of dependents listed above	N/A	N/A
Social security or other government assistance (Specify)		
Pension or retirement income		
Other monthly income (Specify)		
TOTAL MONTHLY INCOME	$9,408.00	N/A
TOTAL COMBINED MONTHLY INCOME		N/A

    **   Income generated from billable hours. Estimated monthly income based on average of most current 6 months of actual income.

FORM 7:
STATEMENT OF FINANCIAL AFFAIRS

UNITED STATES BANKRUPTCY COURT
NORTHERN DISTRICT OF TEXAS
DALLAS DIVISION

In re: I. AM BROKE   §
                         §   Case No. 393-39999-SAF (Chapter 11)
Debtor   §
                         §

STATEMENT OF FINANCIAL AFFAIRS

This Statement is to be completed by every debtor. Spouses filing a joint petition may file a single statement on which the information for both spouses is combined. If the case is filed under chapter 12 or chapter 13, a married debtor must furnish information for both spouses whether or not a joint petition is filed, unless the spouses are separated and a joint petition is not filed. An individual debtor engaged in business as a sole proprietor, partner, family farmer, or self-employed professional, should provide the information requested on this statement concerning all such activities as well as the individual's personal affairs.

Questions 1 - 15 are to be completed by all debtors. Debtors that are or have been in business, as defined below, also must complete Questions 16 - 21. Each question must be answered. If the answer to any question is "None," or the question is not applicable, mark the box labeled "None." If additional space is needed for the answer to any question, use and attach a separate sheet properly identified with the case name, case number (if known), and the number of the question.

DEFINITIONS

"In business." A debtor is "in business" for the purpose of this form if the debtor is a corporation or partnership. An individual debtor is "in business" for the purpose of this form if the debtor is or has been, within the two years immediately preceding the filing of this bankruptcy case, any of the following: an officer, director, managing executive, or person in control of a corporation; a partner, other than a limited partner, of a partnership; a sole proprietor or self-employed.

"Insider." The term "insider" includes but is not limited to: relatives of the debtor; general partners of the debtor and their relatives; corporations of which the debtor is an officer, director, or person in control; officers, directors, and any person in control of a corporate debtor and their relatives; affiliates of the debtor and insiders of such affiliates; any managing agent of the debtor. 11 U.S.C. § 101(30).

1. Income from employment or operation of a business

None

State the gross amount of income the debtor has received from employment, trade, or profession, or from operation of the debtor's business from the beginning of this calendar year to the date this case was commenced. State also the gross amounts received during the two years immediately preceding this calendar year. (A debtor that maintains, or has maintained, financial records on the basis of a fiscal rather than a calendar year may report fiscal year income. Identify the beginning and ending dates of the debtor's fiscal year.) If a joint petition is filed, state income for each spouse separately. (Married debtors filing under chapter 12 or chapter 13 must state income of both spouses whether or not a joint petition is filed, unless the spouses are separated and a joint petition is not filed.)

DATES/AMOUNT(S)	SOURCE
1991 Earnings - $340,000.00	AMC Attorneys
1992 Earnings - $ 99,000.00	ABC Attorneys
1/1/93 - 8/31/93: $0.00	

2. Income other than from employment or operation of business

None

State the amount of income received by the debtor other than from employment, trade, profession, or operation of the debtor's business during the two years immediately preceding the commencement of this case. Give particulars. If a joint petition is filed, state income for each spouse separately. (Married debtors filing under chapter 12 or chapter

13 must state income for each spouse whether or not a joint petition is filed, unless the spouses are separated and a joint petition is not filed.)

DATES/AMOUNT(S)			SOURCE
1991	1/1/91 - 12/31/91	$ 40,000	Leased Commercial Bldg.
1992	1/1/92 - 12/31/92	$ 30,000	leased Commercial Bldg.
1993	1/1/93 - 12/31/93	$ 15,000	leased Commercial Bldg.
1991	1/1/91 - 12/31/91		Rental from Condominium
1992	1/1/92 - 12/31/92	$800,000	Rental from Condominium
1993	$400		Rental from Condominium
1993:	$1,100		Interest in closed bank account at Last Bank & Trust
1993:	$1,400		Sale of stock in Loser Bancshares

3. Payments to Creditors

None

a. List all payments on loans, installment purchases of goods or services, and other debts, aggregating more than $600 to any creditor, made within 90 days immediately preceding the commencement of this case. (Married debtors filing under chapter 12 or chapter 13 must include payments by either or both spouses whether or not a joint petition is filed, unless the spouses are separated and a joint petition is not filed.)

NAME AND ADDRESS OF CREDITOR	DATES OF PAYMENTS	AMOUNT PAID	AMOUNT STILL OWING
Internal Revenue Service, Austin, Texas	1/1/93	$3,000.00	$ 39,000.00
Dallas Savings & Loan	Debt Service Payments @ $1,000/Mo.	$3,000.00	$ 90,000.00
Banking On You	April and May Debt Service Payments at $400.00/Mo.	$ 800.00	$ 80,000.00

None

    b. List all payments made within one year immediately preceding the commencement of this case to or for the benefit of creditors who are or were insiders. (Married debtors filing under chapter 12 or chapter 13 must include payments by either or both spouses whether or not a joint petition is filed, unless the spouses are separated and a joint petition is not filed.)

    4. Suits, executions, garnishments and attachments

None

    a. List all suits to which the debtor is or was a party within one year immediately preceding the filing of this bankruptcy case. (Married debtors filing under chapter 12 or chapter 13 must include information concerning either or both spouses whether or not a joint petition is filed, unless the spouses are separated and a joint petition is not filed.)

None

    b. Describe all property that has been attached, garnished or seized under any legal or equitable process within one year immediately preceding the commencement of this case. (Married debtors filing under chapter 12 or chapter 13 must include information concerning property of either or both spouses whether or not a joint petition is filed, unless the spouses are separated and a joint petition is not filed.)

NAME AND ADDRESS OF PERSON FOR WHOSE BENEFIT PROPERTY WAS SEIZED	DATE OF SEIZURE	DESCRIPTION AND VALUE OF THE PROPERTY
We Are Bankers	Writ of Garnishment filed against Debtor 1/2/92 to collect on unpaid judgment. Judgment was satisfied by Debtor on 4/1/92 and filed with the County Clerk (Dallas County) on 4/2/92.	$100.00 garnished from bank account.

5. Repossessions, foreclosures and returns

None

List all property that has been repossessed by a creditor, sold at a foreclosure sale, transferred through a deed in lieu of foreclosure or returned to the seller, within one year immediately preceding the commencement of this case. (Married debtors filing under chapter 12 or chapter 13 must include information concerning property either or both spouses whether or not a joint petition is filed, unless the spouses are separated and a joint petition is not filed.)

6. Assignments and receiverships

None

a. Describe any assignment of property for the benefit of creditors made within 120 days immediately preceding the commencement of this case. (Married debtors filing under chapter 12 or chapter 13 must include any assignment by either or both spouses whether or not a joint petition is filed, unless the spouses are separated and a joint petition is not filed.)

None

b. List all property which has been in the hands of a custodian, receiver, or court-appointed official within one year immediately preceding the commencement of this case. (Married debtors filing under chapter 12 or chapter 13 must include information concerning property either or both spouses whether or not a joint petition is filed, unless the spouses are separated and a joint petition is not filed.)

7. Gifts

None

List all gifts or charitable contributions made within one year immediately preceding the commencement of this case except ordinary and usual gifts to family members aggregating less than $200 in value per individual family member and charitable contributions aggregating less than $100 per recipient. (Married debtors filing under chapter 12 or chapter 13 must include gifts or contributions by either or both spouses whether or not a joint petition is filed, unless the spouses are separated and a joint petition is not filed.)

8. Losses

None

List all losses from fire, theft, other casualty or gambling within one year immediately preceding the commencement of this case or since the commencement of this case. (Married debtors filing under chapter 12 or chapter 13 must include losses by either or both spouses whether or not a joint petition is filed, unless the spouses are separated and a joint petition is not filed.)

9. Payments related to debt counseling or bankruptcy

None

List all payments made or property transferred by or on behalf of the debtor to any persons, including attorneys, for consultation concerning debt consolidation, relief under the bankruptcy law or preparation of a petition in bankruptcy within one year immediately preceding the commencement of this case.

NAME AND ADDRESS OF PAYEE	DATE OF PAYMENT, NAME OF PAYOR IF OTHER THAN DEBTOR	AMOUNT OF MONEY OR DESCRIPTION AND VALUE OF PROPERTY
Two Guys Who Are Lawyers, P.C.	2/1/93	$1,000.00

10. Other transfers

None

List all other property, other than property transferred in the ordinary course of the business or financial affairs of the debtor, transferred either absolutely or as security within one year immediately preceding the commencement of this case. (Married debtors filing under chapter 12 or chapter 13 must include transfers by either or both spouses whether or not a joint petition is filed, unless the spouses are separated and a joint petition is not filed.)

11. Closed financial accounts

None

List all financial accounts and instruments held in the name of the debtor or for the benefit of the debtor which were closed, sold, or otherwise transferred within one year immediately preceding the commencement of this case. Include checking, savings, or other financial accounts, certificates of deposit, or other instruments; shares and share accounts held in banks, credit unions, pension funds, cooperatives, associations, brokerage houses and other financial institutions. (Married debtors filing under chapter 12 or chapter 13 must include information concerning accounts or instruments held by or for either or both spouses whether or not a joint petition is filed, unless the spouses are separated and a joint petition is not filed.)

NAME AND ADDRESS OF INSTITUTION	TYPE AND NUMBER OF ACCOUNT AND AMOUNT OF FINAL BALANCE	AMOUNT AND DATE OF SALE OR CLOSING
Best Bank, Dallas, Texas	Trust Account - Styled: "I. Am Broke & Assoc., P.C." Cash: $1,000.00 Stock: 2,800 shares of Loser Bancshares sold @ 50C a share - $1,400.00	Liquidated 2/2/93. $1,000.00 $1,400.00

12. Safe deposit boxes

None

List each safe deposit or other box or depository in which the debtor has or had securities, cash or other valuables within one year immediately preceding the commencement of this case. (Married debtors filing under chapter 12 or chapter 13 must include boxes or depositories of either or both spouses whether or not a joint petition is filed, unless the spouses are separated and a joint petition is not filed.)

13. Setoffs

None

> List all setoffs made by any creditor, including a bank, against a debt or deposit of the debtor within 90 days preceding the commencement of this case. (Married debtors filing under chapter 12 or chapter 13 must include information concerning either or both spouses whether or not a joint petition is filed, unless the spouses are separated and a joint petition is not filed.)

14. Property held for another person

None

> List all property owned by another person that the debtor holds or controls.

15. Prior address of debtor

None

> If the debtor has moved within the two years immediately preceding the commencement of this case, list all premises which the debtor occupied during that period and vacated prior to the commencement of this case. If a joint petition is filed, report also any separate address of either spouse.

ADDRESS	NAME USED	DATES OF OCCUPANCY
1100 Commerce Dallas, TX 75242	I. Am Broke & Associates, P.C.	Conducts business from home.
"	Management Company U.S.A.	
"	WLW Joint Venture	

The following questions are to be completed by every debtor that is a corporation or partnership and by any individual debtor who is or has been, within the two years immediately preceding the commencement of this case, any of the following: an officer, director, managing executive, or owner of more than 5 percent of the voting securities of a corporation; a partner, other than a limited partner, of a partnership; a sole proprietor or otherwise self-employed.

(An individual or joint debtor should complete this portion of the statement only if the debtor is or has been in business, as defamed above, within the two years immediately preceding the commencement of this case.)

16. Nature, location and name of business

None

a. If the debtor is an individual, list the names and addresses of all businesses in which the debtor was an officer, director, partner, or managing executive of a corporation, partnership, sole proprietorship, or was a self-employed professional within the two years immediately preceding the commencement of this case, or in which the debtor owned 5 percent or more of the voting or equity securities within the two years immediately preceding the commencement of this case.

None

b. If the debtor is a partnership, list the names and addresses of all businesses in which the debtor was a partner or owned 5 percent or more of the voting securities, within the two years immediately preceding the commencement of this case.

None

c. If the debtor is a corporation, list the names and addresses of all businesses in which the debtor was a partner or owned 5 percent or more of the voting securities within the two years immediately preceding the commencement of this case.

NAME	ADDRESS	NATURE OF BUSINESS	BEGINNING AND ENDING DATES OF OPERATION

17. Books, records and financial statements

None

a. List all bookkeepers and accountants who within six years immediately preceding the filing of this bankruptcy case kept or supervised the keeping of books of account and records of the debtor.

NAME AND ADDRESS	DATES SERVICES RENDERED
Numbers Mann, CPA. 300 Bean Counter Ave. Dallas, TX 75200	Since 1985

None

b. List all firms or individuals who within the two years immediately preceding the filing of this bankruptcy case have audited the books of account and records, or prepared a financial statement of the debtor.

NAME	ADDRESS	DATES SERVICES RENDERED
I. Am Broke	1100 Commerce Dallas, TX 75242	As required.

None

c. List all firms or individuals who at the time of the commencement of this case were in possession of the books of account and records of the debtor. If any of the books of account and records are not available, explain.

NAME	ADDRESS
I. Am Broke	110 Commerce, Dallas, TX 75242

None

d. List all financial institutions, creditors and other parties, including mercantile and trade agencies, to whom a financial statement was issued within the two years immediately preceding the commencement of this case by the debtor.

NAME AND ADDRESS	DATE ISSUED
Banking On You, 6666 Downtown Dr., Dallas, TX 75234	1989 to present, as required.
Dallas Savings & Loan, P.O. Box 77777, Dallas, Texas 75234	1989 to present.

18. Inventories

None

a. List the dates of the last two inventories taken of your property, the name of the person who supervised the taking of each inventory, and the dollar amount and basis of each inventory.

None

b. List the name and address of the person having possession of the records of each of the two inventories reported in a., above.

19. Current partners, officers, directors and shareholders

None

a. If the debtor is a partnership, list the nature and percentage of partnership interest of each member of the partnership.

None

b. If the debtor is a corporation, list all officers and directors of the corporation, and each stockholder who directly or indirectly owns, controls, or holds 5 percent or more of the voting securities of the corporation.

20. Former partners, officers, directors and shareholders

None

a. If the debtor is a partnership, list each member who withdrew from the partnership within one year immediately preceding the commencement of this case.

None

b. If the debtor is a corporation, list all officers, or directors whose relationship with the corporation terminated within one year immediately preceding the commencement of this case.

21. Withdrawals from a partnership or distributions by a corporation

None

If the debtor is a partnership or corporation, list all withdrawals or distributions credited or given to an insider, including compensation in any form, bonuses, loans, stock redemptions, options exercised and any other perquisite during one year immediately preceding the commencement of this case.

[If completed by an individual or individual and spouse]

I declare under penalty of perjury that I have read the answers contained in the foregoing statement of financial affairs and any attachments thereto and that they are true and correct.

Date_____   Signature_____

Date_____   Signature_____
                                              of Joint Debtor (if any)

INDEX